PRACTICAL DREAMER

Volume X in the **Moreshet Series,** Studies in
Jewish History, Literature and Thought

PRACTICAL DREAMER:
Israel Friedlaender and the Shaping of American Judaism

Baila Round Shargel

The Jewish Theological Seminary of America
New York   1985

BM
755
.F7
S52
1985

COPYRIGHT © 1985
THE JEWISH THEOLOGICAL SEMINARY OF AMERICA

Library of Congress Cataloging in Publication Data

Shargel, Baila Round.
  Practical dreamer.

  (Moreshet series; v. 10)
  Bibliography: p.
  Includes index.
  1. Friedlaender, Israel, 1876-1920. 2. Scholars,
Jewish—United States—Biography. 3. Conservative
Judaism—United States. I. Title. II. Series.
BM755.F7S52   1985   296.8′342′0924 [B]   85-8101
ISBN 0-87334-027-2   Rev.

MANUFACTURED IN THE UNITED STATES OF AMERICA

In loving memory of my parents,
Rose and Jacob Round

Israel Friedlaender.

Contents

Part One
The Man

Chapter

Part Two
The Scholar

Part Three
The Public Figure

Foreword

As an agent of creative cultural transmission, Solomon Schechter's rejuvenated Seminary not only brought to North America the critical scholarship and religious Conservatism of German Jewry, but also imbued that dual legacy with some of the diverse expressions of Jewish vitality in Eastern Europe. Under the leadership of Schechter—a scholar of international renown, a superb popular expositor of Judaism, a religious moderate, and a man of culture and charisma—the Seminary quickly became identified with a conception of Judaism that was anti-Reform, multifaceted, responsive to change, and culturally pro-Zionist.

The unfulfilled career of Israel Friedlaender, cut short on a mission of mercy to the Ukraine in 1920, is a tragedy compounded by the tensions spawned by Schechter's vision and example. As this richly documented biography by Dr. Baila Shargel reveals for the first time, Friendlaender's academic career at the Seminary was spent in the torment of reconciling polar opposites. Appointed in 1903 at the age of twenty-seven as professor of biblical literature and exegesis, though trained as an Arabist and student of Islam in Germany, the young academic was never able to generate the kind of Jewish biblical scholarship which Schechter hoped might challenge the "higher anti-Semitism" of many contemporary Christian scholars. Produced without benefit of a model and in an atmosphere rife with religious polemics, his work in Bible could hardly vindicate Schechter's conviction that the recovery of historical truth was best left to the insider.

The absence of a scholarly center of gravity, despite some solid accomplishments as an Arabist, probably accentuated Friedlaender's innate proclivity for communal affairs. Like Schechter and many of the best practitioners of Jewish scholarship in Germany, Friedlaender wholly identified with the scholarly ethos he encapsuled in the apothegm of Leopold Zunz, the founder of the field, that "real learning brings forth great deeds" ("*Wahre Wissenschaft ist tatenerzeugend*"). With courage and credibility, he repeatedly sought to distill and apply the implications of his research to the ideological issues agitating American Jewry in a tumultuous period. His involvement certainly raised the level of public discourse and left a perspicacious legacy, deftly analyzed by Dr. Shargel, but it also shifted imperceptibly the object of his intellectual energy away from sustained scholarship.

Finally, Friedlaender struggled to reconcile his cerebral preference for the elitism and worldliness of Spanish Jewry, which he had absorbed in Germany, with his emotional affinity for the spiritual intensity and cultural vigor of Russian Jewry, from which he hailed. At the same time as Horace Kallen, he defended the right and the need of Russian immigrants to America to retain and cultivate their own cultural ambience, and as the crisis of Jewry in Russia steadily deepened, he labored to mediate its past and ameliorate its present. In the process, he advocated a religious, cultural, and national conception of Judaism, expansive enough to embrace both emancipation and a homeland in Palestine as equally valid and mutually beneficial strategies of survival.

Dr. Shargel has written the first full-scale biography of this gifted, complex, and conflicted man. The research is exhaustive, the analysis contextual, and the text informed by the right questions. As a result, the author sheds new light on Friedlaender's career aspirations and disappointments, on the sources and substance of his thought, and on his dynamic communal role. May this mature and well-crafted assessment serve to redeem his poignant life from the mist of hagiography and to stimulate a new cohort of scholars to study the history of American Conservatism afresh.

ISMAR SCHORSCH
RABBI HERMAN ABRAMOVITZ
Professor of Jewish History
The Jewish Theological
Seminary of America

Preface

In 1945 Rabbi Morris Schussheim publicly deplored the fact that "for twenty-five years the Jewish world has been silent about Israel Friedlaender."[1] A decade later, following the donation of the Friedlaender Papers to the Library of the Jewish Theological Seminary, Rabbi Morris Adler, a well-known Jewish thinker, set out to correct this wrong. During a year's sabbatical in New York, he amassed a sizable collection of memoirs and letters which had not been previously available. Unfortunately and quite ironically, his own life, like that of the man he revered, was also cut off in its prime, in this case by the bullet of a deranged disciple.

In the course of time, the papers collected by Adler were added to the Archives of the Seminary Library, considerably enriching the Friedlaender collection.[2] Recently, there have come to light several personal letters written in 1907 which Friedlaender's dear friend Dr. Harry Friedenwald of Baltimore donated to the library over thirty years ago, with the proviso that they remain unavailable to the public for many years.[3] They deal with a turning point in Friedlaender's life[4] and offer invaluable testimony to his inner conflicts and desired goals. Of equal value to this study are letters exchanged between Friedlaender and Lilian Ruth Bentwich during the periods of their courtship and early marriage and his final journey to Europe. They are in possession of Mrs. Carmel

[1] Morris Schussheim, "Recollections of Israel Friedlaender," *Proceedings of the Rabbinical Assembly* 9 (1945): 170.

[2] See the letter from Irwin Groner to Wolfe Kelman, January 11, 1977, *FP* Box 12. Lilian Friedlaender had donated the Friedlaender papers to the library of the Jewish Theological Seminary in 1950.

[3] See letters from Harry Friedenwald to Alexander Marx: January 9, 1925, *Marx MSS*, and October 31, 1929, *FP*.

[4] I.e., when Friedlaender was considered for a position at the Dropsie College in Philadelphia. In 1978 these letters were placed in the *Friedenwald MSS*.

Agranat, the Friedlaenders' eldest daughter, who graciously let me read them.

Friedlaender left no reminiscences, autobiography, or personal diary worth of the name.[5] For this reason, the letters collected in the Friedlaender Papers have proved indispensable to this study, as have the unpublished essays, notes for lectures, both academic and public, and memoranda of the many organizations to which he belonged. Almost as useful is a set of two scrapbooks containing copies of Friedlaender's published articles, many from journals and newsletters no longer in print and difficult, if not impossible, to obtain.

For granting me access to the Friedlaender Papers as well as the personal *Journals* of his colleague Mordecai M. Kaplan, I would like to thank Dr. Menahem Schmelzer, Librarian of the Jewish Theological Seminary. Thanks are also due to Judith Endelman, former archivist of the Library, for bringing to my attention other riches contained therein, notably the papers of a number of Zionist, communal, and Seminary leaders who were Friedlaender's contemporaries.

Supplementing these sources were data from other archives: the Zionist Archives and Library of New York, under the capable supervision of Mrs. Sylvia Landress, the American Jewish Historical Society of Waltham, Massachusetts, the Central Zionist Archives of Jerusalem, and the Library of the American Red Cross in Washington.

Personal interviews with Friedlaender's students and other associates have been most enlightening. At the inception of this project I received welcome encouragement, good advice, and useful background material from Gerson D. Cohen, Chancellor of the Jewish Theological Seminary of America and Louis Finkelstein, the Chancellor Emeritus. I am also indebted to Dr. Etan Kohlberg of the Hebrew University's Institute of Asian and African Studies for sharing his erudition on Shiism and helping me to clarify Friedlaender's role in the study of this historical phenomenon. I could

---

[5.] The closest thing to an autobiography was a letter, probably to Schechter, written in 1903, containing a résumé of his personal background and academic achievements up to that date. In *FP*, Box 9, is a tiny bound volume, incorrectly marked "Diary of the Late Dr. Israel Friedlaender, January, 1910-July, 1920." In reality, it is little more than a date book of Friedlaender's final journey to Europe, from February 5, 1920 to June 29, 1920. After his death, it was recovered and handed over to James N. Rosenberg, vice-chairman of the JDC, when he visited Moscow.

not have completed this project without the help of Mrs. Anne-Marie Gordon, who graciously donated her time to decipher the German script and translate several letters in the Friedlaender, Steinschneider, and Marx Papers. After reading my manuscript, Dr. Jack Wertheimer offered well-considered comments and constructive criticism, for which I am deeply grateful. I would especially like to thank Professor Ismar Schorsch for training me in the methods of historical research, supporting my decision to pursue this subject, and providing good advice and thoughtful criticism every step of the way.

I have been in contact with all of Friedlaender's surviving children: Herzl Friedlaender, Ben-Zion and Judith Friedlander, and Joy Goldschmidt as well as Mrs. Agranat. All of them have been generous beyond the call of filial duty, volunteering information not otherwise available as well as the financial support that made this publication possible.

For indispensable readership of the work in progress, I am sincerely grateful to my husband, Rabbi Norton Shargel, my daughter Dina Projansky, and my sister Betty Waskow. To them, as well as the younger members of the family, Jonathan, Raphael, and Rebecca Shargel, I owe a debt of gratitude for all their love and support.

Abbreviations

IF Diary	Israel Friedlaender's diary of his mission to the Ukraine, February to June, 1920, *FP*, Box 9.
Kaplan Journals	Journals of Mordecai M. Kaplan, Jewish Theological Seminary Archives.
Marx MSS	Alexander Marx Papers, Jewish Theological Seminary Archives.
Richards MSS	Bernard G. Richards Papers, Jewish Theological Seminary Archives.
Rubenovitz MSS	Herman Rubenovitz Papers, Jewish Theological Seminary Archives.
Schechter MSS	Solomon Schechter Papers, Jewish Theological Seminary Archives.
SE	*Significant Epochs in Jewish History.* A course of six lectures delivered before the Training Class of the Jewish Welfare Board, August 14, 15, and 16, 1918. Outline and nos. 5 and 6 in *FP*, Box 15.
Steinschneider MSS	Moritz Steinschneider Papers, Jewish Theological Seminary Archives.
Wise MSS	Stephen Samuel Wise Papers, American Jewish Historical Society, Waltham, Massachusetts.

Other Abbreviations

AJHQ	*American Jewish Historical Quarterly.*
AJYB	*American Jewish Year Book.*
FAZ	Federation of American Zionists.
HUCA	*Hebrew Union College Annual.*
IF	Israel Friedlaender.
JPS	Jewish Publication Society, Philadelphia.
JQR,o.s.	*Jewish Quarterly Review*, original series, published in England before 1907.
JQR,n.s.	*Jewish Quarterly Review*, new series, published in the United States after 1910.

JRP	Israel Friedlaender, *The Jews of Russia and Poland: A Bird's-Eye View of Their History and Culture*, New York, 1915.
JSS	*Jewish Social Studies*
JTS	Jewish Theological Seminary of America.
MGWJ	*Monatsschrift fuer Geschichte und Wissenschaft des Judentums.*
MJ	*Menorah Journal.*
PAJHS	*Publications of the American Jewish Historical Society.*
PP	Israel Friedlaender, *Past and Present*, New York, 1961. Second edition of the book, somewhat abridged. All citations are from this edition, unless otherwise indicated.
PP (1919)	First edition of *Past and Present*, Cincinnati, 1919.
REJ	*Revue des Études Juives.*
SJ	Solomon Schechter, *Studies in Judaism*.

N.B. Wherever possible, I have followed the Hebrew transliteration scheme suggested in the *AJS Review* 5 (1980): xiii-xiv.

Introduction

On September 9, 1920, a large assembly of Jews met at Carnegie Hall to mourn the premature and violent death of Israel Friedlaender, professor at the Jewish Theological Seminary and prominent Zionist and community leader. Two months before, on July 5, the forty-three-year-old scholar, along with a younger colleague, Bernard Cantor, had been brutally murdered in the Ukraine.

The two men had been sent on a mission sponsored by the Joint Distribution Committee to succor the Jews of that area whose lives had been shattered by a terrible world war and the upheavals which followed it. At the September meeting, seven prominent Jews delivered moving eulogies to an audience of 3,500 to 4,000 people. Today, more than six decades later, the words that are best remembered are those of the reigning *maggid* of New York, Zvi Hirsch Masliansky, who wailed, *"Yisroel, vu-bistu, vu-bistu, akhinu Yisroel?"* (Where are you, Israel, our beloved brother, where are you, Israel, the martyred of the people of Israel?)[1]

In the sixty-four years since Friedlaender's death, Masliansky's query has not yielded a satisfactory response. For despite the shock which pervaded the Jewish community at his death, despite the heat generated by the Carnegie Hall meeting, there resulted a paradoxical situation. Friedlaender has frequently been hailed as an architect of Conservative Judaism; bits and snatches of his felicitous prose are often cited to illustrate one or another plank in its platform, notably its early commitment both to Zionism and to full Jewish participation in American life. Nevertheless, to this date (1984), no one has completed either a full biography of the man or a monograph on his thought. In other words, no one has ventured to

[1]*Memorial Meeting, Israel Friedlaender, Bernard Cantor* (American Jewish Joint Distribution Committee, 1920), p. 41.

answer the question *"Yisroel, vu-bistu?"* in the perspective of history.

To maintain that no inclusive evaluation of Israel Friedlaender has been completed is not to say that none has been ventured. Through the years there have appeared many pieces of varying length and quality on the subject of his life and work. They cover more than half a century in time, beginning with the lengthy record of the 1920 Carnegie Hall assembly. Though the compositions display different styles and focus on different aspects of Friedlaender's life, all of them embrace a common thesis, which can be summarized in these words: Israel Friedlaender was a man who represented a harmonious blending of many diverse elements—Hasidic enthusiasm, mastery of the traditional Jewish texts, training in scientific criticism. This superb scholar and teacher of the Jewish past did not hesitate to plunge into the melee of contemporary Jewish life for the purpose of promoting Zionism and fostering educational efforts on the American scene.

The most complete formulation of the harmony thesis was a commencement address delivered by Rabbi Morris Adler to the graduating class of the Jewish Theological Seminary in 1960. Adler seized upon the popular theme of the two cultures, suggested at that time by the British scientist and literateur C. P. Snow. Snow had deplored the rift between men of letters and men of science. Adler applied Snow's notion of the polarization of knowledge to the contemporary polarization of Jewish life, which, he insisted, was contrary to the spirit of Judaism. To offset this tendency, he suggested the name of Israel Friedlaender, whom he saw as a Jewish *homo universale*, a man whose interests and activities spanned the entire Jewish world. Some of his words bear repeating.

> Three major points on the graph of the life of Israel Friedlaender represent in a vivid way the direction and quality of his fruitful career in our midst—points that were merged and absorbed into his expanding personality. The points were Warsaw, Strassburg and New York. From Warsaw, in the country of his birth, he derived an intensity and enthusiasm which never weakened. Subsequent Western training could not quench the *hitlahavut*, the enkindled spirit and the incandescent heart which Jewish life in Eastern Europe irradiated in him. There he beheld and shared in a vital, deep-delved, rich, rooted community, marked by piety and learning. In Germany, he was inducted into modern scholar-

ship, its discipline and methodology, its spirit of inquiry and research. He revealed in his own academic works the thoroughness with which he had absorbed the new learning. . . . In America, to which he came at the invitation of Dr. Schechter, he glimpsed further horizons. He throbbed to the opportunity which the youth, the expansiveness, the power and the freedom of the New World made available to the Jew.

Not blind to its brashness and materialism, he was moved by a deep faith in its possibilities. He believed that America, unscarred by the bitter memories, struggles and hates of Europe opened vistas of achievement and fulfillment not to be found in the Old World. . . . The theory of Dubnow, rejecting as it did the negations of assimilation and upholding the collective personality of Jewish life found a place in the philosophy of this Chassid, disciple of Juedische Wissenschaft, American teacher and impassioned Zionist. For he aspired, to use his own words, to attain "that synthesis of Jewish life which combined in a higher unity the essential elements of the doctrines formerly believed to be exclusive of one another." The points on the graph of Israel Friedlaender's life drew near and joined to form a line.[2]

How can we describe the scene in which the "fruitful career" of Israel Friedlaender unfolded? The emerging American Jewish community of the early twentieth century was fragmented physically and troubled spiritually, split into what Jacob Marcus has called "two disparate, yet parallel Jewish cultures."[3] The primary culture was that of the Jews who had emigrated from Central Europe since the middle of the nineteenth century, in time to benefit materially from the rapid industrial development that followed the Civil War. Their cultural baggage included an intense ambition and drive, an abiding love for their native language and culture, and a haunting fear of the accusation of dual loyalty. At the turn of the century, it was their leaders, notably Isidor and Oscar Straus, Adolph Lewisohn, Louis Marshall, and Jacob Schiff, who represented American Jewry; it was their religious expression, Reform Judaism, which dominated the American synagogue.

Challenging their hegemony and, as many of them saw it, their hard-won social status as well, were the masses of Jews from Eastern Europe, now streaming into the country in unprecedented numbers. Although Russian and Polish Jews had been coming to

[2]This essay is found in *FP*, Box 12.
[3]Jacob Marcus, "The Periodization of American History," in *Studies in American Jewish History* (Cincinnati, 1969), p. 10.

this country since the eighteenth century, they had arrived in smaller numbers than their German co-religionists before the assassination of Czar Alexander II in 1881. When Alexander III adopted a draconian Jewish policy of severe economic restrictions, combined with the threat, and often the reality, of violence, the migration of Jews increased dramatically. Within a few years, the "Russian" Jewish population overtook that of the Germans. The newcomers, who hailed from Hungary and Rumania as well as the czar's swollen empire, settled mostly in the port cities of the East and Midwest, with the greatest numbers inhabiting New York's crowded Lower East Side.

Their displacement was both physical and spiritual. Many former storekeepers, innkeepers, and agricultural agents eked out a living as workingmen in the needle trades, with little prospect of improving their own lot, but with high hopes for their children. In the face of economic necessity and psychic dislocation, religious observance became the exception rather than the rule among the younger Jews. A staggering variety of cultural modalities emerged to replace religion; Bundism, anarchism, socialism, and Yiddishism were the most prominent. Weaker than any of them was the Zionist movement. The FAZ (Federation of American Zionists), under the leadership of Richard Gottheil, Harry Friedenwald, and Stephen Wise, attracted a small membership.

To the "uptown Jews" (as the acculturated Jews of German background came to be called), these were dangerous trends. To counteract these ideologies by anchoring the "downtown Jews" to firm religious moorings and orienting them to American modes of life, they established the Educational Alliance on the Lower East Side. There they conducted lessons and religious services on the Reform model and offered classes in the domestic sciences, the arts, English, and naturalization. The immigrants' response was to attend the People's Synagogue and Sunday School in small numbers, even as their participation in the other activities grew from year to year.

It was evident that the Reform religious and educational institutions could not capture the souls of the immigrants. For this reason, a group of forward-looking uptown Jews decided, in 1901, to revive a moribund traditional religious institution. This was the Jewish Theological Seminary, a rabbinical school founded in New York City in 1886 and modeled after an institution of the same name in

Breslau, Germany. Like its European namesake, the American seminary accepted the world view of what was then called "Historical Judaism." This moderately reformist branch of traditional Judaism adopted a developmental approach to Judaism even as it insisted upon the binding character of Jewish law. Judaism, in the eyes of the historians who founded the movement, was a national and religious culture rather than a confessional creed.

The lay leaders who funded the venture, Jacob Schiff, Leonard Lewisohn, Mayer Sulzberger, Daniel and Simon Guggenheim, and Louis Marshall,[4] were wealthy and prominent members of New York's prestigious Temple Emanu-el. Some of them still cherished traditional ceremonials, but all of them were embarrassed by Jewish ethnicism. Nevertheless, they conducted an extensive search for a charismatic leader committed to Historical Judaism[5] and found him in the person of Solomon Schechter, reader in rabbinics at Cambridge University. In 1902 Schechter came to New York to assume the position of president of the Jewish Theological Seminary of America. His first obligation was to discover like-minded European Jewish savants willing to cast their lot with an American rabbinical seminary. First to be engaged was Louis Ginzberg, a promising young talmudist already residing in America. Schechter then initiated the search for a professor of biblical literature and exegesis. After offering the position to the noted Polish-Jewish scholar Samuel Poznanski,[6] Schechter sailed to Europe in the summer of 1903. When Poznanski decided to reject the offer, he turned to Israel Friedlaender, with whom Ginzberg had been in contact since May.[7] The two men had studied at different times with the noted orientalist Theodor Noeldeke at the new German University of Strassburg; Noeldeke, in fact, initially recommended Friedlaender to Ginzberg.[8] Schechter engaged both Friedlaender and another young scholar, Alexander Marx, an historian and bibliographer associated with the venerable Moritz

---

[4]See Cyrus Adler, *I Have Considered the Days* (New York, 1945), pp. 243-244.
[5]See Abraham J. Karp, "Solomon Schechter Comes to America," *AJHQ* 53 (September 1963): 42-62.
[6]Abraham Yaari edited the correspondence between Schechter and Poznanski on this issue and published it in Hebrew under the title *Solomon Schechter's Letters to Samuel Poznanski* (Jerusalem, 1943).
[7]Louis Ginzberg to Israel Friedlaender, May 12, 1903, June 25, 1903; Israel Friedlaender to Louis Ginzberg, June 25, 1903. In *FP*, Box 1.
[8]Ibid., May 12, 1903.

Steinschneider. Marx assumed the position of professor of Jewish history and literature and chief librarian of the Seminary.

Thus Friedlaender was one of a trio of promising scholars, all in their late twenties, chosen by Schechter to train rabbis and educators for the immigrant masses. The three young men had much in common. All of them accepted the developmental approach to Jewish history; all were punctilious in their observance of Jewish law; all harbored strong feelings for the Jewish nation and culture. Together, they represented the different branches of Ashkenazic Jewry: Friedlaender, son of a Polish *maskil* who had flirted with Hasidism in his youth; Ginzberg, collateral descendant of the Gaon of Vilna, the archetypical *mitnaged;* and Marx, the Jewish polyhistor from Koenigsberg in East Prussia. Most importantly, they came to New York as fully qualified and highly respected scholars, graduates of the prestigious German universities of Strassburg, Heidelberg, and Koenigsberg.

Marx and Ginzberg would contribute materially to Jewish scholarship for a full half-century and, in the process, train two generations of American rabbis. Friedlaender's early death makes him a more remote figure. Yet of the first faculty of the reorganized Jewish Theological Seminary, Friedlaender alone labored not only for the Jewish community but actually in its midst. With great eloquence, he imparted the messages of religious revival and Hebraic renewal learned from his German-Jewish predecessors Graetz and Frankel and his Russian-Jewish contemporaries Ahad Ha-am and Dubnow. Selflessly, he donated precious hours of his time to the education and Americanization of the immigrants and their children. For the Zionist cause in particular he exerted the most arduous efforts of mind and body.

Friedlaender's years in New York were those of American Jewry's bumptious adolescence. The community had nearly attained full physical and numerical strength, but was subject to frequent feverish upheavals. Friedlaender's calls for reason and compromise were all too often drowned in the clanging din of competing interests. This long-overdue study of the man, his thought, and his communal endeavor is intended to further understanding of a critical and formative period of American Jewish history.

Part One
THE MAN

Chapter 1

America—"Land of Wonder and Terror"

In the brief span of his life, Friedlaender traveled a winding road. It was a circuitous route, which led him from east to west, and ultimately returned him to his native land. All too often his life reflected the condition described by the title of Ahad Ha-am's famous collection of essays. On six separate occasions he stood uneasily "at the crossroads." Five of the six crises molded his personality and his outlook; the sixth one sealed his fate.

From earliest youth Friedlaender displayed both a unique talent for absorbing and retaining a large store of facts and a singular capacity for deep, heartfelt emotion. He was the eldest of four children, born in Wlodwa, Poland, on September 8, 1876, to a sixteen-year-old mother, Gittel, and Pinchas, a devoted father, who made a better than average living as a cattle dealer specializing in horsehair. In his fourth year, the family moved to Praga, an eastern suburb of Warsaw, where he was raised. Even as a young boy educated in a traditional *ḥeder*, which, characteristically, emphasized talmudic study, Friedlaender demonstrated unusual brilliance. He mastered the traditional biblical commentaries and committed large portions of the Bible to memory; in later years his lectures and writings would be peppered with quotations from Scripture. He also received private instruction in modern Hebrew, acquiring a literary skill in this idiom that he would exercise throughout his life, even after he mastered a number of Near Eastern and European languages.

High school attendance on the Sabbath was mandatory in Praga; for this reason Israel's parents provided him with home tutors in secular subjects. The youth completed the curriculum of the Russian gymnasium at age fifteen, then embarked upon serious study of the German language and literary classics.[1] There was little opportunity for socializing with his peers; Friedlaender found emotional satisfaction and perhaps also an opportunity for adolescent rebellion against his "enlightened" father, by seeking out Hasidic rabbis. To his parents' chagrin, he donned the *kapota*, the Hasidic robe, which he proudly wore until his departure from Poland.[2]

Friedlaender journeyed to Berlin in his eighteenth year, in order to obtain the European education that his talents demanded. After a short period of preparation, he enrolled in both Berlin University and the modern Orthodox Hildesheimer Rabbinical Seminary, with the intention of pursuing a rabbinical career. This ambition was not fulfilled as Friedlaender intended it; he soon decided to devote his life, instead, to Semitic scholarship. In a larger sense, however, he became "rabbi" to several generations of young people. First in Germany and later in the United States, he served as the teacher and inspiration of many Jewish students who required spiritual sustenance even as they pursued secular studies. In Berlin, Friedlaender initiated a series of courses in Hebrew and Jewish history for the organization of Jewish students *(Verein Juedischer Studenten)*. Here he demonstrated a precocious inclination for rhetoric and pedagogy.

Disappointing encounters with assimilated German Jewish students convinced Friedlaender of the urgent necessity of imparting the message of national and cultural revival to a wider audience. To accomplish this purpose, he boldly initiated correspondence with two important East European thinkers, Simon Dubnow and Ahad Ha-am, whose ideas were as yet unavailable to Western Jewry. Upon receiving their approval,[3] the twenty-one-year-old student

[1]Most of this information is culled from the letter which I have designated "Autobiography, 1903."

[2]Moshe Ha-Levi [Morris D. Levine], "Ha-shalem Be-midotav," *Ha-Toren* 7 (July 30, 1920): 3.

[3]See Simon Dubnow's obituary on Friedlaender, *Ha-aretz* 4 (8 Elul 5682); Ahad Ha-am, *Igrot ahad ha-am*, 6 vols. (Jerusalem, 1923), 1:212 (April 24, 1898).

translated into German Dubnow's *Essay on the Philosophy of History* and Ahad Ha-am's *Sacred and Profane*. (A full volume of his translations of Ahad Ha-am's essays into German was later published in two editions, 1904 and 1913.)[4] These and other early works demonstrated Friedlaender's mastery of the literary craft. A charming Hebrew poem celebrating the twenty-fifth anniversary of the *Rabbiner Seminar* in the meter of the Beethoven Ninth Symphony chorale, reflected the good humor and light touch which would endear him to many acquaintances. An essay tracing the development of spoken and written Hebrew from earliest times to the nineteenth-century *Haskalah* was an early example of Friedlaender's facility in turning dry-as-dust chronicle into lifelike reality.[5] These amateur adventures, for which the serious student sacrificed his leisure time, were further indications of his "rabbinical" tendency to utilize Jewish learning for the purpose of stirring strong resolution in the hearts of the listeners.

Nevertheless, in 1899 Friedlaender's young life underwent its first decisive upheaval; he decided to pursue an academic career in the field of Semitics. For an East European Jew who had never attended a proper gymnasium to embark on this course of action was a display of extreme audacity; the German establishment was loath to accept even native-born Jews as university professors. Yet Friedlaender naively and eagerly followed his inclinations and interests, repairing to Strassburg to complete his oriental studies with Theodor Noeldeke, "the Nestor of Orientalists."[6] Friedlaender soon became an expert philologist, studying half a dozen Semitic languages and thoroughly mastering three. His minor subjects were Persian and philosophy, the latter under the instruction of the famous Wilhelm Windelband. His doctoral dissertation, completed in 1901, investigated Maimonides' utilization of the Arabic languages; a second thesis, qualifying him for an academic position, dealt with Shiite heresies. After receiving the Ph.D. degree, he undertook an intensive study of Moslem historiography and produced a penetrating comparative analysis of the messianic idea within the three monotheistic religions. Not abandoning his

[4] Printed in Berlin under the title *Am Scheidewege.*

[5] "Die Hebraische Sprache," published in *Israelitischer Lehrer und Cantor* 9:45-46 and 10:53-54 (Berlin, 1899). Translated and printed in *PP* under the title "The Hebrew Language," pp. 95-111.

[6] From Noeldeke's obituary in the *London Times*, December 30, 1930, p. 9.

Lilian Ruth Friedlaender.

Israel Friedlaender.

Jewish interests, he researched *geniza* fragments in the library of Frankfurt-am-Main. The most ambitious project initiated during the Strassburg years (1899-1903) concerned the rich religious folk-lore dealing with the notion of eternal life. It would take him ten years to complete this study.

Noeldeke was one of the few German savants free of bias against Jewish students. He not only encouraged Friedlaender's aspirations toward a university career; he hoisted him onto the bottom rung of the slippery academic ladder. For two semesters Friedlaender served as a *privatdozent* (instructor), teaching Arabic and Syriac philology and giving two courses in Jewish philosophy.

The academic year 1902-1903 culminated in the second turning point of his life. For as it drew to a close, Solomon Schechter invited Friedlaender to come to New York to serve as professor of Bible at the reorganized Jewish Theological Seminary. Discouraged by the rampant assimilation and defection of Jewish professors at Strassburg,[7] and realizing the near impossibility of academic advancement in Germany, the twenty-seven-year-old instructor accepted the position.

The ocean voyage of September 1903 proved stormy, though relieved by occasional bright and sunny days,[8] a harbinger of life in America. For two years Friedlaender roomed with his friend and colleague Alexander Marx, in an apartment near the Seminary. In the summer of 1904 Friedlaender returned to Europe to pursue some scholarly projects initiated at Strassburg. While laboring in the Bodleian Library, he visited the home of Herbert Bentwich, a prominent British Zionist. There he made the acquaintance of Bentwich's eldest daughter, the winsome Lilian Ruth. The court-ship developed swiftly during the course of the summer. The custom of the day permitted written correspondence only between a lady's suitor and her parents. After his return to America, Friedlaender observed this formality, in the process securing a strong personal relationship with Herbert Bentwich. However, he also took advantage of special occasions, such as birthdays and Jewish holidays, to write to Lilian directly[9] and send her small gifts

---

[7]He later would write that thirty-one out of thirty-three Jewish professors at Strassburg had their children baptized. See his article "Judaism in Western Europe," *American Hebrew* 90 (New York, February 9, 1912): 442.

[8]IF to Marx, September 25, 1903, *Marx MSS*.

[9]See letters from IF to Lilian Bentwich, January 10, March 10, and April 14, 1905, *Agranat MSS*.

as tokens of his affection. The letters offered an account of Friedlaender's efforts to become an English gentleman. Characteristically, he immersed himself in the study of English literature and history; uncharacteristically, he strove to adopt the sporting style of tennis, gymnastics, rowing, and long walks. His persistence was well rewarded when Lilian accepted the proposal of marriage communicated in his eloquent Passover letter. Immediately after Seminary classes were completed, Friedlaender hastened to England, to be married on September 26, 1905.

Even before his marriage to the Englishwoman, Friedlaender displayed almost the same remarkable facility in the English language that marked his German speech and writing. During their first months in America, the three new Seminary professors received instruction in English from Henrietta Szold. Each of them, Friedlaender, Marx, and Ginzberg, eventually mastered the written language sufficiently to publish the results of his scholarship in lucid English prose. However, Friedlaender's spoken English was more grammatical and idiomatic, less accented—in short, more understandable than that of the others.

Friedlaender's success as a teacher was attributed to additional factors as well. Slight of build, of medium stature and regal bearing, meticulously groomed, he was a fine figure of a man. A short, dark beard framed a straight-featured, bespectacled face that was almost handsome. To young men from old-fashioned homes he was the epitome of courtliness and grace. Yet he did not remain aloof from his students in the style of the typical European professor; instead he displayed concern for their welfare. Early in his career he assumed the obligation of channeling financial aid to needy seminarians, a duty which he dispatched with kindness and tact for a period of sixteen years.[10] At a time when most students commuted by subway to Morningside Heights, it was Friedlaender who suggested that a dormitory be built, very much to the chagrin of the budget-conscious Cyrus Adler.[11]

Inside and outside of the classroom, the young professor was eager to give more of himself than was expected. His assignment was to instruct rabbinical students in the literature of the Bible, the history of the canon, and medieval Jewish philosophy, and later to

---

[10]*FP* contain many letters to IF seeking financial aid and thanking him for dispensing it to students. See also IF to Cyrus Adler, October 16, 1916, *Adler MSS.*

[11]See the letter from Harry A. Cohen to Morris Adler, July 27, 1955, *FP*, Box 12.

The faculty and class of JTSA, 1918.

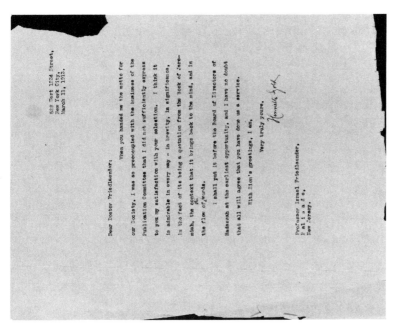

532 West 123d Street,
New York City,
March 11, 1913.

Dear Doctor Friedlaender:

When you handed me the motto for
our Society, I was so preoccupied with the business of the
Publication Committee that I did not sufficiently express
to you my satisfaction with your selection. I think it
is admirable in every way - in brevity, in significance,
in the fact of its being a quotation from the Book of Jeremiah, the context that it brings back to the mind, and in
the flow of words.

I shall put it before the Board of Directors of
Hadassah at the earliest opportunity, and I have no doubt
that all will agree that you have done us a service.

With Zion's greetings, I am,

Very truly yours,

Henrietta Szold

Professor Israel Friedlaender,
Palisade,
New Jersey.

Letter from Henrietta Szold acknowledging Friedlaender's selection of "the healing of the daughter of My people" from Jeremiah, for the Hadassah motto.

Courtesy of the Library of the Jewish Theological Seminary

Friedlaender (right) with a tennis partner, Maurice Meltzer, 1916.

Courtesy of Herman Dinkin

impart his knowledge of Jewish history to undergraduates in the Teachers Institute. A natural pedagogue, he spoke almost without notes and injected humor and warmth into his lectures. In addition to his regular classes he also offered extracurricular lessons in the Arabic language and modern Hebrew literature, focusing on the essays of his favorite author, Ahad Ha-am.

Moreover, he deliberately established friendly relations with his students, who were periodically invited to one or another of the Friedlaender homes in New York City and Palisade, New Jersey, where the family lived between 1911 and 1918. There they were enchanted by the graciousness of his beautiful wife and amused by the mischief of his increasing brood of children. To cement relationships with his students, the professor would sometimes go out of his way to walk with them on the street or accompany them on the subway and even visit their homes in times of crisis. At the time of their graduation from the Seminary, Friedlaender would try his utmost to see the young rabbis settled in secure positions.

This extraordinary quality of deep concern extended far beyond the Seminary community. For Friedlaender considered it his sacred duty to serve the largest migration of Jews in all history. Unlike many European Jewish intellectuals who regarded American Jewry with condescending disdain, Friedlaender was optimistic about its potentiality. On one occasion he told a student, "Perhaps it takes a stranger to come into a community and feel its strength."[12] However, he was equally familiar with its shortcomings and the dangers to Jewish survival posed by American freedom.

> The expansion of American Judaism is not an organic growth from within, but a mechanic addition from without. Its gain, to use a Biblical simile, is the gain of one who puts his earnings into a bag with holes. As long as the earnings exceed the holes, the bag seems constantly to swell. But no sooner will the earnings have stopped than the bag will begin to shrink and will finally collapse.[13]

He therefore resolved to awaken a spirit of Jewish renewal in the hearts of the new settlers. Tirelessly, he preached the message of Dubnow and Ahad Ha-am, which he had already translated for

[12]Morris Schussheim, "Recollection," p. 173.
[13]*PP*, p. 165.

Central European Jewry. A Zionist from his student days, he became active in the Federation of American Zionists soon after his arrival in this country.

As a participant in the organization's inner councils, he met two men who would figure prominently in his life. Richard Gottheil, the first president of the organization, was professor of Semitics at Columbia; with him he shared a common academic interest. Harry Friedenwald, the ophthalmologist and medical historian from Baltimore and president of the Zionist Federation from 1904 to 1910, became his lifelong friend and confidant.

Friedenwald's efforts on his behalf created the third major trial of Friedlaender's life. It occurred in May 1907, eight months after his thirtieth birthday, and indicated that he had never resolved the inner conflicts over his life's direction. It will be recalled that at the first critical juncture of his life, he had embarked upon a career of oriental scholarship. At the second, when he decided to join the Seminary faculty as professor of Bible, Schechter assured him that the new position did not demand abandonment of his primary academic interests. He dangled before the young man the prospect of long summer vacations free for scholarly research.

And, indeed, Friedlaender did seize the opportunity. Notwithstanding the birth of four children during the prewar years, the family spent three summers in Europe. There Lilian and the children, Herzl, Ben-Zion, Carmel, and Judith, enjoyed the hospitality of the Bentwiches; their husband and father repaired to the archives of Oxford and the Continent.

Despite this apparently satisfactory arrangement, Friedlaender was not content with his position as professor of Bible. What had initially appeared to be an admirable arrangement turned out to be a disconcerting one. Even as Friedlaender energetically pursued his oriental studies, he knew that he was not fulfilling his initial promise to Schechter: to contribute to biblical scholarship. That Friedlaender was uncomfortably aware of the schizophrenic character of his academic life was indicated in a letter written to Harry Friedenwald in 1907, in which he complained: "The chair I occupy is not the one for which my previous studies and inner inclinations fit me best."[14] He was convinced that "the endeavors to combine both [biblical and Semitic studies] have only had an injurious effect

[14]IF to Harry Friedenwald, May 22, 1907, *Friedenwald MSS.*

upon my productivity as a scholar."[15] It was for this reason that he decided at that time to follow Friedenwald's advice and associate himself with a project that was still on the drawing boards. Two years before, the philanthropist Moses Dropsie had died; he had willed his fortune to the establishment of a Jewish institution of higher learning in Philadelphia. Friedlaender applied for the chair of Semitic languages at the new Dropsie College for Hebrew and Cognate Learning. Schechter encouraged the move, with the proviso that he continue to teach at the Seminary as well. Because of a plan which envisioned Dropsie College, Graetz College, and the Jewish Theological Seminary as branches of a single university, this did not seem farfetched. In discussing the matter with Friedenwald in a letter dated May 22, 1907, Friedlaender did not rule out this possibility, even though he realized that such an arrangement "would only augment the split of energy of which I complain even now."[16]

A second letter, dated May 27, gave Friedlaender's response to his nomination for the presidency of the new Dropsie College. Suppressing his obvious pride and excitement, he modestly suggested two alternatives, either a self-governing faculty "similar to the Berlin Hochschule or the Breslau Seminary" or a lesser title for head of the college, "secretary, registrar, everything which would enable him to help in the practical work of the institution."

Details of what happened after that are unavailable. It is clear, however, that when the Dropsie College opened in 1908, Cyrus Adler was its undisputed president.[17] Friedlaender bore the disappointment with good grace, writing Adler a congratulatory note in March of that year and receiving the self-effacing reply, "[I] am glad that you have more faith in me than I have in myself."[18] In a note to Friedenwald written at that time, Friedlaender insisted that he retained his ambition to assume "higher responsibility than I have at present." For the time being he continued to be tortured by the lack of "a clear individual goal for my activity."[19]

With no well-defined single objective, Friedlaender undertook a

---

[15]Ibid.

[16]Ibid.

[17]In a letter to Simon Wolf, dated July 9, 1908, Adler claimed that no other scholar-administrator was available, *Adler MSS.*

[18]Cyrus Adler to IF, March 20, 1908, *FP.*

[19]IF to Friedenwald, March 17, 1908, *Friedenwald MSS.*

number of projects, literary and communal. Between 1908 and 1914 he completed all of the Semitic studies that he had initiated during his years at Strassburg, some of which he translated and edited for his new English-speaking audience. In addition, he contributed the results of new research in Jewish law, philology, and history to the *Jewish Quarterly Review* (JQR), then edited by Schechter and Adler, as well as several *Festschriften* published in Europe. Nor did he abandon his first literary love, the Hebrew revival; he contributed occasional articles to the fragile American Hebrew press and expatiated upon the theme of the old-new language in articles and lectures delivered before lay audiences. With great enthusiasm, he supported Eliezer Ben-Yehudah's fund-raising trip to America and all but convinced Ahad Ha-am to journey to this country in order to deliver a series of lectures at Dropsie College.[20]

Out of fear for his health, well-wishers such as Marx, Asher Ginsberg, and even Cyrus Adler warned him to slow down.[21] Stubbornly, he heeded none of these warnings. In addition to his scholarly labors and continuing support of the Hebrew renaissance, he also plunged headlong into public life.

He was an early supporter of the efforts of Judah Magnes to create a community marked by "order, unity and a popular base."[22] The New York Kehillah, or Jewish Community of New York, came into existence in the spring of 1909, under the leadership of Magnes and with the financial backing of the Jewish notables of New York, led by Jacob Schiff. At every stage of its short-lived existence, Friedlaender championed the organization. Before its establishment, he aroused interest in its cause by lecturing on the need for well-run bureaus to supervise ritual slaughter, prevent crime, and organize philanthropy.[23] Until his final journey to Europe, he served on its executive committee. His best efforts, however, were reserved for the Bureau of Jewish Education, the organization's most successful organ. Vehemently, he argued the bureau's merits before opponents on the right and on the left,

[20]Ahad Ha-am, *Igrot Ahad Ha-am* 4:188-190 (January 4, 1911); 5:60-62 (June 3, 1913).

[21]Marx to IF, August 28, 1910, *FP*; Ahad Ha-am, *Igrot* 4:156-157 (October 20, 1910); Adler to IF, November 1, 1909, *FP*.

[22]Arthur A. Goren, *New York Jews and the Quest for Community: The Kehillah Experiment, 1909-1922* (New York, 1970), p. 56.

[23]Box 9, *FP*, contains an outline of a speech entitled "Religious Problems in New York City," which deals with this problem.

defending its position even when it was challenged by the Seminary administration. To inform the wider public of the new system, Friedlaender composed a lengthy report on the subject of elementary Jewish education for the U.S. Department of the Interior.[24]

At the same time Friedlaender joined organizations dedicated to raising the Jewish consciousness of older students. One was the Menorah movement, which served college youth. Friedlaender solicited books for this organization from uptown magnates,[25] contributed articles to its journal, and lectured extensively on college campuses. He performed similar services for the Intercollegiate Zionist Federation. Not only did he join existing youth organizations; he also created new ones. In 1909 he became the founding president of Young Judea, an amalgam of several Zionist youth groups; with Mordecai Kaplan he helped to establish Young Israel in 1912 to perpetuate traditional religion among the downtown Jews.

Nor did he overlook the adult Jewish public. Like Masliansky, Friedlaender can be characterized as a member of the first generation of American *maggidim* (of whom Maurice Samuel was the best example of the second). They were Jews of identifiable East European origin who usually lectured in English, charismatic speakers who set out to educate general audiences on topics of contemporary Jewish interest.

Friedlaender was at his best in delivering public addresses.[26] The size of the forum did not concern him; he addressed a national convention of a large organization and a local branch of the New York Public Library with equal verve. His eloquent prose charmed the members of youth organizations and lay audiences of Russian immigrants but sometimes alarmed the zealous Americanizers who controlled the Educational Alliance and the American Jewish Committee. Not a spellbinder like Stephen Wise, he spoke informally, in conversational tones which were always serious but never solemn. His lectures were studded with biblical allusions,

---

[24]Under the title "The Problem of Jewish Education in America and the Bureau of Education of the Jewish Community of New York City," *Report of the Commission of Education for the Year Ended June 30, 1913*. Part of the report was reprinted in *PP* (1919), pp. 279-307.

[25]Warburg to IF, April 20, 1912; Schiff to IF, November 1, 1915, *FP*.

[26]See testimonials collected by Morris Adler, *FP*, Box 12; corroborated from personal interviews by this writer with Solomon Grayzel and Simon Greenberg.

abounded in stories and jokes, and often referred to contemporary issues.

A 1917 lecture, for example, compared the existence of European Jewry before the Emancipation to life in the trenches of World War I in France.[27] Another popular address delivered during the same period described Jewry after the Emancipation as a household of sisters who had always been devoted to their old "mother Zion."

> They were happy in their unity, they were happy in their affection. Then came emancipation, and one after the other the sisters began to leave their home to join the larger life of the world around. And the married daughters sometimes forgot their old mother and the sisters they had left behind. They would send an occasional contribution towards the upkeep of the old home, but absorbed by their new duties and fascinated by new attractions, they would care but little for what was going on within its walls.[28]

In this case, the metaphor was no mere figure of speech, but a description of the personal situation of many in his audience. It is easy to imagine the sense of nostalgia tinged with guilt which it evoked.

Friedlaender's public addresses always drew a crowd; many were subsequently published. An article which appeared in one organ of the Anglo-Jewish Press, the *Baltimore Jewish Comment*, for example, would find its way into another, the *Philadelphia Exponent* or the *American Israelite* of Cincinnati. In his later years, Friedlaender became a respected spokesman for the Zionist cause and the Russian-Jewish condition in leading secular publications. The *New York Times*, *New York Post*, and *Century* magazine printed his articles; his book reviews and short columns became a standard feature of the *Nation*. A lover of travel, Friedlaender frequently journeyed to Boston to address the very active Menorah Society of Harvard University. He would often spend a weekend in more distant cities, returning more than once to such places as Detroit and New Orleans.

To appreciate the intensity and vigor of the man, let us examine his administrative and communal activities during the academic

[27] *Aspects* IV, 3.
[28] *PP*, p. 325.

year 1910-1911, when Friedlaender was thirty-five years old. The Seminary had acquired a second branch, a Teachers' Institute, in 1909, adding to his duties as professor and chairman of the Student Loan Fund the responsibilities of training future Jewish educators. Friedlaender's interest in the education of the very young led to his assumption of the role of chairman of the board of trustees of the Bureau of Jewish Education. As we previously noted, he was already a member of the Kehillah Executive and, as a consequence, of the American Jewish Committee as well.

In 1910-11 Schechter took a leave of absence. During this time, Friedlaender served as his deputy, keeping in close touch with the Seminary president, but also making important decisions on his own, such as setting into motion the creation of the United Synagogue.[29]

During the same period, Friedlaender became the official leader of American Zionism. The very week when his second son, Ben Zion, was born (on July 4, 1910), Friedlaender was in Pittsburgh, accepting the chairmanship of the executive committee of the Zionist Federation (FAZ). In this capacity he served for a year, with only Henrietta Szold and Judah Magnes to aid him.[30] At the same time, he continued his service as secretary of the short-lived but important Achavah Club, a forum for intellectuals committed to the renascence of Jewish national life.[31]

All of these activities left Friedlaender with insufficient time to continue his Semitic studies. In the course of time, he completed the scholarly projects initiated in Germany, but undertook no new ones. Gradually his attention shifted to the East European milieu which he had abandoned in his youth. A major undertaking during the period of the First World War was his three-volume translation of Dubnow's *History of the Jews of Russia and Poland*. Friedlaender's public lectures of the period dealt with a matter of major concern to

---

[29]In the *Rubenovitz MSS*, Box 1, are several letters from Friedlaender on this subject. Herman and Mignon Rubenovitz published two of them in their book, *The Waking Heart* (Cambridge, Mass., 1967), pp. 126-127, 132-133. See also Herbert Rosenblum, "The Founding of the United Synagogue of America" (Ph.D. diss., Brandeis University, 1970), pp. 151-181.

[30]He acknowledged the help of these great and dear friends in his closing speech to the FAZ, which was delivered in Yiddish. See *Dos Yiddishe Folk*, May 26, 1911.

[31]Using documents from *FP*, Box 8, Moshe Davis has published the records of the Achavah Club, under the title "Israel Friedlaender's Minute Book of the *Achavah* Club (1909-1912)" in *Mordecai M. Kaplan Jubilee Volume* (New York, 1953), pp. 157-213 (hereafter cited as "Minute Book").

Jewish immigrants from Eastern Europe, the fate of their relatives living in what had become the war's eastern front. He buoyed their spirits with recitals of Polish Jewry's past achievements and dreams of a brighter future for both the American and Russian branches of the common stem.

It was Friedlaender's fruitless endeavor to establish peace within fractious American Jewry that generated the fourth major crisis of his life. This one, unlike the previous three, was protracted, extending for more than a year (1915-1916). Moreover, it involved no fewer than three issues that were dear to his heart: Jewish education, the Americanization of the immigrants, and the creation of an American Jewish Congress. Later chapters of this study will treat each of them in depth. Here it is sufficient to recount that Friedlaender produced a long and serious analysis of each situation, proposing reasonable solutions to each problem. However, in each case, he was disappointed by the tepid reaction to his proposals. The following mordant observation dealt with the Congress issue; it revealed his feelings about the others as well.

> I am glad you liked my article on the present situation in American Jewry. It shares the fate of virtuous women who are best thought of when they are least spoken of. I had hoped that my analysis might lead to a fruitful discussion of the present crisis and help to relieve the unbearable tension in our public life. But thus far the only response noticeable has been that of complete silence.[32]

Friedlaender's response to the silence was to resign from the Bureau of Jewish Education, the Educational Alliance, the American Jewish Committee, and the Provisional Zionist Committee (PC). Such was his commitment to public life, however, that he soon resumed a role, albeit a more modest one, in each of the organizations.

The year 1915-1916 produced yet another heartache. Friedlaender's relations with Cyrus Adler had always been correct and cordial, but never close. Although the two men worked together in preparing publications for the JQR and the JPS, their views on several issues were not compatible. In June 1915, Friedlaender hotly defended two causes which Adler had attacked publicly, the communal organization of Jewish education and the right of a

[32]IF to Professor Joseph Jacob, January 18, 1916, *FP*.

nonpracticing Jew, Louis Brandeis, to head American Zionism.[33] Several months after this bitter exchange, on November 20, 1915, Schechter died unexpectedly. Adler was soon afterwards selected to serve as acting president of the Jewish Theological Seminary, even as he continued to serve Dropsie College in the same capacity. For Friedlaender, this change not only thwarted a personal ambition; it also put him in the uncomfortable position of serving an institution under the leadership of a man whose perspective on Jewish life differed dramatically from his own.

Of the unfortunate events of 1915-1916 it was the personal slight by the Zionist leaders that cut most deeply. We have seen that Friedlaender registered his disapproval with the policies of various organizations by resigning from membership. In doing so, he was playing a role in a charade known to all. According to the rules of the game, the next step was for the organization to select a committee which would then draft a resolution imploring the resignee to reconsider. Whether or not the person then withdrew his resignation, the game had been played to the finish. When Friedlaender resigned from the Provisional Committee on July 3, 1916, however, no resolution appeared. On August 11, Jacob de Haas, a confidant of Brandeis and Wise, leaders of the organization, wrote him a letter of apology. The note informed him that the PC had indeed appointed a committee (of three) to compose a letter urging him to withdraw his resignation. De Haas claimed that he himself had prepared the draft but Wise had mislaid it, thinking a copy had already been transcribed and duly remitted.[34] Subsequently, Friedlaender consented to rejoin the PC,[35] unaware that this distasteful incident prefigured things to come.

Friedlaender smarted under the unforeseen and undeserved rebuffs of 1915-1916, yet such was his sense of "present crisis" in American Jewish life that he never considered abandoning public service. Aware that the European war was weakening the bonds he had helped to forge between the "Yidn" and the "Yahudim," he resolved to continue to function as a link between the two communities, as instructor and exemplar. To Samuel Strauss, his opponent on the issue of Americanization, he wrote: "From the very beginning of my association with the [Educational] Alliance I

[33]IF to Adler, June 7, 1915, *FP*.
[34]Jacob de Haas to IF, August 11, 1916, *FP*.
[35]See IF to Friedenwald, May 8, 1917, *FP*.

conceived it as my particular function to pave the way for a better understanding between the powers that be at our Institution and the constituency which it is called upon to serve."[36] To Lee Kohns, another of the uptown magnates, he explained why he considered himself a mediating influence between the two groups: "The fact that I had had to undergo in my life two or three times a complex change in environmental language and that I have had in my scholarly career an opportunity of thinking various modes of human thought . . . has enabled me not only to understand but also to appreciate ideas and associations radically different from my own."[37]

Friedlaender was equally proud of his East European background and his German university education, equally comfortable with the denizens of the ghetto and the members of the Seminary's board of trustees. Unlike most East European intellectuals, he cultivated the friendship of upper-class Jews sympathetic to the cause of Jewish life, lawyers such as Julian Mack and Louis Marshall, and businessmen such as Jacob Schiff and Nathan Straus. Yet, despite the admiration which he inspired among the uptown leaders, they never considered him one of their own. The issue was one of substance rather than style. Though Friedlaender quoted Goethe with the best of them, they considered his proposals for retaining the ancient modes of prayer and socialization to be retrogressive. Though his letters were peppered with German expressions, his spirited defense of Zionism only strengthened their fear of dual loyalty. This probably explains why they ignored his reasoned proposal for resolving the dispute over the creation of an American Jewish Congress, even though he actually supported their position.

Friedlaender was more welcome in East European circles; it was primarily Russian Jews who constituted his lecture audiences and reading public. However, his ideas did not reflect the prevailing tendencies of the Lower East Side. Its residents were more interested in preserving Yiddish than in promoting Hebrew education, more attracted to radical social movements than to Zionism. Hyman Grinstein has noted, "At a time when the Socialists could have filled to overflowing the square in front of the *Forward* building, on

[36]January 8, 1917, *FP.*
[37]November 5, 1918, *FP.*

New York's lower East Side, the Zionists could hardly have filled a small hall in the same neighborhood."[38] Even within the Zionist movement, Friedlaender found scant camaraderie. Though he retained the respect of all Zionists and continued to produce useful Zionist pamphlets even after his resignation from the executive position, few of his fellow workers shared or even understood his Ahad Ha-amist point of view.

It seems that no aspect of Friedlaender's multiple communal activity yielded unqualified personal satisfaction. Why, then, didn't he follow the advice of his faculty colleagues and abandon the public forum? The answer must lie in the character of the man, which was molded in his early years. However, in the absence of any data whatsoever about his childhood and youth, it is impossible to deliver a psychological profile of our subject. What we do know is that he was endowed with a penetrating critical acumen and an equally strong emotional impulse and was determined to exercise both in the service of Judaism.

Evidence of his deeply passionate nature were his visits to Hasidic rabbis during his adolescence and his attraction to the leading philosopher and historian of Jewish national revival during his student days. Even his choice of subject matter for scholarly analysis bears witness to this distinguishing characteristic. Periods of religious history marked by restless longing for salvation and unbounded messianic enthusiasm enlisted Friedlaender's attention, placing him outside of the rationalist *Wissenschaft* tradition and inside the camp of the neoromantic historians.

Also confirming the young scholar's deeply emotional nature is the following excerpt from the letter which he wrote to Schechter, officially accepting the position of professor of Bible at the Jewish Theological Seminary.

My responsibility to my students is to impart to them a basic knowledge of the Bible, knowledge which will awaken in them the *love* of Bible. I do not intend to treat the Bible as a document of the past, of mere antiquarian interest. Instead, in the spirit of historical Judaism, I will demonstrate how it will form the basis of the Judaism of the present and the future.[39]

---

[38]In "The Efforts of East European Jewry to Organize Its Own Community in the United States," *PAJHS* 49 (December 1959): 84.

[39]IF to Schechter, August 7, 1903, *FP* (his emphasis).

That knowledge was greater than book learning was a thesis popular with turn-of-the-century German philosophers, among them Wilhelm Windelband, Friedlaender's teacher. It became a theme of many of his public lectures. In 1915, he informed a college group:

> Jewish knowledge to me is valuable in the sense in which the word "knowledge" is employed in Hebrew. For "to know" in Hebrew (*yada*) does not merely mean to conceive intellectually, but expresses at the same time the deepest emotions of the human soul; it also means to care, to cherish, to love. It is remarkable indeed that the only Hebrew expression which in any way approaches what in modern languages we call religion is *daath elohim*, the knowledge of God. . . . We want to be frank about our Judaism, we want to be clear about our faults, we want to remedy our faults whenever we can, but at the same time we want to have the sympathy that goes with knowledge.[40]

Behind Friedlaender's activities on behalf of Jewish religion, education, and Zionism was the desire to instill into the young American Jewish community "the sympathy that goes with knowledge." The problem was that if these undertakings satisfied the emotional side of Friedlaender's nature, they also consumed time necessary for scholarly pursuits. That this troubled him deeply is evident from his correspondence. A letter to Schechter written in 1911 complained: "The pressure of work, perhaps still more, the strain of responsibility, has indeed been very great, and I am going to return to my literary work, which I have greatly neglected."[41] For Dubnow Friedlaender described America as "the land of wonder and terror . . . [where it is] difficult to work without interruption."[42]

At the time of his feud with the trustees of the Educational Alliance, he gave a bitter account of the high cost of public service. "Every meeting," he informed Richard Gottheil, "involves loss of sleep and food, not to speak of the loss of time which I can ill afford."[43] Nevertheless, in the very next paragraph he answered his correspondent's request to do some (unspecified) work for the University Zionist Society with these words: "It does not permit of

[40]"From a Menorah Address," in *MJ* 1 (January 1915): 38.
[41]IF to Schechter, February 16, 1911, *Schechter MSS.*
[42]In "Jewry, East and West (The Correspondence of Israel Friedlaender and Simon Dubnow)," ed. Moshe Davis, *YIVO Annual of Jewish Social Science* 9 (New York, 1954): 31; from *FP* Box 9.
[43]January 9, 1917, *FP*.

a refusal. I am entirely in your hands. I hope you will be merciful."[44]

In actuality, it was Friedlaender who was unmerciful to himself, as the aforementioned statement to Dubnow signified. At first America seemed a "land of wonder," offering a secure academic position unavailable in Europe, a favorable chance for scholarly achievement, and the opportunity for public service. Yet even before war clouds from Europe began to darken the sunny American skies, Friedlaender learned that America was also a "land of terror." His fervent ardor for Jewish revival, fueled with a Dickensian conviction that he was living in the worst of times, rendered exclusive concentration on scholarship an impossibility.

Nevertheless, as Friedlaender approached his fortieth birthday, the mishnaic "age of understanding,"[45] in September 1916, he could anticipate a promising future both for himself and for the community which he so diligently served. The birth of Joy Nechama in 1915 had enlarged the family once again: now he was the proud father of five handsome children. As far as his personal goals were concerned, if he had not as yet advanced beyond the status of professor at a small rabbinical seminary, he could be proud of his reputation as a scholar of unusual intellectual and moral stature, a lecturer and writer of note. If the problems of Russian Jewry on both sides of the Atlantic consumed his attention during wartime, he retained his hopes of a postwar resumption of the research on several Maimonides manuscripts from the Seminary's *geniza* collection. Offsetting the personal disappointments which he had suffered was the near-achievement of goals for which he had long labored. Discomfiture over his own reduced role in American Zionism was counterbalanced by the welcome fact that the movement was finally securing a large following. And, indeed, as compensation for the poor response to his analysis of the Congress controversy, he could rejoice in the settlement of the dispute that very month.

Basically optimistic, Israel Friedlaender could reasonably reckon upon several decades of continued academic accomplishment, and of participation in the growth and development of his own young family, the Seminary, the Zionist movement, New York Jewry, and the American Jewish community at large.

[44] Ibid.
[45] *Abot* 5:24.

Chapter 2
Crisis, Death, and Transfiguration

While our heart is aroused over the martyrs that fell by the hands of violent mobs, we witness with indifference the disappearance of that for which they became martyrs.

—*Israel Friedlaender*

Israel Friedlaender's life was a microcosm of Jewish existence in the early twentieth century. He belonged to a cohort of talented young men from traditional Jewish homes introduced to Western culture through the medium of the German university. At the time when the young scholar sought direction for his life, an entire generation of Jewish youth was caught up in cross-currents of enlightenment and national revival and the search for cultural and religious authenticity. It was not only students and scholars like Friedlaender, but a considerable portion of East European Jews, who traveled westward—to Germany, to England, and, in largest numbers, to the United States—for the purpose of bettering their lot in life.

The enormous migration of 1890 to 1910 created the largest urban concentration of Jews in all history; a million Jews inhabited New York City. Their problems loomed so large that Friedlaender never assumed the position of a narrow specialist; instead he became a leader concerned with the broad scope of Jewish experience. By the second decade of the new century, it seemed that

Jewish communal life, having survived the hazards of organization, was beginning to flourish. Friedlaender proved himself equally resilient; he bore the rebuffs of Zionist and communal leaders with equanimity, resolving to continue his labors on behalf of American and world Jewry.

Neither Friedlaender nor the American Jewish community was allowed to ripen slowly into maturity; the Great War catapulted both into positions of prominence. Because this country was neutral for the first two and a half years of the war, it became the hub of world Jewish activity. It served as the *Nachtasyl* for European and Palestinian workers as diverse as Shmarya Levin, David Ben-Gurion, Eliezer Ben-Yehudah, and Aaron Aaronsohn. The Provisional Executive Committee for General Zionist Affairs, under the leadership of Louis Brandeis, became the center of world Zionism. Furthermore, because American Jewry was the only important Jewish community physically untouched by the war, it assumed the staggering burden of administering aid to needy brethren in the Old World. In the course of time, the three major relief organizations, representing different ideological and sociological divisions in the community,[1] established a combined effort, the American Jewish Joint Distribution Committee, commonly known as the "Joint."

Palestine and European relief were issues which dominated Friedlaender's life during the war and its aftermath; indeed, they generated the final two crises of his life. At first, the "relief" which he proffered was spiritual rather than material. He strongly believed that the immigrant community could plot its course into the future only if it thoroughly understood its past. His portrayal of the history of East European Jewry took several forms: a three-volume translation of Dubnow's history of that group, a one-volume summary of that history, shorter magazine pieces, and numerous lectures.

Although Friedlaender served on the Provisional Committee,[2] most of his efforts on behalf of Zion were also of a theoretical nature. Frequently, he was called upon to produce a position paper on a Zionist issue or to deliver a lecture on the foundations of the movement to an elite group or a mass meeting. At one point, he

---

[1]They were the American Jewish Relief Committee, organized by the magnates, Orthodoxy's Central Relief Committee, and the People's Relief Committee, representing labor.
[2]As its recording secretary and archivist.

almost convinced Jacob Schiff to abandon the position of "non-Zionist" for that of "Zionist."[3] As a lifelong Zionist, Friedlaender greeted news of the Balfour Declaration with exhilaration, expressing the feeling in two ways. He increased his literary output on the subject and named his third son and sixth child, Daniel Balfour, in honor of the British foreign secretary.

All Zionists welcomed international recognition of their movement in what seemed to be a facsimile of Herzl's "Charter." Unfortunately, the actual situation of the Jewish community of Palestine offered little cause for rejoicing. The war had all but destroyed the economic and demographic base of the *yishuv*. Turkey, an ally of Germany, demanded that Russian Jewish settlers, now enemy aliens, either depart the country or take on Turkish citizenship. Many left; those who did not were conscripted either into the beleaguered Ottoman army or the infamous local labor battalions. Both groups were subjected to back-breaking labor, malnutrition, and impossibly poor living conditions. To add to the misery, the Turkish policy of requisitioning farm animals, agricultural tools, and foodstuffs reduced the Jewish settlements to destitution. As long as the United States remained neutral, however, it was able, through the good offices of Henry Morgenthau, Sr., its (Jewish) ambassador to Turkey, to bring in occasional supplies of food and currency and thereby stave off total starvation.[4]

Precipitating the penultimate crisis in Friedlaender's life was his interest in the dispensing of relief to Palestinian Jews. Unfortunately, joyous anticipation of an opportunity to serve them was followed by a last-minute rebuff, which turned national recognition into public humiliation. It began with his appointment to a relief mission in February 1918.

This mission must be seen in the larger context. During the previous autumn General Allenby had launched the British invasion of Palestine. His triumphal march into Palestine had taken place in December, yet parts of the north would remain in Turkish hands for another ten months. To observers it was obvious that assistance could not wait for the final victory. No fewer than three

---

[3]Jacob Schiff to IF, January 7, 1918, *FP*.
[4]See Howard M. Sachar, *A History of Israel from the Rise of Zionism to Our Time* (New York, 1976), pp. 89-90, and Ronald Sanders, *The High Wall of Jerusalem* (New York, 1983), pp. 139-140.

bodies were created to render aid. The first was a Zionist Commission organized in London under the leadership of Chaim Weizmann. As long as a state of hostilities existed in Palestine the State Department would allow no American to join it. It did, however, permit the organization of two relief missions in the United States. One was a Hadassah Medical Unit, under the direction of Alice Seligsberg. Overriding Secretary of State Lansing's objection, President Wilson authorized both the mission and its new insignia, a red Star of David. The other was a relief mission created by the American Red Cross under the sponsorship of the President's War Council. The Red Cross invited the Joint Distribution Committee, which had already performed important relief work, to select one or two Jewish members for this project.[5]

By the time these commissions were organized, most U.S. citizens supported the British conquest of Palestine in particular and the Allied war effort in general. This endorsement however required a disavowal of sentiments which many Americans had previously held. At the inception of hostilities in 1914, the majority had favored neutrality; as late as 1916, Wilson had campaigned on the slogan "He kept us out of war." The early position of most American Jews had also been neutral, but with a tilt to the Central Powers. How could they support England and France, which were allied with czarist Russia, the persecutor of their European brethren? For them it was providential that the United States declared war on Germany in April 1917, a few weeks after revolution toppled czardom: now they could wholeheartedly sustain the Allied cause.

America's entry into the war created new problems. As masses of young men trained to fight in the European theater, a spirit of war hysteria stalked the land. Many citizens became fanatical anti-Germans. Friedlaender's involvement in the Red Cross Commission sheds an unfavorable light upon the emotional state of an immature nation peremptorily embroiled in world war and a minority community struggling for legitimacy.

His adversaries were two important Zionists with whom he had previously maintained cordial relations. Richard Gottheil, a fellow Semitics scholar, had once labeled Friedlaender "the foremost

---

[5]That the number of Jewish members was unclear was later revealed in contradictory testimony before the JDC. See below, p. 31.

Arabist of this country."[6] Stephen S. Wise, who became chairman of the Provisional Committee after Louis D. Brandeis' appointment to the Supreme Court, had recommended Friedlaender to deliver the important Adolph Lewisohn Lectures explaining Conservative Judaism in 1917.

On February 14, 1918, at the suggestion of Louis Marshall, the Executive Committee of the JDC invited Friedlaender to go to Palestine as the Jewish representative on the Red Cross expedition.[7] Hesitating only to obtain his wife's consent, he eagerly accepted. He later wrote:

> The ease with which I reached a decision, fraught with grave possibilities and responsibilities both of a public and private nature, was due to the fact that the prospect of assisting, however humbly, in the establishment of the Third Jewish Commonwealth appeared in my eyes as the realization of a dream fondly cherished by me since the days of my childhood, and as the consummation of a life and training which seemed to have been a continuous preparation for the task in store for me.[8]

On February 27, Friedlaender went to Washington. First he contacted Cornelius N. Bliss of the War Council. After answering questions about the loyalty of the Friedlaender and Bentwich families to Bliss's apparent satisfaction, Friedlaender received what he considered to be official confirmation of his appointment.[9] There followed a meeting with Brandeis in which Friedlaender received the imprimatur of the Zionist office. The following morning, Dr. Ward, chairman of the expedition, conferred upon him the rank of

[6]See Louis Finklestein's Introduction to *Past and Present*, p. x. In a personal interview on March 15, 1978, Finklestein confirmed that it was Gottheil who described Friedlaender with these words.

[7]See the correspondence between Louis Brandeis, Stephen Wise, and Jacob de Haas during February 1918, *de Haas MSS*, *Brandeis MSS*, and *Wise MSS*.

[8]Herbert Parzen published the documents pertaining to Friedlaender's involvement in the Red Cross Commission in the *Herzl Yearbook* 6 (1964-65): 321-368, under the same title as his study in *JSS*, "Conservative Judaism and Zionism." See p. 328 for this part of Friedlaender's testimony.

[9]In reality, this was not the case. As Rudolph A. Clemen, Jr., information specialist of the Library of the American Red Cross, informed me in a letter, dated August 16, 1979. "An ironic aftermath of this matter is the fact that Dr. Friedlaender had been granted a commission, but it was not approved by the War Council until a year later on February 27, 1919, the day before the War Council was discontinued, when his name was submitted with thirty-six others for approval. Obviously, his name should not have been on this list, since he did not serve, but he may have received a commission certificate at that time because of this error."

major. Friedlaender quickly returned home to make the necessary
arrangements for the long journey.

In New York Friedlaender accepted the congratulations of
friends and acquaintances. Even Cyrus Adler bestowed his
guarded approval, at the same time warning the immigrant professor, "Your name and foreign birth render the greatest discretion
upon your part, which I am sure you will not fail to exercise."[10]
Then suddenly, in the midst of final preparations, Friedlaender
incurred a last-minute rebuff, which turned joyous anticipation
into extreme distress. At a farewell party arranged by his students,
he received an alarming phone call; a newspaper reporter introduced him to highly disturbing charges. First was the claim that
Friedlaender's appointment created a "rift" in the Zionist ranks.
Even more serious was the report of the double-barreled assault by
Richard Gottheil, who had informed the reporter that pro-German
forces in New York had imposed Friedlaender upon the Red Cross
Commission. Gottheil had also insisted that Friedlaender was
unsuitable in his own right, "having been outspokenly pro-German
prior to the war and ominously silent since then."[11]

Despite Friedlaender's furious disclaimers, Gottheil's statement
appeared in the *New York Sun* the following morning, March 7,
1918. That afternoon Bliss telephoned Felix Warburg the news that
opposition to Friedlaender's appointment had "developed from a
highly placed source" and that for this reason, his appointment had
to be "kept in abeyance."[12] Upon learning of this, Friedlaender
submitted his resignation to Bliss on March 8, even as he protested
the groundlessness of the charge. Nevertheless, on the same day an
article appeared in the *New York Times*, under the heading "Appointment of Dr. Friedlaender to Palestine Red Cross Mission
Meets with Opposition."[13] It reported an interview of the previous
evening in which Stephen Wise stated that he had never considered
Friedlaender a suitable candidate for the commission. At the time
the name was first suggested, he insisted,

> I earnestly urged the members of the Committee including Mr. War-
> burg, not to designate Professor Friedlaender on the ground that he was

[10]Adler to IF, March 4, 1918, *FP*.
[11]These were the words used by Gottheil in the *New York Sun* article of March 7. See
Parzen "Conservative Judaism" *(Herzl Yearbook)*, p. 321.
[12]Ibid., p. 332.
[13]*New York Times*, March 8, 1918, p. 11.

widely suspected of pro-German sympathies prior to our advent into the war, and that, moreover, it had been reported that a protest would be lodged against Professor Friedlaender's designation if it should be made.

The Committee which had the matter in charge was apparently undisturbed by the possibility of such a protest and proceeded to procure the designation of Professor Friedlaender. No question has been raised with respect to the integrity of Professor Friedlaender as a man or of his pro-American sentiments at this time. The only question that was raised was whether it was fitting to send anyone in the name of the Red Cross to a territory occupied by the British military authorities who had failed to be outspokenly pro-Ally prior to America's entrance into the war.[14]

Thus did the official leader of American Zionism support the innuendos of the jingoistic professor.

Every chronicler of Friedlaender's life has dealt with this incident,[15] yet no one has answered or even asked the most fundamental question which it raises: What was the origin of the "highly placed source" ultimately responsible for Friedlaender's dismissal? Our research has not culminated in a definitive solution to the problem. But it has uncovered several facts that point in a certain direction.

Richard James Horatio Gottheil, the English-born academic, abandoned scholarly objectivity for the duration of the war in order to ferret out German sympathizers. He pressed the Zionist organization to censor several writers, and personally cast aspersions on Alice Seligsberg's loyalty, which Brandeis hotly defended.[16] Apparently, his protests crossed the ocean; when the Hadassah Medical Unit reached England, it was not allowed to proceed to Palestine until British authorities investigated charges against its leader. Gottheil's suspicious disposition made him a willing conduit of innuendo against anyone who appeared lukewarm about the war effort. It is true that before the United States entered the war,

[14]Parzen, "Conservative Judaism" *(Herzl Yearbook)*, p. 323.

[15]The most extensive treatment of the issue was made by Herbert Parzen in his "Conservative Judaism and Zionism (1896-1922)," *JSS* 23 (October 1961): 253-258, and the chapter on Friedlaender in his book *Architects of Conservative Judaism* (New York, 1964), pp. 180-187. Though highly detailed and informative, they are not analytical, nor do they use archival sources not found in the Library of the Jewish Theological Seminary.

[16]*Letters of Louis D. Brandeis*, ed. Melvin I. Urofsky and David W. Levy, 5 vols. (Albany, 1971-78), 4:340-341.

Friedlaender, like most American Jews, had not supported the Allies. Moreover, even after April 1917, he took pains to distinguish between the kaiser's aggressive militarism, which he abhorred, and German *Kultur*, which he admired. For the chauvinistic Professor Gottheil, this civilized and balanced attitude must have offered proof of Friedlaender's unsuitability for a sensitive position in British-occupied territory. Nevertheless, it is almost certain that Gottheil did not initiate the objections to Friedlaender, for a letter written to Wise late in 1918 clearly indicates that it was Wise who introduced him to "the Friedlaender business": "[You] put me up and egged me on to taking a stand in the matter."[17]

This raises the more serious question of Stephen Wise, who, like Gottheil, was also a superpatriot, but with a different background. From the outbreak of hostilities in Europe, he had opposed Wilson's policy of "preparedness," i.e., rearmament. As late as February 12, 1917, two months before the United States entered the war, he had been an ardent pacifist, appealing to German-Americans to help overthrow militarism by resisting military service. After April, however, he performed a complete about-face, speaking at Carnegie Hall in praise of Wilson's declaration of war, denouncing the neutralists with whom he was once allied, supporting the draft, even deprecating "treasonable use of free speech by alien anarchists."[18]

All of this notwithstanding, intense chauvinism was probably not responsible for Wise's press release of March 8. Nor did Stephen Wise bear Friedlaender any personal ill will. As the leader of American Zionism, he was, in all likelihood, governed instead, by feelings of Zionist pique.

From a letter written by Jacob de Haas to Brandeis[19] we learn that the Zionists feared that the Red Cross Mission would detract attention from the two Jewish-sponsored groups. It is possible that Wise's statement to the press attempted to discredit the American expedition by impugning the suitability of its Jewish member. It also furnished an effective weapon against the JDC, which had solicited permission from the Red Cross to designate the Jewish

[17]Richard Gottheil to Stephen Wise, November 27, 1918, *Wise MSS*. He also made the same claim in an earlier letter, dated July 29, 1918, *Wise MSS*.

[18]Friedlaender collected those and other data on this matter. See *FP*, Box 6; also Zosa Szajkowski, *Jews, Wars and Communism I* (New York, 1972), chap. 7.

[19]March 6, 1918, *de Haas MSS*.

member of the expedition. In the opinion of the Zionists, their organization, rather than the Joint, should have been granted this privilege. All through the war the Zionists had felt that the JDC and its most important constituent body, the American Jewish Relief Committee, had short-changed Palestinian relief.[20] In the very month when the Red Cross Expedition was being formed, the two organizations had reached a fresh agreement on this issue,[21] now jeopardized by the Friedlaender appointment. Furthermore, to discredit Friedlaender was to tarnish Warburg and Marshall, who had recommended him to Cornelius Bliss. These two men, as well as Magnes, Friedlaender's good friend who was an outspoken pacifist, and Friedlaender himself, had opposed Wise and Brandeis on the Congress issue.

Nevertheless, it is unlikely that Wise would have challenged Friedlaender's nomination unless authorized to do so by a higher power, either in the Zionist movement or the American government. Two bits of evidence indicate the probable British source of the objections to Friedlaender. One was Wise's own testimony before the committee which investigated the debacle. He stated then that it was a cabled query from the *London Daily Mail* to the *New York Sun* which raised the question of Friedlaender's loyalty to the Allied cause.[22] What stimulated the British newspaper to initiate the inquiry? Herbert Bentwich offered a hint in a second piece of evidence, a letter which he wrote a month after Friedlaender's dismissal[23] in which he chastised his son-in-law for not cabling him during the crisis. Had this been done, he assured Friedlaender, he might have been able to override objections to his appointment through personal contacts in the Foreign Office and the War Ministry.

The objections may have originated from an incident which took place three summers before; it would have been amusing had it not been carried out in so unpleasant a fashion.[24] When war erupted in Europe, the Friedlaender family was vacationing in the Bentwich

[20]See Urofsky, *American Zionism*, pp. 157-159.

[21]See Yonathan Shapiro, *Leadership of the American Zionist Organization, 1897-1930* (Urbana, Ill., 1971), p. 121.

[22]See Wise's testimony, Parzen, "Conservative Judaism" *(Herzl Yearbook)*, p. 343. Records of the *London Daily Mail* and the *Jewish Chronicle* were destroyed or lost during the Blitz; hence no corroboration from that side is presently available.

[23]Dated April 9, 1918, *FP*.

[24]Recounted in a letter from Herzl Friedlaender, July 18, 1982; see also Margery and Norman Bentwich, *Herbert Bentwich, the Pilgrim Father* (Jerusalem, 1940), pp. 89-91.

country home in Birchington, Kent. At that time an order was issued demanding the extinguishing of all lights at sunset in houses facing the Channel and the Thames estuary. Absent-mindedly, the Bentwich family cook, herself a German woman, left one light burning. Soon a squad of soldiers appeared at the door, searched the building, questioned every inhabitant, and subjected Friedlaender to house arrest. Herbert Bentwich soon straightened out the matter, enabling the Friedlaenders to return to America, yet there is no question that a military report was issued. In Herzl Friedlaender's opinion, it undoubtedly stated that the foreign-born son-in-law possessed documents "in strange codes, i.e. Hebrew, Arabic, Russian, and German."[25]

It is possible that an interested party could have dredged up the military report of 1914 and leaked it to the press in 1918. The question remains: who possessed the motive for such an action? Bentwich believed the culprit to be Chaim Weizmann ("C.W."). According to his letter, Weizmann had only learned on February 14 that America had withdrawn support from the Zionist-sponsored mission and decided instead to establish another one under the auspices of the American Red Cross. Bentwich's letter implied that the British Zionists, then preparing their own expedition to Palestine, wanted to discredit or at least slow down the American government-sponsored mission. Insinuations about Friedlaender would have served this purpose admirably.

What remains unclear is the means by which Wise received the directive. Four facts, however, are instructive. First, Warburg later claimed that when Friedlaender was suggested in February, Wise first questioned his suitability and later acquiesced to his nomination.[26] We must therefore assume that Wise received new intelligence early in March which caused him to take action.

The second fact is that Wise visited Washington at that time.[27] Thirdly, we now know that the list of commissioners approved by the War Council on March 7 did not include Friedlaender's name.[28] Thus Wise's statement of March 8 could not have been a *cause* of Friedlaender's dismissal; it was, rather, a vindication of a decision

[25] These are Herzl Friedlaender's words.
[26] Parzen, "Conservative Judaism" *(Herzl Yearbook)*, p. 354.
[27] Jacob de Haas to Louis D. Brandeis, March 1918, *de Haas MSS.*
[28] Documented in the letter from Clemens. See above, n. 9.

already made by government officials transmitted to Wise during his visit to Washington.

And finally, when the JDC responded to Friedlaender's resignation by passing a resolution blaming his withdrawal on "unfounded rumors," not only Wise but also Judge Julian Mack voted against it.[29] Mack was, next to Brandeis, the American Jew closest to the source of power in Washington. A judge on the U.S. Court of Appeals, he had outlined the standards for conscientious objectors. Wise was an intimate associate of Brandeis, consulting with him on almost a daily basis. Since none of these harbored a personal grudge against Friedlaender, it is likely that they were aware of a British communication to the American government unavailable to the others.

After Friedlaender resigned from the commission, many private individuals and public organizations expressed their regrets. The FAZ, the JDC, and Hadassah passed resolutions expressing confidence in his loyalty,[30] while the PC set up hearings to air both sides of the story.[31] None of these actions satisfied Friedlaender, who felt that the Zionist movement had betrayed him. He was particularly distressed by Wise's statement in the course of the PC hearings that another man, the social service executive Dr. Morris Waldman, had been designated *the* Jewish executive on the commission, and that he (Friedlaender) was to have functioned only as "his aide and interpreter," or as Wise indelicately termed him, "a good Kosher Zettel."[32] He was equally offended by the fact that none of the rather mild resolutions passed by the Zionist organizations appeared in the *Maccabean*, their official organ. To explain this, Zionists pointed out that Wise had threatened to resign his position as head of the PC were the issue to be publicized. Harry Friedenwald and Henrietta Szold, intimate friends of Friedlaender and, like him, ardent Zionists, urged him to abandon the matter for the good of the movement.[33]

Swallowing his disappointment, Friedlaender returned to the classroom and lecture hall. In 1919 he edited and published the only anthology of his popular writings, *Past and Present*, which was

[29]Parzen, "Conservative Judaism" *(Herzl Yearbook)*, pp. 348-349.
[30]JDC and PC resolutions, March 14, 1918, *FP*; Hadassah resolution, April 16, 1918, *FP*.
[31]Parzen, "Conservative Judaism" *(Herzl Yearbook)*, pp. 327-355.
[32]Ibid., p. 338.
[33]Henrietta Szold to IF, May 28, 1918, *FP*; Friedenwald to IF, May 12, 1918, *FP*.

very well received. No longer active in Zionist organizational work, he nonetheless continued his apologetics for the Jewish national movement. In the last two years of his life he promoted a fresh cause, that of Arab-Jewish cooperation in the new Palestine.

Nevertheless, the feeling of "failure" of which he complained to his father-in-law[34] persisted. It was the need to overcome a general sense of inadequacy and lack of direction, exacerbated by the humiliation of 1918, which created the sixth and final crisis of Friedlaender's life, the disaster of 1920. Like the fifth crisis, the Red Cross imbroglio, it was played upon the stage of global conflict.

The end of the Great War did not bring relief to beleaguered Eastern Europe. The area of Jewish settlement continued to serve as a battlefield; one observer estimated that fourteen wars raged there simultaneously.[35] As the new Polish government contested border areas with the Soviet Union, then embroiled in war with White forces, Ukrainian bands despoiled the land, fomenting brutal pogroms. Jewish suffering was so acute that the Joint Distribution Committee planned a mission to Poland to dispense badly needed funds and find missing relatives of American Jews. The U.S. State Department granted grudging permission, but made it clear that the commissioners proceeded at their own risk.[36] Friedlaender, at the time, was chairman of the JDC's Committee on Russia; the position had been granted him as compensation for his rejection from the Red Cross expedition. When he volunteered to serve on the second commission, the leaders of the organization were constrained to accept his offer.

On January 20, 1920, shortly after the bar mitzvah of his firstborn son, Herzl, Friedlaender took leave of his wife and six children. The JDC delegation spent the month of February in the Warsaw area, dispensing mail from relatives and sorely needed funds from several organizations. Friedlaender's eagerness to serve was almost immediately blunted by the attitude of his colleagues. The social service executives in charge of the expedition regarded

[34]To which Bentwich alluded in his letter of April 9.

[35]See Moshe Davis, "The Human Record: Cyrus Adler at the Peace Conference, 1919," in *Essays in American Jewish History to Commemorate the Tenth Anniversary of the Founding of the American Jewish Archives under the Direction of J. R. Marcus* (New York, 1975), p. 483.

[36]See the report of Friedlaender's death, which appeared on the front page of the *New York Times*, July 11, 1920.

him as unfit for the job because of his lack of experience in social welfare and even his commitment to religious observance. For this reason he regretfully declined an invitation to visit the remarkable Jewish school system of Lodz, lest his absence from the office be construed as reneging on the job. To add to the frustration, the American delegates were soon ordered out of Poland and compelled to bide their time in Western Europe. For the rest of the winter and into the spring, Friedlaender traveled back and forth, meeting officials in Copenhagen, Paris, Rotterdam, and several German cities.[37] Among them were members of the Jewish delegation to the peace talks. From the safety and boredom of the west, a frustrated Friedlaender complained to his wife of "the waste of five months of my life."[38]

It was at this juncture that Friedlaender rose to the challenging but dangerous opportunity that presented itself. In late spring the JDC representatives learned that the Poles, having secured a military victory, had opened the border between Galicia and Podolia. Straightway, Friedlaender secured an appointment to a three-man JDC delegation sent to the Ukraine to dispense funds to Jewish victims of war and pogrom.

Marking the second journey to the east were a few pleasant experiences: a visit with friends of his parents and the venerable physician of his childhood, chats with important Jewish scholars such as Samuel Poznanski,[39] the rescue of the family of a colleague. Yet, he wrote his daughter Carmel some five weeks before his death, it seemed that "the sun has stopped shining."[40] For the bright spots only slightly relieved the horrors of the final months of his life. From the time that he returned to the land of his birth, he was confronted with the destruction of Jewish institutions, the personal suffering of friends and acquaintances, and harrowing eyewitness accounts of pogroms.

These outrages spurred Friedlaender on to bolder actions. On July 4, he bribed a Ukrainian chieftain to call off a pogrom.[41] The following morning, he left a relatively safe area to venture into the

[37]Alfred Kahn, currently of New York, recalls meeting Friedlaender in Cologne at this time.
[38]June 4, 1920. *Agranat MSS.*
[39]*IF Diary, FP.*
[40]A. Marx, "Israel Friedlaender, Zionist and Scholar," *Maccabean*, August 1920, p. 33.
[41]Leon S. Blatman, ed., *Kamenetz-Podolsk: A Memorial to a City Annihilated by the Nazis* (New York, 1966), p. 73. Blatman, a young Jewish student who served as the mission's Ukrainian translator, traveled with Friedlaender during the final weeks of his life.

Friedlaender and two American officials with a Jewish family in the Ukraine, June, 1920.

Courtesy of Dr. Louis Finkelstein

אמעריקאנער הילף־אויף, נאראלניצעך ביית אמת

ביז 5 1920

Tombstone placed over the graves of Friedlaender and Cantor; the photograph was incorrectly dated and marked: "a shvarzer khuppah at the cemetary of Yarmolinetz."

still-unsecured territory around the cities of Kiev and Kamenetz-Podolsk.[42] With him in the car driven by a Polish chauffeur was a young Reform rabbi, Bernard Cantor, newly arrived from Warsaw with additional funds. The rest of the JDC delegation traveled in another direction. In an area situated near the town of Yarmolinetz, the car was ambushed, the two Americans brutally murdered. It was first reported that a Red Army patrol had performed the terrible deed.[43] No one disputed the fact that the assassins were clothed in the uniforms of the Soviet army, which was then pushing a counteroffensive. Some American Jewish officials believed that the perpetrators were Red partisans who mistook Friedlaender and Cantor for Polish officers.[44] The report issued by the driver of the car inadvertently supported the suspicion that the uniforms indicated neither the identity of the murderers nor their motives.

> He, the chauffeur, was driving Professor Friedlaender and Dr. Cantor in an automobile. When they came near Yarmolinetz, three individuals dressed in Bolshevik uniforms stepped out of the forest, ordered the car to stop and commenced to search the passengers. The chauffeur, who speaks Russian, made an effort to persuade the searchers to let the party alone, telling them that they were Americans. When however, they continued taking no notice of his plea, he jumped from the car and commenced to run. When he was some distance away he heard a shot and, looking back, saw one of the Americans fall to the ground.[45]

The second man, undoubtedly, then received the same treatment.

From the outset, few people believed the chauffeur's story. The Yiddish newspaper *Forward* asked,

> How did Bolshevik soldiers penetrate into territory which had for so long been under Polish occupation? How did the chauffeur manage to escape so easily from the hands of three armed soldiers? And how was it possible for him to have seen who fell when the shooting commenced if he was in the course of running off?[46]

[42]Ibid., p. 74; *Statement by Dr. M. Leff before the American Joint Distribution Committee*, March 21, 1921. Dr. Leff was a member of the three-man Joint delegation to the Ukraine.
[43]Blatman, *Kamenetz-Podolsk*, p. 75; Leff, *Statement*.
[44]Reported to Ben-Zion Friedlander by a HIAS official in 1940.
[45]From a report on Friedlaender and Cantor's deaths, which appeared in the *Forward*, July 12, 1920.
[46]Ibid.

The article arrived at the conclusion that it was probably the chauffeur who contrived the assassinations with members of Petlura's band or of some group following another Ukrainian brigand. Such outlaws often masqueraded in Bolshevik uniforms. As JDC emissaries were known to possess large sums of money intended for relief, there was soon a consensus that the motive behind the double murder was neither political nor racial; it was, rather, simple robbery.[47]

The deaths of Friedlaender and Cantor were not immediately confirmed, since their bodies had been stripped of all clothing. After their identity was determined, the Jewish population of Yarmolinetz gave them a decent burial.

Clearer details about Friedlaender's death will, in all probability, never be obtained. Nor, at this point, do they seem to matter. The outstanding fact of the matter is that a talented scholar, writer, and lecturer met a violent death in his forty-fourth year, having neither reached his full potential nor resolved his inner conflicts.

More significant for our understanding of the man is the question of his plans for the future. Members of his family and some of his acquaintances have maintained that he planned to resettle his family in the newly restored Zion under what still promised to be benevolent British administration. Several pieces of evidence point in this direction. The first is a letter which he wrote to his brother-in-law Norman Bentwich in 1913. Complaining about his situation at the Seminary in particular and the condition of New York Jewry in general, Friedlaender concluded "All this makes me feel that . . . I am not the right man in the right place."[48] He asked Bentwich, who was then living in Cairo, whether he knew of a university chair that he could occupy, perhaps at the Haifa Technion.

A second piece of evidence is the soul-searching letter sent to his wife shortly before his death, in which he resolved to limit his prodigious activity in favor of "concentration."

No one can be a Jack of all trades. I certainly have not the capacity of being one. I shall from now on strive for depth and not for breadth. It is

---

[47]The *New York Times* (July 13, 1920, p. 10) and other press reports concurred on this matter. Only Margery Bentwich disagrees, upholding the supposition that "in their uniforms they were taken for American spies," *L. R. Friedlander*, p. 73.

[48]Ibid., p. 35.

Lilian Friedlaender with her five older children.

גן ע״ש ישראל פרידלנדר

(ע״ח אלול תרט״ו - י״ט תמוז תרפ״א)

חוקר המקרא, מפרש תרבות ערב מבוני החינוך היהודי ביהדות אמריקה
ומהוגי הציונות והמדינה היהודית

מת מות קדושים באוקראינה על משמר פעולתו למען עמו

──────────

גן זה נחנך בשנת תש״א

כתרומת תלמידי המוסד לחינוך בוגרים ע״ש ישראל פרידלנדר

מוקדש מחדש במלאות חמישים שנה למותו

בשוב האוניברסיטה העברית למכונה על הר הצופים

**Memorial plaque for Friedlaender on Mount Scopus
campus of Hebrew University.**

Courtesy of the Library of the Jewish Theological Seminary

Zionism of a personal kind. For Zionism means concentration against the decentralization and breadth of the dispersion.[49]

The question remains: how literally is the word "Zionism" to be taken? We know that Friedlaender exerted a concerted effort to visit Palestine between the projected ending of his European mission and his return to America. On March 5, 1920 he met in Paris with Chaim Weizmann, who urged him to undertake the journey[50] and later secured a British visa for him.[51] After this, however, despite strenuous efforts on the part of Friedlaender, his wife Lilian, and Judah Magnes,[52] no one was able to convince the JDC to allow him to go.

In order to determine the incentives behind Friedlaender's efforts to reach Palestine, it is necessary to examine his own statements. Letters written from Europe indicated two types of motivation, private and public. First, such a journey would provide personal compensation for the aborted venture of 1918. To Lilian he expressed the need "to go there and thereby wipe out the stain which has been resting upon me for the last two years."[53]

At the same time Friedlaender perceived the presence of another stain, one which was damaging the fabric of life in his beloved Zion. This was the deepening Arab rejection of the Jewish presence in Palestine, dramatically demonstrated in the attacks on Metulla and Tel Chai in February 1920 and the violence at Nebi Musa in April of that year. News of these harrowing events stung Friedlaender to the quick, arriving as they did during what he termed his period of "enforced idleness"[54] in Western Europe. Uselessly vegetating in Copenhagen, he longed for an opportunity to utilize his lifelong training as an Arabist: "Again and again I feel how very congenial the task would be to help in establishing the proper relation between the Jews and the Arabs, for it is only upon the basis of such a mutual understanding that the future of Jewish Palestine can be built up."[55]

[49]IF to Lilian, June 9, 1920, *FP* and *Agranat MSS;* also quoted by Margery Bentwich on p. 73 of the biography of her sister.
[50]*IF Diary*, March 5, 1920; IF to Lilian, March 5, 1920, *Agranat MSS.*
[51]IF to Lilian, May 12, 1920, *Agranat MSS.*
[52]See letters from IF to Lilian, May 5 and 12, 1920, and Lilian to IF, March 23, 1920, *Agranat MSS.*
[53]March 5, 1920, *Agranat MSS.*
[54]IF to Lilian, April 18 and 29, 1920, *Agranat MSS.*
[55]Ibid., May 12, 1920.

This statement to his wife, repeated in a letter to Julian Mack,[56] conveyed the resolve to settle permanently in Palestine. Yet it remains unclear just how the intention was to have been implemented. It has been suggested that Weizmann offered Friedlaender a position on the faculty of the nascent Hebrew University. Yet neither Friedlaender's personal diary nor any of his letters written from Europe mention such a proposal, nor did they indicate a plan to remain in Palestine for an extended period of time. In the correspondence of 1920, it was Lilian rather than Israel Friedlaender who introduced the issue of permanent settlement in the land of the fathers.[57] Indeed, after her husband's death she did just that, after lengthy consultation with her father.[58]

However, the actions of the widow must not be confused with the intentions of the husband. For if Palestine was really Friedlaender's goal, why did he travel there by the circuitous and hazardous route of the wartorn Ukraine? We can speculate that he journeyed far from his family and American associations in order to make up his mind about the future. Like the mythological creature, he needed to touch the *terra firma* of the old homeland, in order to gather strength for his next venture in life. By the time he wrote from Warsaw to Lilian and to Mack, he had decided to emigrate. It is more plausible, however, that despite the sentiments expressed in the letters to his relatives and friends, which may have been ephemeral in character, he planned to remain in the United States. He certainly undertook the mission in the spirit of service to American as well as Russian Jewry.

Discouraged by the slow pace of progress since his optimistic predictions of 1907, he felt that American Judaism needed a reviving stimulus from the old center. While he was in the process of deciding to take the journey, he wrote to his wife, "In spite of years of war and pogrom, I believe there is a spark there it is my duty to kindle—to create that current so necessary to the future of American and Russian Jewry, and by my mere observation to that end I will come back and show them here the policy they must consider."[59]

[56]Reported by Mack at the *Memorial Meeting for Israel Friedlaender and Bernard Cantor*, p. 47.
[57]Lilian to IF, March 23, 1920: "I still more than you desire to go to Palestine permanently," March 23, 1920; Lilian to Herbert Bentwich, June 27, 1920: "I feel that [Palestine] is the place for us and for our children." *Agranat MSS.*
[58]Margery Bentwich and Norman Bentwich, *The Pilgrim Father*, pp. 215-217.
[59]Bentwich, *L. R. Friedlander*, p. 71.

There is no reason to believe that the other letters just cited contradicted this intention. Moreover, his thwarted expectations of 1907, 1915, and 1918 are likely to have inhibited any radical decision.

* * * *

In his own day Friedlaender was celebrated as a phrasemaker whose lucid, incisive prose uncovered the reality that lay beneath the surface of contemporary Jewish life. It is therefore fitting that he unwittingly composed his own epitaph. In his important essay "The Problem of Judaism in America," he lamented, "While our heart is aroused over the martyrs that fell by the hands of violent mobs, we witness with indifference the disappearance of that for which they became martyrs."[60]

This dry and penetrating observation evokes the double irony of his own death and life. After his death he finally received the appreciation not granted him in life. Every organization with which he had been associated passed and circulated resolutions honoring his memory. Friedlaender's ghost did not share the obscurity of the "virtuous women" to whom he had likened himself in 1916.

Yet the mass meeting convened in his honor at Carnegie Hall on September 9, 1920 was, like his personal fate, distinguished by a certain unpleasantness. Before the gavel sounded, his father raced to the podium, whereupon he tearfully (and unnecessarily) requested financial assistance.[61] Furthermore, the person chosen to chair the assembly was none other than Cyrus Adler, the very symbol of his frustrated hopes and ambitions. Witnesses reported that Adler conducted the meeting with his customary icy efficiency.[62]

During his life, as we have seen, his ambitions were constantly thwarted, his common-sense suggestions either ignored or, worse,

[60]*PP*, p. 168.
[61]Letter from Ben-Zion Friedlander to author, July 19, 1983. Also related to this writer by the late Rabbi Israel M. Goldman, March 27, 1978, and the late Dr. Solomon Grayzel, March 7, 1979, and corroborated in a letter from Marx to Friedenwald, September 11, 1920, *Friedenwald MSS*. After Friedlaender's death, a memorial fund was established for Lilian and the children under the trusteeship of Marshall, Warburg, and Magnes. It is doubtful, however, that Israel's father was included. That Mrs. Friedlaender subsequently provided for her father-in-law's needs, however, is indicated in a letter from Magnes, February 14, 1922, *FP*.
[62]Ibid.

waved as a banner but not implemented. This resulted in an accretive sense of failure. Indicating a feeling of inferiority are his files, which contain reviews of his own books and articles, all of them favorable, and a small battery of weapons to be used against his detractors—for example, a list of Stephen Wise's pacifistic activities from the pre-April 1917 era. Contributing to Friedlaender's sense of inadequacy were two discordant factors. One was a heartfelt conviction that since Judaism was in mortal danger of "disapperance," he was compelled to labor unceasingly on its behalf. The other was a lofty innocence about the ways of man. Friedlaender assumed that others, like himself, labored only for Judaism, not personal aggrandizement and political machinations. From this naiveté stemmed the thwarted expectations of 1915-1916 and 1918 and the tragedy of 1920. In the first instance, Friedlaender produced penetrating analyses of the Congress-Committee dispute and the Americanization and education issues, which were ignored by individuals and groups engaged in a power play. After the Red Cross fiasco, Friedlaender could not achieve personal vindication at a time of war hysteria and communal pressure. And, finally, the decision of the Joint Distribution Committee to assuage the previous insult by accepting Friedlaender as a participant in the mission to the Ukraine resulted in a series of injuries. Even before the mission's tragic climax, Friedlaender impatiently endured the delaying tactics of government officials and the derision of the JDC social workers.

To observe that in each of these instances ambition outweighed accomplishment is not to concur with Friedlaender's sense of failure. His successes in the final analysis, however, arose not from his relief work, but from his intellectual endeavors as scholar, publicist, and lecturer. He left a thin but sturdy shelf of books and articles on Semitics, Jewish history, and the new social sciences, which offered fresh insights on the medieval past and current life. To this day, his writings remain valuable sources for students of early-twentieth-century Jewish historiography, American sociology, New York history, Zionism, and Conservative Judaism. Equally valuable was his role as a transmitter of ideas imported from Europe and adapted to the American setting. A generation of rabbis and educated laymen became familiar with the thought of Dubnow and Ahad Ha-am through Friedlaender's trenchant analyses of the past and pungent observations on the present. Most important was his optimism about the future of Judaism in the New World, which contrasted sharply with the despair of most East European intellectuals. Like Martin Luther King in 1963, Friedlaender had a dream in 1907, a hauntingly optimistic dream of a magnificent future for his people in America. It has never been superseded.

Part Two

THE SCHOLAR

Chapter 3

The Sabato Morais Professor of Biblical Literature and Exegesis

> Jewish learning, distorted by bias and prejudice, has been brandished as a weapon against Judaism. We realize more clearly than ever before that we are the natural and rightful guardians of our own vineyard.
>
> —*Israel Friedlaender*

When Friedlaender matriculated in the universities of Berlin and Strassburg, the scientific study of history had long prevailed in the German academy. Scholars unearthed forgotten historical documents and examined them, as well as more familiar data, from a critical standpoint. They applied the evolutionary hypothesis to society, which they perceived as a living, dynamic organism, continuously changing in response to internal and external forces.

Moreover, the newer disciplines of philology and archaeology were called into the service of history. Philologists analyzed sources into their component parts, distinguishing between earlier and later documents; they also demonstrated how each author's point of view affected his statement of fact. Archaeologists unearthed, then systematically examined, a wealth of artifacts: clay tablets from Mesopotamia, the contents of Egyptian pyramids, monuments with Hittite inscriptions, gigantic winged bulls from ancient Assyria, delicate colored frescos from Persian palaces.

These, it became clear, helped define the world of the Bible. In a secular age, Scripture became the record of an ancient civilization and consequently grist for the historian's mill. Bible scholars divided the Pentateuch into a series of documents, which could be separated and dated. Once they changed the order of the documens, the critics reconstructed a history of the Israelite religion which deviated significantly from the views long maintained by the Western religions.

Their interest in the origins of religion awakened, historians then turned to the rise of Islam. Mohammad became a popular subject of investigation, followed by the various Moslem and pre-Moslem traditions. When Jews entered the ranks of European scholars, the medieval world of Islam rather than the biblical period became their area of specialty. Discouraging traditionally educated Jews from critical Bible study was the widespread notion that this discipline undermined the very foundation of Judaism. They were loath to contribute to a branch of knowledge to which Solomon Schechter would later apply the epithet "higher anti-Semitism." Encouraging them to investigate the Islamic world were three significant factors. First, their prior knowledge of two Semitic languages, Hebrew and Aramaic, facilitated mastery of a third, Arabic. Secondly, they brought to their studies an understanding of the Jewish concepts of a Written and an Oral Law, which paralleled the Islamic Koran and *ḥadith*. And finally, they knew that Jews had played an important role in medieval Arabic culture.

The German university, however, made no distinctions between students of the ancient and the medieval Middle East. All "orientalists," as these scholars were called, were considered laborers in a common field.

This helps to explain why Schechter was willing to appoint as professor of Bible a young man who had established a reputation in the medieval rather than in the biblical arena. The selection of Friedlaender also demonstrated another conviction absorbed from German scholarship and sometimes utilized in Schechter's polemic against Reform Judaism. The Jews, he argued, were orientals;[1] it followed that the study of Judaism was a function of scholars trained as orientalists. Moreover, he knew that even though Friedlaender had not concentrated on the history of the ancient Near

---

[1] *SJ* 2, pp. 150, 183; *Seminary Addresses*, p. 5.

East, he had attended the lectures of the famous Friedrich Delitzsch and even given lectures on *Babel und Bibel* to Jewish students.[2] He had also studied Bible with David Hoffmann, the only
Jew to have offered a rebuttal of the Wellhausian hypothesis.[3]

When Israel Friedlaender accepted the position of Sabato Morais
Professor of Biblical Literature and Exegesis at the Jewish Theolog-
ical Seminary of America, he acknowledged his limitations as a
Bible scholar and pledged to remedy the situation.

> I take upon myself the personal obligation ללמוד על מנת ללמד to learn in
> order to teach others. I shall seek to familiarize myself with the
> problems of Biblical scholarship in order to be able to present them to
> my students. In cooperation with other scholars who deal with these
> problems, I intend to make a modest contribution to their clarification
> and solution.[4]

Friedlaender's meager output in biblical scholarship indicates
that he did not fulfill his pledge to Schechter; he neither clarified
major issues nor did he offer solutions to the problems raised by
biblical criticism. For this there were several reasons. In the first
place, unlike Schechter, he clearly differentiated between the areas
of biblical and medieval scholarship, placing himself firmly in the
latter field. In addition, his unstinted devotion to communal activity left him little energy for a secondary academic interest. Finally,
and most fundamentally, he was uncomfortable with the trend of
current biblical criticism. In his opinion, it reflected a haughty
disdain for the Jewish religion and its sacred books, the Masoretic
text and the traditional glosses on them.

Yet this did not reduce Friedlaender's distinction as professor of
Bible. His contributions, however, are best described as didactic
rather than critical. Through his lectures and essays, he came into
contact with current leaders of American Jewry as well as future
rabbis and teachers. By virtue of his position as professor in a
traditional rabbinical seminary, his statements on biblical topics
were stamped with authenticity. For this reason, he paved the way
for the acceptance of certain features of modern biblical scholarship
which had heretofore been suspect.

[2]IF, "Autobiography, 1903." These lectures are, unfortunately, lost.
[3]David Hoffmann, *Die wichtigsten Instanzen gegen die Graf-Wellhausensche Hypothese*, 2 vols.
(Berlin, 1904, 1916).
[4]IF to Schechter, August 7, 1903, *FP*.

For example, although he scrupulously and frequently reiterated his respect for the medieval Jewish commentators, he carefully distinguished between their insights and the plain meaning of the biblical text. Thus his description of "Maimonides as an Exegete" sympathetically explained the great philosopher's allegorical treatment of the Bible, indicating both its appropriateness for the twelfth century and its inappropriateness for the twentieth. Maimonides resorted to allegory, declared Friedlaender, when confronted with a section of the Bible that neither advanced the narrative nor formulated tutelary ideas. "He cannot conceive, for instance, that the genealogical table of the descendents of Noah has a value in itself, in fact, is one of the most valuable documents of antiquity, and he is therefore on the lookout for philosophical reasons to justify its place in the Bible."[5] Friedlaender's selection of Genesis 10, the importance of which has been manifest only to modern critics, is a firm endorsement of a second trend in modern biblical scholarship, the utilization of archaeological findings from civilizations contemporary to ancient Israel.

Scattered throughout his writings are references to recent discoveries, such as the Moabite Stone and the El Amarna letters. To convey the usefulness of modern archaeology in advancing knowledge of the biblical milieu, Friedlaender summoned a striking literary image.

> The marvelous discoveries of the last century which have raised the ancient Orient from its grave have taught us that Israel was not, as was formerly thought, a sort of Robinson Crusoe living in an island of its own, working out its destinies apart from the rest of the world; it was a very small and insignificant part of a vast humanity which in point of civilization and material achievement was endlessly superior to it.[6]

The science of archaeology uncovered ancient artifacts and utilized them to explain the biblical world. Friedlaender accepted its findings as well as those of other branches of curent scholarship in ancient history. But on the issue of biblical interpretation, he defined his standpoint as "scientific" rather than "critical."[7] As an example of the latter he offered the very cryptic Hosia 6:5:

[5]*PP (1919)*, p. 201.
[6]*Aspects* I, 6.
[7]See "The New York Theological Seminary. Interview with Dr. Israel Friedlaender," *Jewish Chronicle* (London), June 22, 1906, p. 21.

That is why I had hewn down the prophets,
Have slain them with the words of My mouth:
And the day that dawned [brought on] your punishment.[8]

The Septuagint offers a version of the text different from the traditional one; this citation, therefore, demonstrated a willingness to consult translations and other non-Masoretic documents which would help unravel the meaning of a difficult text. As a modernist and historian, Friedlaender also accepted another premise of current biblical scholarship, that the Bible is a series of texts which, though sacred, have been edited by human hands. Implied in this was the recognition of editorial omission or error. Thus he did not hesitate to refer to Deutero-Isaiah,[9] nor did he shrink from minor biblical emendation. In Seminary students from traditional homes, this aroused some excitement, as one of them indicated years later. "We seemed to be galloping along in a grand adventure of discovery. Some of us found misplaced commas, others misplaced periods. We changed letters and we moved words."[10]

Another student recalled Friedlaender's use of a correction made by Samuel David Luzzatto to a verse from Ezekiel (3:12). This emendation changed the meaning of an important liturgical text from "Blessed be the Presence of the Lord from His place" to "When the glory of God rose from its place."[11]

In his only scholarly article on a biblical subject,[12] Friedlaender addressed another problem in the same mildly critical fashion. It dealt with the magnificent Prophecy of Peace, found both in Micah and Isaiah, which contains the famous:

They shall beat their swords into plowshares
And their spears into pruning hooks:
Nation shall not take up

[8]Ibid., p. 22. It is interesting that his friend Samuel Poznanski had written briefly on this subject in the Hebrew periodical *Ha-goren* 3 (1902): 114. Many years later another JTS professor would claim that this difficult verse was, as his title would indicate, a "prophetic attestation to the Decalogue." See Shalom Spiegel's article in the *Harvard Theological Review* 22 (April 1934): 105-144.

[9]"New York Theological Seminary. Interview with Dr. Israel Friedlaender," p. 21.

[10]Morris Schussheim, "Recollections," p. 171.

[11]From an interview with Max Kadushin, November 8, 1978. See Morris B. Margolies, *Samuel David Luzzatto: Traditionalist Scholar* (New York, 1979) on Luzzatto's biblical exigesis. I have used his translations of the biblical verse and Luzzatto's emendation, p. 121.

[12]Entitled "The Present Position and the Original Form of the Prophecy of Eternal Peace in Isaiah 2:1-5 and Micah 4:1-5," in *JQR* n.s.6 (1916): 405-413.

Sword against nation:
They shall never again know war.[13]

Friedlaender refused to pose the obvious question of how two men could have uttered identical words; he examined only the structure of the prophecy and its position in the two biblical books. Accepting the assumption of the fluidity of the biblical text current in *Juedische Wissenschaft* since the time of Geiger, Friedlaender reconstructed an original text which combined all of the verses in both prophecies with a few that follow. The reader puts down the article with a sense of satisfaction at the resolution of the issue in a way that enhances rather than detracts from the beautiful text. However, upon reflection, he realizes that it makes no attempt to deal with questions which a bolder analysis would have raised.

Textual rearrangements and random emendations marked the limits of Friedlaender's biblical scholarship. From the outset of his career, he followed a program intended more to promote ideas than to extend the frontiers of criticism. His letter accepting the Seminary position informed Schechter of the young professor's desire to awaken love of the Bible in the hearts of his students. As his audience expanded to include members of the community at large, he pursued this objective with alacrity. Reinforcing his message were reprints in his anthology; seven of the first eight pieces in *Past and Present* dealt with biblical subjects. Both in conception and tone, these essays differed noticeably from the analysis of the Prophecy of Peace. Although studded with learned allusions and scriptural citations, they were not works of disinterested scholarship. For the purpose of analysis, Friedlaender's writings on biblical themes may be grouped into two categories, "literary" and "polemical."

Dominating the first group were two essays on the Hebrew prophets, "The Prophet Jeremiah" and "The Political Ideal of the Prophets."[14] If they borrowed freely from Ahad Ha-am, they nonetheless indicated a definite independence of mind. To understand their deviation from Ahad Ha-am, it will be useful to recall two important essays on the subject of prophecy written by "The Sage of Odessa."

---

[13]Isaiah 2:4; Micah 4:3.
[14]*PP*, pp. 67-94; 1-34.

In his treatment of Moses, Ahad Ha-am asserted that he was not concerned with the "archaeological Moses," the lawgiver, soldier, and statesman about whom new historical data may one day be uncovered. What interested him was the "historical" figure, the Moses of what he understood as Jewish tradition. His essay was a deliberate search for an archetype. "This ideal—I reason—has been created in the spirit of the Jewish people; and the creator creates in his own image."[15]

A related essay, "Priest and Prophet," did not refer to any priest or prophet by name; Ahad Ha-am regarded both as types rather than individuals. The prophet, for him, represented forthrightness and truthfulness.

> A certain moral idea fills his whole being, masters his every feeling and sensation, engrosses his whole attention. He can only see the world through the mirror of his idea; he desires nothing, strives for nothing, except to make every phase of the life around him an embodiment of that idea in its perfect form.[16]

This definition reminds the reader of the new sociology of Ahad Ha-am's famous contemporary Max Weber, who also portrayed the prophet as an archetype, an "ideal type."[17] If Ahad Ha-am's prophet was a Weberian model, endowed with charisma, then his priest was the individual responsible for the routinization of charisma.

> He appears on the scene at a time when Prophecy has already succeeded in hewing out a path for its Idea, when that Idea has already had a certain effect on the trend of society, and has brought about a new harmony or balance between the different forces at work. The Priest also fosters the Idea, and desires to perpetuate it; but he is not of the race of giants. He has not the strength to fight continually against necessity and actuality; his tendency is rather to bow to the one end and come to terms with the other. Instead of clinging to the narrowness of the Prophet, and demanding of reality what it cannot give, he broadens his outlook, and takes a wider view of the relation between his Idea and

[15]Ahad Ha-am, "Moses," in *Nationalism and the Jewish Ethic: Basic Writings of Ahad Ha-am*, ed. Hans Kohn (New York, 1962), p. 209.

[16]Idem, "Priest and Prophet," in *Selected Essays of Ahad Ha-Am*, trans. and ed. Leon Simon (New York, 1970), p. 130.

[17]Max Weber, *The Sociology of Religion*, trans. Ephraim Fischoff (Boston, 1964), chapter on "The Prophet," pp. 46-59.

the facts of life. Not what *ought* to be, but what *can* be, is what he seeks.[18]

Ahad Ha-am's appraisal of Hebrew prophecy permeated Friedlaender's thought. Yet the younger man's essay on Jeremiah was separated from Ahad Ha-am's discourse on Moses not simply by the gap of the few hundred years between the lives of the two protagonists, but by the chasm that separated the world view of the historian from that of the philosopher. For Friedlaender, laboring under the constraint of German historiography, experienced what Butterfield has called "a joy in detail as such, and a desire to participate in it wherever it comes—a passion for human beings in themselves, love of events in their very uniqueness."[19] Armed with an extraordinary command of the merest detail of the biblical text as well as an easy familiarity with the archaeological data so summarily rejected by Ahad Ha-am, he sketched a moving portrait of the prophet Jeremiah. He presented a man for all seasons yet of his own time, a participant in the events of his day as well as a critic of them. His Jeremiah, "the sublimest of the prophets," was also a frail and troubled human being, who argued with and berated the people whom he loved yet by whom he was despised, who suffered and cried and believed.

If Friedlaender delighted in the idiosyncrasies of human beings and the uniqueness of historical periods, he also accepted a second dictum of *Wissenschaft*. "The historian must have an eye for generalities."[20] Thus, he characterized the Hebrew prophet in this fashion: "His *soul* is full of the spirit of the Lord, and the Divine word is shut up in his bones as the scorching fire—not that flickering harmless flame which lights the hearth, but that raging fire of God which splitteth the rock."[21]

To describe the nature of prophecy in general without losing sight of the qualities which mark the individual prophet, Friedlaender wrote: "The Divine element, the consciousness of God, the communion with God, are common to all the prophets, but every one of them has a sharply marked individuality in which he differs

---

[18]Ahad Ha-am, "Priest and Prophet," p. 131.
[19]Herbert Butterfield, *Man on His Past: The Study of the History of Historical Scholarship* (Boston, 1955), p. 104.
[20]Ibid.
[21]*PP*, p. 3 (Friedlaender's emphasis).

from all the others, this difference being determined, as is the case with every man, by place, time, and environment."[22] If this analysis suggested a broadly historical perspective, it also demonstrated a noticeable departure from the rationalism of Friedlaender's predecessors in Jewish scholarship. They, like Ahad Ha-am, concentrated on the prophets' ethical message; he insisted that the Jewish people had always revered them in equal measure for their ability to commune with God. Nor was Friedlaender, like Ahad Ha-am, a radical evolutionist convinced that the perception of the divine was a phenomenon confined to the distant beginnings of Israel. To the contrary, he presented spirituality as a feature which also distinguished later Jewish religious leaders: scribes, Pharisees, and rabbis.

This principle animated Friedlaender's lectures and essays on biblical subjects which were polemical in intent. They were, to a large extent, directed against the view of scholars who accepted, in whole or in part, the findings of the Wellhausen School, which dominated the scientific study of Scripture during his lifetime. In his attempt to reconstruct Israelite history from an evolutionary standpoint, Wellhausen proposed a documentary hypothesis of the structure of the Pentateuch. He built upon the findings of an earlier scholar, K. H. Graf, and placed the prophets at the center of Israel's religious development. According to the Graf-Wellhausen thesis, the heights of prophetic religiosity and morality were followed by marked decline. Priests and scribes set the agenda for the religion which came to be known as Judaism. The former instituted a sacrificial cult that had been unknown to previous generations. They were followed by the Pharisees, heirs to Ezra the Scribe, who formulated a religion of ritual that left no room for the spirit.[23] Under their guidance, the Jewish people became exclusivist to the point of misanthropy. It was against this background that Jesus emerged, revived the older "Israelite" ideals of humility, righteousness, and humanitarianism, and pursued them to new heights, culminating in a sublime act of personal sacrifice for the salvation of humanity.

In the early years of the twentieth century, leading Reform Jewish scholars accepted Wellhausen's hypothesis about the origins

---

[22]Ibid., p. 73.
[23]Julius Wellhausen, *Prolegomena to the History of Ancient Israel* (New York, 1957), p. 410.

of the Pentateuch even as they drew different conclusions about the later development of Judaism. Kaufmann Kohler, president of the Hebrew Union College, and for Schechter "His Majesty's Opposition,"[24] proclaimed Reform Judaism the true heir to Hebrew prophecy. Never subject to the magical elements of Christianity and "emancipat[ed] from the yoke of dead [Jewish] ritualism,"[25] this movement, he believed, would lead the world to a universal religion.[26] Julian Morgenstern, the American-born, German-educated Bible scholar who would later succeed Kohler, understood biblical ceremonialism and nationalism as passing phases manifestly outgrown in the unfolding of Jewish history.[27]

Unlike his Reform counterparts, Friedlaender did not address the Graf-Wellhausen hypothesis, with which he was undoubtedly familiar. He had listened to its proponents at the Berlin University and its boldest Jewish opponent, David Hoffmann, at the Hildesheimer Seminary. That he did not inject this issue into his Bible classes at the New York Seminary can be partially explained by the fact that he never taught a class in the Pentateuch; mastery of its text and some of the commentaries was a prerequisite to admission to the institution. Yet his colleague Louis Ginzberg supported the documentary hypothesis in articles intended for the broad public,[28] in marked contrast to Friedlaender, who never introduced the issue into either his scholarly or his popular writings. How can we account for this? Friedlaender's own words provide the answer. "Jewish learning, distorted by bias and prejudice, has been brandished as a weapon against Judaism. We realize more clearly than ever before that we are the natural and rightful guardians of our own vineyard."[29]

More than any other statement, this *cri du coeur* expressed Friedlaender's personal frustration at the current state of biblical criticism. Convinced that it was less the objective study it pur-

---

[24] See Schechter's essay under this title in his *Seminary Addresses and Other Papers* (New York, 1959), pp. 239-244.

[25] Kaufmann Kohler, *Studies, Addresses and Personal Papers* (New York, 1931), p. 221. (This is a compilation of Kohler's papers over many years.)

[26] Ibid. See also his essay "The Mission of Israel," pp. 177-200.

[27] Morgenstern summarized the history of Reform theology in a remarkable article, "The Achievements of Reform Judaism," *Central Conference of American Rabbis Yearbook* 29 (1925): 247-281. Jewish universalism is the thesis of Kohler's essay "Backwards or Forwards" in his *Studies*, pp. 201-235.

[28] See his article "Law, Codification of," *Jewish Encyclopedia* 7 (1904, 1910): 635-647.

[29] *PP*, p. 205.

ported to be than a series of poisoned arrows aimed at the heart of traditional Judaism, he claimed the position of "guardian." As professor of Bible in a traditionalist institution established to train a new generation of Jewish religious leaders, it was his self-assumed duty to nurture the old "vineyard," not to plant new ones. As an authentic champion of the Hebrew Bible, he would protect the precious fruit from the ravages of the higher criticism.

The best defense, as every military commander knows, is a strong offense. In a series of polemical essays, Friedlaender attacked the critics, sometimes employing uncharacteristically abrasive language. The most disputatious of all Friedlaender's writings was "A New Specimen of Modern Biblical Exegesis (1907),"[30] his analysis of *A Critical and Exegetical Commentary on the Book of Psalms*, written by the respected American Bible critic, Charles A. Briggs. In the attempt to discredit Briggs's *Commentary*, Friedlaender's review essay drove home several points. It argued that the work violated the elementary requirements of scholarship, knowledge of the language of the text under consideration and the literature of the same period. A lumbering descent into the lower criticism, it was, for Friedlaender, also a precipitate flight into the higher criticism, drawing conclusions from the Wellhausen hypothesis undocumented in the Psalms themselves. Furthermore, it displayed a pro-Christian tendency inappropriate to disinterested scholarship.

> We constantly stumble against lucubrations and interpretations of an avowedly Christological nature, which may testify to the author's loyalty to his faith . . . but can have no place in a critical inter-confessional commentary which is supposed to be free from polemical and ecclesiastical bias. . . . The author is in all earnestness convinced that Psalm ii (as well as Psalm cx) "find their only realization in the resurrection, enthronement and reign of Jesus Christ." . . . Our author discusses the question whether the coincidence of the Psalmist's description with the sufferings of Christ is accidental or due to "prophetic anticipation."[31]

Finally, Friedlaender insisted, the *Commentary* reflected a shocking lack of respect for Jewish scholarship bordering on dishonesty.

[30]*PP (1919)*, pp. 113-137.
[31]Ibid., pp. 115-116.

For, although Briggs never utilized the insights of the traditional Jewish commentators, he nevertheless cited the names of the medieval exegetes in his bibliography. Friedlaender himself held their findings in great respect. Even as he introduced rabbinical students to modern techniques of scholarship he offered the following admonition: "Criticism is fine, but take my advice and stick to Kimche, Rashi and Ibn Ezra."[32]

In the area of modern Jewish criticism, he particularly valued Arnold Ehrlich, going so far as to fault Briggs for failing to consider his analysis of the Psalms. Like Friedlaender, Ehrlich was a lower critic, but of a more radical inclination, an expert in emending and rearranging texts. Many years after writing his "New Specimen of Modern Biblical Exegesis," Friedlaender would eulogize him as a biblical scientist whose conclusions, unlike those of many Christian critics, were grounded in "a proper understanding of the text," and of the "linguistic and cultural environment" of the New East.[33]

This principle, of course, formed the basis of sound investigation of every historical epoch. It is noteworthy that even as Friedlaender took the critics to task for their disdainful attitude toward Jewish exegesis and their wild conjectures about biblical texts, he accepted other axioms which governed their investigation of the biblical period. As a modern scholar, Friedlaender too searched for mundane factors to explain the events of Israel's past and did not venture theological interpretation of events. Moreover, like most early-twentieth-century thinkers, he accepted the notion of the evolution of all historical phenomena. He believed, with them, that Jewish monotheism during the postexilic period was totally different from the paganism practiced by most preexilic Israelites. Finally, like his Christian and Reform opponents as well as his mentor Ahad Ha-am, he visualized the prophets as the culmination of Jewish religiosity.

Friedlaender was one of the first American Jewish scholars to expound these conceptions in the service of traditional Judaism. His most extensive anti-Reform polemic, "Aspects of Historical Judaism," submitted the thesis that the development of Judaism was based upon three intertwined factors, monotheism, nationalism, and ceremonialism, each of which achieved its essential form

---

[32]Schussheim, "Recollections," p. 141.
[33]IF, "A Great Bible Scholar, Arnold B. Ehrlich," *Nation*, January 10, 1920, p. 41.

during the time of the Babylonian exile. As we have just indicated, Friedlaender accepted the prevailing notion that the preexilic popular religion of the Israelites was pagan. He was convinced that monotheism only became the "unshakable foundation" of Judaism at the time of the Babylonian destruction of the Temple and the Jerusalem political center. At this time, the prophetic idea of one universal God who demands human perfection clashed with the popular conception of a national god who controlled only the destiny of Israel and who was only one force among a multiplicity of forces. Out of the crisis of exile emerged a new system of faith which was true monotheism, the belief in one God "over and above nature and humanity."[34]

According to his analysis, classical Jewish nationalism, the second "aspect" of Historical Judaism, like monotheism, the first, emerged out of the crisis of the Babylonian destruction. In the preexilic period, Israelite and Judean nationalism was indistinguishable from that of the surrounding nations; both tiny polities strove for political supremacy over their neighbors. To prove that this was a necessary if rudimentary stage in national development, Friedlaender penned several additional essays. One was an angry response to Julian Morgenstern, professor of Bible at the Hebrew Union College, who had observed,[35]

> The history of Israel and Judah . . . is on the whole a gloomy record of bad government, tyranny and oppression, such as has been characteristic of every little Oriental state from the beginning of history. It is the most incontrovertible proof that Israel's genius does not lie in the field of self-government, that from first to last as a nation Israel was a most dismal failure.[36]

Against this theory, Friedlaender protested that the ancient Judeans demonstrated considerable ability in self-government; after all, the Davidic dynasty survived for three hundred years. It is obvious that he was not debating an historical issue but a contemporary one. It was not *ancient* Judea's political adequacy or inadequacy that kindled his passion. It was, rather, the attempt of the

[34]*Aspects* I, 8. We shall call this series of lectures "The Temple Emanu-el Addresses." See below, Chapter 6.

[35]In "The Significance of the Bible for Reform Judaism in the Light of Modern Scientific Research," *CCAR Journal* 18 (1908): 217-248.

[36]IF quoted this statement from Morgenstern's article, *PP*, p. 39.

Reformers to preempt the prophets to promote the notion that the Jewish genius was always religious and never political. The implication, of course, was that Zionism is a modern aberration rather than an outgrowth of an essential biblical idea.

For this reason Friedlaender took great pains to portray the prophets as patriots who supported Israelite and Judean sovereignty until the bitter end. Never did they relinquish hope, he argued, even in the face of mighty world empires. What they did, however, was to change the content of the political ideal by "transferring Israel's claim to superiority from a sphere where it was bound to crumble at the slightest contact with reality to a domain where it was unassailable and indestructable: they accomplished it by turning the *political* superiority of Israel into *religious*, or *spiritual* supremacy."[37]

In all the centuries of exile, Jews prayed for the day when they would return to Zion in the very mundane sense of the earthly city of Jerusalem. But this was not to be a Zion that would outfit armies or contract alliances in order to conquer other nations. Zion is valuable only as the seat of Israel's spiritual supremacy. The lesson for modern times is that only a small remnant, equipped to live the prophetic ideal, should return to Palestine in order to reestablish Zion as the spiritual center of the Jewish people.

This was also the thesis of "The Political Ideal of the Prophets,"[38] an essay which used biblical history to promote the Spiritual Zionism of Ahad Ha-am. Methodologically, it adhered to the dialectical principle of interpretation which underlay Friedlaender's conception of the origin of Jewish monotheism, namely, that new forms are created out of the conflict between an outmoded idea and a new political reality. When the old notion of political supremacy was challenged by the reality of the destruction of national sovereignty, a new kind of Jewish nationalism emerged. From the Babylonian exile onward, spiritual nationalism would be the second fundamental element of historical Judaism.

Former students remember Friedlaender best for his endorsement of spiritual Zionism. One rabbi maintained that this was the

[37]Ibid., p. 15 (emphasis added).
[38]*PP*, pp. 1-34. This essay, which bears the subtitle "A Study in Biblical Zionism," is noteworthy as one of very few Zionist tracts originally written in English and then translated into Hebrew. It was published twice in that language. See p. 1, n. According to "Bibliograph" (Kressl), M. H. Zelden helped to formulate the Hebrew translation. *Hadoar* 61 (December 24, 1976): 123.

essential message of all his classes, whether the subject matter was ostensibly one of the books of the Prophets or the Hagiographa, ancient or medieval Jewish history, or even the history of the canon. He recalled that the gentle professor loved to interpret this verse from Isaiah 28:12

זאת המנוחה הניחו לעיף וזאת המרגעה

to mean "not physical battle but spiritual striving."[39] Isaiah's advice not to embark upon political adventure justified Friedlaender's conviction that the goal of Jewish nationhood was spiritual elevation rather than political power.

For this reason, Friedlaender found it difficult to accept parts of the Bible that reflect a different perspective. Another of his students remembered his comment about Psalm 137, the familiar dirge in which the Judeans, weeping by the rivers of Babylon, hung up their harps, unable to sing on alien soil. Brooding over the last two lines of the psalm, the professor declared that he would willingly have sacrificed ten years of his life had he been able to eradicate its redoubtable ending: "a blessing on him who seizes your babies and dashes them against the rocks."[40]

Soon after the Babylonian exile and the return to Zion half a century later, prophecy came to an end. How could the people maintain prophetic ideas in the face of these changes? Friedlaender submitted that new leaders, aware of the gap between the uncompromising standards of the prophets and the practical realities of human nature, took up the challenge. Ezra "understood that prophetic Judaism was indispensible as an ideal, as a stimulus, as a guidance, but that it was too lofty and exalted to serve as a lever in the grey everyday existence of man, and he, therefore, proceeded to turn the solid gold bars of prophecy into small coin."[41] These "small coins," the Written Law of the Pentateuch and the Oral Law, commentaries on it, were studied and observed by the entire people. Thus "ceremonialism" served as the third aspect of historical Judaism.

Continuing his defense of traditional Judaism, Friedlaender surveyed the whole of Jewish history. He divided his people's past into

---

[39]Interview with Max Kadushin.
[40]Interviews with Simon Greenberg, March 28, 1978 and November 18, 1981.
[41]*PP*, p. 94.

two uneven parts—before and after the Emancipation. Before that watershed, Jews lived a life of their own, whether in Palestine or the diaspora; afterwards, they began to participate in the life of the nations around them. The "natural" long line separating the two epochs of the first period was the year 70 C.E. Until that time, Jews "were centered in Palestine" and lived a "normal" national life; afterwards came dispersion and the "suspension" of national functions.

To make Emancipation the modern watershed was to emphasize the hazards which it harbored. In contrast to the *Juedische Wissenschaft* scholars of the nineteenth century, who directed their research toward the goal of achieving Emancipation, Friedlaender used scholarship to illuminate the dangers which arose as a result of Emancipation, dangers which his generation regarded as a threat to the survival of Judaism.

What is strange about his selection of the year 70 C.E. as the first line of demarcation in Jewish history is that, while he professed to accept that date, his historical survey selected another, 586 B.C.E. For it clearly indicated that each of the three "aspects" of historical Judaism was born out of the destruction of the First, not the Second, Temple. Within Friedlaender's system there was also a second watershed, the year 444 B.C.E., when Ezra and Nehemiah, having achieved Jewish separation, established the Torah as the guide for Jewish "ceremonialism."

This new periodization struck a blow at both the Christian and Reform perceptions of Judaism. For Christians the year 70 was more than a watershed in Judaism; it was not a mere comma, but a full stop. With the destruction of the Second Temple, the Jews, having rejected Jesus, ceased to be a force in world history and culture. The promoters of the "mission" theory adapted the Christian periodization to their own purposes. For them, the destruction of the Second Temple affected Jewish life on two levels, external and internal. Externally, the Jews went out into the world, on their great "mission" of spreading the message of ethical monotheism to the nations. Within the Jewish people, however, a stifling rabbinism replaced the political state. Ambitious rabbis were responsible for a proliferation of religious regulations, which obscured rather than promoted the exalted ideals of the prophets.

By adopting 586 B.C.E. rather than 70 C.E. as the turning point of Jewish history, Friedlaender attempted to refute these defamations of rabbinism. For he argued that rabbinism had its origin in the Bible itself in the person of Ezra, the bearer of an unbroken chain of tradition from the classical prophets. Friedlaender disarmed his opponents by accepting their evaluation of the prophets. He agreed that their ideals of religion and morality are valid for all time, that the period in which they flourished was a Golden Age by which all subsequent ages must be judged. However, their age was "golden" in a limited sense. For the prophetic ideals did not immediately filter down to the people. "Down to the Babylonian exile, the Jews as a whole were a chosen people only potentially. It was only during the Babylonian exile that the Jewish people received the new heart and the new spirit and finally realized their exalted mission."[42]

If the age of classical prophecy was a Golden Age, then the period of Ezra and Nehemiah was a Silver Age. Friedlaender knew that by ascribing great significance to the fifth century B.C.E. Restoration, he was following both an ancient tradition and contemporary scholarly opinion. In rabbinic tradition, Ezra was the savior of Judaism, the second Moses.[43] With this opinion, Christian scholars did not argue; however, many ascribed to this phenomenon a negative value. Friedlaender noted Eduard Meyer's "sneering" remark that the age of Ezra was the "genesis of Judaism,"[44] by which he implied a break with the prophetic tradition. Other Christian historians and Bible critics portrayed Ezra and Nehemiah as the founders of "Nibdalism." Their acts of rejecting the Samaritans and banishing foreign wives became the prototype of inhumane exclusiveness.

For this reason they were an embarrassment to Reform Jewish thinkers who maintained that universal ethical monotheism was the essential idea of Judaism. Friedlaender hated the term "Nibdalism," but accepted it and transvalued it, turning a necessity into a virtue. In his opinion, the rulers of Restoration Jerusalem enforced isolation for an exalted purpose. Their concept of a holy, distinctive people following a spiritual calling enabled the Jews to preserve the religious, moral, and ethical message of Hebrew prophecy for

---

[42]*Aspects* III, 4.
[43]Cf. this statement from the Babylonian Talmud, *Sukkah* 20b: "In ancient times when the Torah was forgotten from Israel, Ezra came up from Babylonia and established it."
[44]*PP*, p. 31.

themselves and all mankind.[45] Against the Christian theologians as well as his Reform colleagues, he contended that Jewish ceremonialism, like "Nibdalism," was not a retrogressive step. To the contrary, it was the application of the prophetic ideal to a new historical situation.

This argument was calculated to appeal to an American audience living in the age of Dewey and James. In the second decade of this century they were inclined to judge a man's actions by concrete results. Friedlaender insisted that Ezra's activities were commendable because they applied great principles to everyday life, thus passing the pragmatic test. The average citizen had little use for gold bars stored at Fort Knox, but he knew that gold coins were acceptable everywhere as legal tender.

On the scholarly level, this chain of reasoning challenged the repudiators of Jewish tradition by drawing upon the disciplines in which modern critical scholarship is grounded. We have seen how Friedlaender utilized his philological expertise to indicate the Christian critics' inadequate mastery of the biblical idiom and thought. We have observed how this nationalist historian inveighed against the Jewish Reformers' failure to place biblical events in their proper setting. Most remarkable was Friedlaender's ability to marshal evidence from archaeology to demonstrate how that new science could be utilized to support tradition rather than undermine it.

What he never realized was the fact that some of the arguments which he advanced against others could have been used to discredit his conception of biblical and postbiblical history. What were they? To begin, Friedlaender mocked his opponents' tendency to read their own preconceived notions into the biblical text. Yet it is obvious today that this professor of biblical "exegesis" (i.e., extrapolating from the text of Scripture), no less than the men he criticized, was a master of eisegesis (which means reading one's own ideas into a text). This is evident in his discovery of "spiritual Zionism" in the sayings of the prophets, ignoring the fact that concepts such as "nationalism" and "Zionism" would have been foreign to anyone living before the nineteenth century C.E.

Moreover, if Friedlaender drew upon the data uncovered and deciphered by archaeologists, he did not always consider their

---

[45]This is the thesis of "Nationalism and Assimilation in Biblical Times," *PP*, pp. 35-38.

implications. As a student of Friedrich Delitzsch he acknowledged ancient Israel's debt to her neighbors on the material level. However, without citing any evidence, he postulated Israel's exceptionalism in spiritual matters. Following Ahad Ha-am, he always insisted that her exalted notions of monotheism, law, and morality were *sui generis*, creations of the Hebrew spirit alone.

Furthermore, since Friedlaender did not deal with the Pentateuch, he never explained the origin of these concepts. One would have expected this student of David Hoffmann to have asserted that the ideas came from God, through Moses. He could have repeated Hoffmann's arguments against the Wellhausian reconstruction of the Pentateuch. Since he never did either, the reader is left with the impression that, much as he would have liked to have done so, he could not honestly dismiss the documentary hypothesis any more than he could embrace it.

Finally, as we have already noted, he openly adopted some of the conceptualizations of the higher criticism, if only to transvalue them. The problem remains that, because he did not discuss the origins of Israelite religion, he sometimes advanced arguments that conveyed implications which he probably never intended. Consider his thesis that Jewish ceremonialism is the practical application of the ideals of classical prophecy. Jewish tradition has always maintained that its laws and customs derive ultimately from the Torah, not the literary prophets. Friedlaender's gold-bars-into-gold-coins metaphor implies a Wellhausian conception which is anathema to any defender of Jewish tradition, namely, that the prophets preceded and were in part responsible for the composition of the Pentateuch.

How then can we summarize Friedlaender's contribution to biblical scholarship? First, we must admit that as a biblical "scientist" he was competent, but exceedingly timid. As a critic of the critics, on the other hand, he was incisive, advancing the Jewish response to Wellhausen several steps beyond Hoffmann. He did more than unmask contradictions; he revealed the ideological bent of the higher criticism, which distorted evidence in order to demonstrate foregone conclusions. However, because of the contradictions within his own thought—his inability to reconcile the notions that he absorbed from contemporary biblical scholarship with the traditional values which he cherished—he did not extend the frontiers of biblical knowledge. What he did was to utilize biblical ideas to promote cultural Zionism and to defend Jewish ceremonial law.

It is impossible to take leave of Friedlaender's biblical scholarship on a negative note. Let us close by contrasting it with the work of his contemporaries. In the opinion of H. L. Ginsberg, currently Sabato Morais Professor Emeritus in Biblical History and Literature, many scholars of Friedlaender's day "were devoting far too much time to an ever more minute dissection of the books . . . of the Bible into documentary 'sources,' and far too little to the study of their content and its utilization for history."[46]

To turn from their books to Friedlaender's *Past and Present* and "Aspects of Historical Judaism" is to move from dry-as-dust, picayune, highly speculative source criticism to bright and readable, if tendentious history. The greatness of the Bible has always been its ability to speak to people of all ages. There is no question that it really did convey to Friedlaender the message of spiritual Zionism and the vindication of Jewish law. It is also true that the professor made no attempt to conceal his biases. In the process, he produced writings that engage the mind and awaken the emotions sixty-four years after his death.

[46]H. L. Ginsberg, "New Trends in Biblical Criticism," p. 297.

Chapter 4
The Semitist

I belong in Semitic Studies, not Bible studies.
                        —*Israel Friedlaender to Harry Friedenwald*

The relation between Judaism and Islam . . . is based on
reciprocity; because it does not consist of mere giving or taking,
but is permeated by the principle: *do ut des*.
                        —*Israel Friedlaender*

Throughout his life, Israel Friedlaender regarded himself as an
orientalist rather than a Bible scholar. Scattered throughout his
correspondence are indications of this self-description; the first of
the above quotations offers its clearest illustration. Friedlaender's
conception of himself as an orientalist can be traced to his university training. It is true that he studied under Friedrich Delitszch
and David Hoffmann, who dealt, in quite different ways, with the
world of the Bible. Yet his scholarly inclinations were to a far
greater extent sharpened by two medievalists, Moritz Steinschneider and Theodor Noeldeke.

Steinschneider, Friedlaender's teacher at the *Veitel-Heine-
Ephraimsche Lehrenstalt*, is best known for his comprehensive critical
bibliographies which encompassed the entire spectrum of Jewish
literature. Dominating his work were several conceptions upon
which Friedlaender's historical perspective rested. Steinschneider
maintained that Jewish literature was the product of the tension
between an inner dynamic and external circumstance. Moreover,
he demonstrated the abiding worth of diaspora Jewry. Medieval

Jews he argued, were not only consumers of Arabic culture; they were also the producers and transmitters of ideas which affected Moslems in equal measure. Finally, his definition of Jewish literature was broad, including not only philosophical, theological, and halakhic works, but also books and manuscripts dealing with science and mathematics.

Equally significant in the development of Friedlaender's academic interests and historical perspective was Theodor Noeldeke, the Strassburg professor who directed his research, strongly recommended him for three academic positions,[1] and remained his correspondent long after his emigration to America.[2] Friedlaender felt a particular closeness to Noeldeke; on one occasion he asserted that he valued his teacher's humanity even above his outstanding scholarly accomplishments.[3]

Through Noeldeke, Friedlaender was exposed to the newer academic trends as well as the biases of contemporary French and German scholarship. Noeldeke was the paradigmatic philologist. Expert in all the languages of the Near East, he specialized in Arabic, Syriac, and Persian grammar. A peer of Steinschneider in devotion to scientific criticism, he nevertheless operated under several different assumptions. Steinschneider considered pedantic erudition as sufficient unto itself. Noeldeke did not; philology became a springboard from which to attack historical problems.

The two scholars also displayed divergent perceptions of the proper reading public for historical writing. Steinschneider censured such men as Graetz and the editor Ludwig Philippson for popularizing historical ideas. Noeldeke, on the other hand, published several books and many articles on Arabic culture and Islamic religion which were deliberately intended for the educated layman.

Distinguishing Noeldeke's point of view from that of Steinschneider and other Jewish scholars were certain presuppositions of German romantic historiography. One was the definition of history as past politics. Another was the racialist principle of

---

[1]I.e., his first position as *privatdozent* at the University of Strassburg, his Seminary professorship, and the Dropsie position mentioned in the correspondence between Friedenwald and Friedlaender, May 22, 1907, *Friedenwald MSS*.

[2]There is a large packet of letters from Noeldeke, dated 1903 to 1916, in *FP*, Box 10.

[3]See notes to unpublished address "Theodor Noeldeke as a Personality and as a Teacher," delivered at the Oriental Club, March 6, 1906. *FP*, Box 14.

historical interpretation, a curious mixture of romantic nationalism, comparative philology, and the new discipline of anthropol-
ogy. One of the issues with which Friedlaender had to deal was
Noeldeke's understanding of "Semites" and their religion. The
Strassburg orientalist maintained that Semites, i.e., people whose
ancestors spoke Semitic languages, were endowed with certain
indelible qualities: unreflective simplicity, a strong sense of moral
demand which often resulted in narrowness and fanaticism, and a
predilection for formalized religion.[4] Few of them cultivated a close
relationship with the living God. Christianity, though a daughter
religion of Judaism, borrowed its most exalted features from the
Greeks. "My studies as an Orientalist have been the very means of
increasing my philhellenism and I think that the same experience
will befall anyone who makes a serious but open-minded attempt to
acquaint himself with the nature of Eastern peoples."[5]

From Noeldeke, Friedlaender learned the techniques of close
philological analysis as well as the methods of drawing historical
conclusions from philological evidence. However, because of his
personal background and religious inclinations, he did not adopt
his teacher's *de haut en bas* attitude toward the religions and cultures
of the Near East. To the contrary; he brought to his Semitic studies
a predisposition in their favor. When the historical data under
consideration were of Jewish origin, this was strikingly evident.

An example was his doctoral dissertation, entitled *Der Sprachgebrauch des Maimonides*.[6] It was a philological study of the vocabulary,
syntax, and word usages employed by the great Jewish philosopher
in his *Guide to the Perplexed*. To the extent that the *Sprachgebrauch*
dealt with the language employed by Maimonides, it was a work of
disinterested scholarship. Careful philological analysis led to the
conclusion that Maimonides wrote the pure Arabic commonly
spoken by the educated Jews and Moslems of his day. However,
the analysis did not stop there. Friedlaender then examined the
language of Maimonides' Moslem contemporaries, arriving at the
conclusion that their literary expression, unlike his, was impure.

[4]See Noeldeke's *Sketches from Eastern History*, trans. John Sutherland Black (London and
Edinburgh, 1892), pp. 6-10, 45.
[5]Preface to Noeldeke's *Aufsätze fuer persischen Geschichte*, quoted in *Historians of the Middle
East*, ed. Bernard Lewis and P. M. Holt (London, 1962), pp. 309-310.
[6]The full title was *Der Sprachgebrauch des Maimonides. Ein lexikalischer und grammatischer
Beitrag zur Kenntnis des Mittelarabischen* (Frankfurt am Main, 1902). This was actually the first
half of the dissertation; the second half remained unpublished.

For, in order to embellish their writings with words and "anti-
quated" expressions deriving from the already archaic Koran, these
authors actually "repudiated the living language" of contemporary
discourse.[7] Unequivocally, this conclusion suggested the superiority of the Jewish philosopher to his Moslem contemporaries.

After his immigration to the United States, Friedlaender continued to devote special attention to Maimonides, examining a number of *geniza* fragments relating to his work in Fostat, including one
written in his own hand.[8] Among the *geniza* documents which he
transcribed were responsa, not only of Maimonides[9] but also of two
other halakhists, Shmuel ben Hofni[10] and Isaac ben Reuben.[11] The
most ambitious of Friedlaender's *geniza* ventures initiated in America concerned Maimonides' famous *Letter to Yemen*. His comparison
of three Arabic manuscripts to the extant Hebrew version was,
unfortunately, incomplete at the time of his death.[12]

Friedlaender's devotion to Maimonides stationed him in the
rationalistic tradition of earlier Jewish scholarship. No historical
figure was more venerated by committed Jews struggling to enter
European society than this symbol of Jewish rationality and urban-
ity, who functioned successfully in two cultures.

Another subject which engaged the concern of Jewish *Wissenschaft* scholarship was the political situation of medieval Jews
dwelling in Islamic lands. Dealing with this issue were three
articles which Friedlaender contributed to the *Jewish Quarterly
Review*. The first study, which sparked controversy with Louis
Ginzberg,[13] asked whether a certain *geniza* fragment was, as its title
indicated, "The Arabic Original of the Report of R. Nathan
Hababli,"[14] heretofore available only in Hebrew. To support his

[7]See excerpt from IF, *Selections from the Arabic Writings of Maimonides*, Semitic Studies
Series no. 1, edited by Richard Gottheil and Morris Jastrow (Leyden, 1909), p. xiv.

[8]"Ein Gratulationsbrief an Maimonides," in *Judaica, Festschrift zu Hermann Cohen's Siebzigsten Geburtstage* (Berlin, 1912), pp. 257-264. In 1916 Friedlaender paraphrased a section from
this congratulatory letter to Maimonides (probably on the latter's appointment as head of the
Egyptian Jewish community), sending it to Louis Brandeis on the occasion of his nomination
to the United States Supreme Court (*FP*, January 30, 1916).

[9]See "A New Responsum of Maimonides concerning the Repetition of the Shemoneh
Esreh," *JQR*, n.s. 5 (1914): 1-15.

[10]"Lessons from *Sefer Ha-shutafut* of R. Shmuel ben Hofni," (Hebrew), in *Festschrift zum
Siebzigsten Geburtstage David Hoffmann's* (Berlin, 1914), pp. 83-97.

[11]"Notiz. Zum *Sha-are Shevuot* des R. Isaac ben Reuben," in *MGWJ* 55 (1911): 501-502.

[12]The project was later assumed by Abraham Halkin, who published it under the title
Moses Maimonides' Epistle to Yemen (New York, 1952).

[13]Louis Ginzberg, *Geonica* (New York, 1909). See the section entitled "The Language of
Nathan Hababli's Report," pp. 22-29.

[14]*JQR*, o.s. 17 (1905): 747-761.

affirmative answer, Friedlaender advanced two kinds of arguments. The first were philological, based on the actual wording of the manuscript. The others were historical; Friedlaender drew inferences from the data to demonstrate how certain historical problems were illuminated at precisely the point at which the Arabic original deviated from the extant Hebrew text: the duration of Kohen Zedek's presidency, the identity of the sons of Netira, the chronology of the events under consideration.

Two shorter articles dealt with the continuance of Jewish settlement in Arabia after the Islamic conquest.[15]

Friedlaender's argument that Jews remained on the Arabian peninsula long after the time of Mohammad introduced a thesis of his more extensive Semitic studies: Jewish life and thought were not only a significant factor in the *origins* of Islam (a point made by Geiger at the inception of *Juedische Wissenschaft*);[16] they also figured in the *development* of the younger faith. In similar fashion, he would insist that Jewish religious and cultural creativity did not cease with the ascent of its daughter religions onto the plane of history.

Even as Friedlaender pursued conventional areas of Jewish scholarship, he also pondered a newer issue. This was the relationship between Judaism, Christianity, and Islam, not in the high culture of philosophy and official piety, but in the previously unexplored regions of messianism and sectarian heterodoxy. Inherent in the young man's decision to deal with these phenomena was a rejection of the rationalist bias of *Wissenschaft des Judentums*. Here he revealed himself a man of his time. For Friedlaender flourished during the period when scholars, influenced by the philosophical retreat from positivism,[17] initiated a sympathetic reexamination of historical phenomena previously regarded as outré: mysticism, chiliasm, and the popular culture of the unlettered *Volk*. Jewish historiography, to some degree, followed suit as some scholars reevaluated the Jewish past. Pitting themselves against the Reform Jews, who retained their allegiance to Enlightenment values, they deliberately immersed themselves in periods of time when Judaism embraced values that were emotional rather than intellectual. On the literary

---

[15]"The Jews of Arabia and the Gaonate," *JQR*, n.s. (1910): 249-252, and "The Jews of Arabia and the Rechabites," ibid, pp. 252-257.

[16]See his famous prize essay "Was hat Mohammed aus dem Judenthume aufgenommen?" (Baden, 1833).

[17]Cf. H. Stuart Hughes, *Consciousness and Society: The Reorientation of European Social Thought* (New York, 1958), chap. 1.

level, Hasidism, the object of Graetz's disdain, presented an appealing demeanor in the form of charming tales ingeniously reconstructed by Peretz and Buber. Younger adherents of the Historical School produced monographs on Hasidism, Kabbalah, and related aspects of Jewish mysticism. Among them were Friedlaender's mentor Simon Dubnow, who composed a sympathetic history of Hasidism,[18] his colleague Louis Ginzberg, the archetypical *mitnagged*, who nevertheless wrote a fine piece on Kabbalah,[19] and Solomon Schechter, who glorified the saint alongside the scholar.[20]

If his two colleagues on the Seminary faculty did not ignore the affective side of Judaism, it is nevertheless true that they concentrated their most protracted efforts upon rabbinic scholarship. Clarifying Ginzberg's position on the place of Halakha in Jewish historiography was the following statement: "No one will doubt except those who are given over to philological trifles or theological sophisms that it is the Halakah alone which gives us a true mirror of that time."[21]

We have already noted the several occasions when Friedlaender glanced into the halakhic mirror. But his wider choice of subject matter indicates that he relentlessly sought other reflections of medieval times, non-Jewish as well as Jewish. There is no question that he delighted in the "philological trifles" and the "theological sophisms" held in contempt by his colleagues. In contrast to Ginzberg and Schechter, most of Friedlaender's scholarly interest focused upon popular movements, not elitist philosophies, religious enthusiasm rather than conventional piety, heterodoxy more than orthodoxy. Moreover, despite the fact that he was a Jewish nationalist, and in contrast to all of the scholars mentioned above, he was drawn to ideas which adherents of the monotheistic creeds held in common.

It was Noeldeke who guided him along the path of comparative religion. After accepting the dissertation on Maimonides in 1901, he convinced the young scholar to carry on postdoctoral study of a manuscript by the eleventh-century Moslem historian Ali b. Aḥmad ibn Hazm, which dealt with the various heterodoxies of

---

[18]*Voskhod*, 1888-93; *Ha-Pardes*, 1894; *Ha-Shiloah*, 1901.
[19]"Cabalah," *Jewish Encyclopedia* 3:456-479.
[20]See "The Chassidim," *SJ* 1, pp. 1-45; "Safed in the Sixteenth Century—A City of Legists and Mystics," *SJ* 2, pp. 202-285.
[21]*Geonica*, p. ix.

Islam. This short period of research set the agenda for all of Friedlaender's major contributions to the field of Islamic and Judeo-Arabic historiography. By the time that Friedlaender sailed for America in September 1903, he had initiated projects on the following subjects, all of which grew out of his exploration of this document: the messianic idea in Islam, Moslem philosophies of history, the role of Abdallah b. Saba in the foundation of Shiism, Ibn Hazm's perspective on the Shiite heresy, the contributions of Shiism toward the growth of eighth-century Jewish messianism, and Khadir, the quasi-messianic figure of Moslem myth.[22]

Broadly speaking, the Semitic studies which engaged most of Friedlaender's attention dealt with a single significant issue: messianism. To legitimize his interest in an historical phenomenon eschewed by his rationalistic predecessors, he suggested that messianism expresses the universal longing for justice as well as salvation. What was the source of this movement, which so strongly influenced all three monotheistic religions? "The messianic belief of the Jews . . . emanated, like everything else that is great and original in ancient Israel, from the Jewish prophets."[23] In all three religious systems, the messianic impulse found its most fervent expression outside the religious establishment. Friedlaender treated two such phenomena. One was folklore, where popular imagination tended to dwell on proto-messianic figures from a large and interrelated literature. The other was heterodox sectarianism. He maintained that it was through the sects, rather than the traditional "churches," that the tremendous energy inherent in the prophetic-messianic idea was discharged.

To investigate sectarianism in the monotheistic religions, Friedlaender wrote four important monographs. The thesis of "The Messianic Idea in Islam"[24] was simple: Shiite messianism was rooted in Jewish messianism and a heterodox Christian belief. Evidence of its profound debt to Hebrew prophecy was its very terminology, which echoed the prophets' awareness of the wrongs of this world and their dreams of a just future for mankind. Shiites look forward to the return of their Mahdi, or messianic redeemer,

[22]"Autobiography, 1903."
[23]*PP (1919)*, p. 141.
[24]Ibid., pp. 139-158. A translation of *Die Messiasidee in Islam*, reprinted from *Festschrift zum 70 Geburtstage A. Berliner's* pp. 116-130 (Frankfurt am Main, 1903). The editors of the 1961 edition of *PP* apparently considered this valuable article too "technical" to be included in this volume. See the Editorial Note by Marvin S. Wiener.

who will one day "fill the earth world with justice, even as it is filled with injustice."[25]

A second study[26] suggested that the founder of this heterodox sect was Abdallah b. Saba, a dark-skinned Jew from Yemen or Ethiopia, who became a fanatical follower of Ali, son-in-law to Mohammad. Upon hearing the news of his leader's death, he refused to believe it but rather insisted that a substitute had died in his place. He was convinced that Ali would one day return to earth, resume his rightful position as head of Islam, and put an end to all earthly injustice. In Friedlaender's opinion, this doctrine was linked to the beliefs of the Christian Docetist sect, with whom Ibn Saba had come into contact. Docetists borrowed an ancient Gnostic dogma and maintained that the person nailed to the cross was not Jesus of Nazareth but a substitute who assumed his features. Jesus himself had not died, they proclaimed, but had ascended to heaven, whence he would one day return to earth.

The Docetist idea is one of the concepts analyzed in Friedlaender's most extensive study of Shiism, "Shiitic Elements in Jewish Sectarianism."[27] Its conclusions, like those of the monograph on Ibn Saba, were based upon the writings of medieval Jews and Moslems, such as Qirqisani and Ibn Hazm.[28] Friedlaender utilized evidence from Qirqisani as a foil to the view of Sharastani. Gerson D. Cohen points out that this piece demonstrated "the chronological, geographic, linguistic, and doctrinal affinities between Muslim Shiite beliefs and Jewish sectarian behavior and messianology in the eighth century."[29] Here Friedlaender observed that active medieval messianism first surfaced in eighth-century Persia. Followers of the Jewish and Alid messianic pretenders used similar terms to describe them. More significantly, they ascribed to them qualities, such as immortality and the ability to "hide" for centuries and then to reappear, that originated in Gnostic Docetism. Subsequently, with the defeat of the Persian Alids and the Jewish Isaunians, these ideas went underground. During the following

[25]Ibid., pp. 146, 149, 151, 156, 158.

[26]"Abdullah b. Saba, der Begruender der Si'a und sein juedischer Ursprung," *Zeitschrift fuer Assyriologie und Verwandte Gebiete* 23 (1909): 296-327; 24 (1910): 1-46.

[27]*JQR*, n.s. 1 (1910-11): 183-215; 2 (1911-12): 481-516; 3 (1912-13): 235-300.

[28]His essay "Qirqisani's Polemik gegen den Islam" was published in the *Zeitschrift fuer Assyriologie und Verwandte Gebiete* 26 (1911): 93-110.

[29]In "The Reconstruction of Gaonic History," Introduction to Jacob Mann's *Texts and Studies in Jewish History and Literature*, 2 vols. (New York, 1972), 1:lxii.

millennium they reappeared sporadically as new Jewish messianic pretenders and different would-be Muslim Mahdis arose upon the historical scene.

If the first two studies uncovered Jewish and Christian contributions to Shiism, the third suggested that once Shiism was established in certain areas, it made its mark upon Jewish messianism, which was revitalized in lands where it prevailed. The lesson was obvious; influences did not flow in one direction, but from Judaism and Christianity to Islam and then back again to Judaism. This essay conveyed a notion that would later become associated with the contemporary scholar Shelomo Dov Goitein: during the medieval ascendance of Islam, there were times when Moslems and Jews achieved a symbiotic relationship. In Friedlaender's words: "The relation between Judaism and Islam is of such particular attraction to the student, because, like every other healthy relation, be it between individuals or communities, it is based on reciprocity; because it does not consist of mere giving or taking, but is permeated by the principle: *do ut des.*"[30]

Rounding out his investigation of medieval sectarian messianism was a translation and commentary on Ibn Hazm's *Kitab al-Milal wa'n-Nihal.*[31]

Friedlaender's Semitic studies sustained some assumptions held neither by his predecessors nor his contemporaries. Consciously, he struggled against the mind-set of the medieval Moslem chroniclers who furnished his evidence as well as modern Western orientalists. The former, he argued, nourished a prejudice against all heresy and bent to the necessity of outlining their subject according to koranic specifications. The latter, he knew, internalized the European prejudice against Semitic spirituality. French and German scholars, especially, tended to explain religious schism in racialist terms. Edgar Blochet, for example, writing in 1903, explained the original rupture between Sunnites and Shiites as "the rivalry between the Iranian genius and the Semitic spirit."[32]

[30]*JQR*, n.s., 1:183-184.
[31]Published in two consecutive issues of the *Journal of the American Oriental Society* 27 (1907): 1-80 and 29 (1908): 1-183, under the title "The Heterodoxies of the Shiites in the Presentation of Ibn Hazm." Under the same title, it was published in book form by Yale in 1909. Previous to this, in a *Festschrift* article in honor of Noeldeke's seventieth birthday, entitled "Zur Komposition von Ibn Hazm's *Milal wa'n Nihal*" (Giessen, 1906), pp. 267-277, Friedlaender had explained the plan of his book and how he would carry it out.
[32]*Le Messianisme dans l'héterodoxie Musulmane* (Paris, 1903), quoted in *RÉJ* 40 (1903): 137.

Utilizing the same sources as his French and German colleagues, Friedlaender boldly disputed their findings. Shiism, he maintained, did not originate in Persia; its founders were "Arabs of the purest water."[33] This sect first developed in Iraq under "heterogeneous influences," Greek, Jewish, and Christian, "which came to bear upon the young Islam."[34] According to Friedlaender's account, Persians adopted Shiism for reasons which had nothing to do with race. Their action reflected, instead, the political condition of a proud people forcibly subjected to a younger civilization and their resultant emotional and cultural needs. Shi'at Ali, the party of Ali, sustained their conviction that the wrong people were in power. In promising the restoration of Mohammad's true heir, converted by Ibn Saba into a messianic figure, it also offered solace to this downtrodden nation. In addition, Shiism cultivated such ideas as the hereditary nature of royalty, which conformed to their rich Iranian heritage and thereby established continuity with their own national past.

It was more difficult to explain the Jewish messianic rebellion of Abu Isa of Isfahan. To account for its limited success, Friedlaender drew attention to the general ambiance of eighth-century Persia, "a seething cauldron of anarchy and revolution,"[35] and the type of men it produced, "adventurers and men of pluck."[36] Friedlaender knew that Shiism had captured the loyalty of many Moslems in Iraq. Why, then, he inquired, didn't Abu Isa attract Iraqi Jews to his cause? After considerable investigation, he concluded that "Babylonian Jewry was too strongly imbued with the Talmudic spirit and too firmly ruled by the authority of the Exilarch and the Geonim to submit to new-fangled doctrines of extravagant non-Jewish sectarians."[37] The Exilarchate and the Gaonate were political and religious institutions which strongly supported talmudic law. Like Louis Ginzberg, Friedlaender placed Halakha at the center of Jewish life and agreed that whenever it has been strong, it has successfully resisted countervailing pressures.

From these studies, it is clear that Friedlaender advanced a theory of multiple causation that was more complex and sophisti-

---

[33]*PP (1919)*, p. 150.
[34]"Heterodoxies," p. 5.
[35]Ibid., p. 205.
[36]Ibid. Here he quoted Wellhausen directly.
[37]Ibid., p. 208.

cated than those of many European orientalists. Implicitly rejecting race as a determining circumstance, he suggested that, in addition to political elements, such factors as *sitz im leben*, personality, and culture must be taken into consideration.

Of all Friedlaender's contributions, it is his four studies of medieval sectarianism that have proved most fruitful for twentieth-century research. Many of Friedlaender's insights have borne the test of time, but some details of his work have been called into question. Especially controversial were his bold assertions about Abdallah b. Saba. His analysis of this shadowy figure elicited acute criticism which has not abated with the passage of time. However, it should be noted that Friedlaender himself was aware of the speculative nature of his thesis, as his friend Alexander Marx noted.[38]

Other scholars have detected flaws in Friedlaender's "Shiitic Elements," which made extravagant claims in establishing fifteen points of contact between Moslem and Jewish sectarianism. Salo Baron, for example, has noted that there is no real compatibility between Abu Isa's *five* messengers and the number *seven* prominent in Jewish and Moslem soteriology.[39] And Gerson Cohen, who praised the work as a "major contribution,"[40] found another problem. He pointed out that Friedlaender "offered no new explanation of the genius and growth of Karaism."[41] This leaves the present writer to wonder why he did not apply to the Jewish sect his generalization about the Shiites—that they enacted their own Oral Law after rejecting the authority of the establishment.

The great contemporary analyst of Jewish messianism, Gershom Scholem, was unable to find any historical connection between Docetist doctrine and Shiitic beliefs.[42] However, this writer would like to point out that Friedlaender's analysis revolved around the Gnostic origin of Docetism, which Scholem also detects at the heart of Jewish messianic mysticism.

I would like to venture a few additional observations. Here and there Friedlaender's reasoning strikes me as unmethodical, his claim to enter the mind of his protagonists presumptuous. One

---

[38]See "Friedlaender the Scholar," p. 349.
[39]*A Social and Religious History of the Jews* (Philadelphia, 1957), vol. 5, p. 376.
[40]Gerson Cohen, "Reconstruction," p. lxii.
[41]Ibid.
[42]See Scholem's *Sabbatei Ṣevi* (Princeton, 1973), p. 605.

example is his analysis of "the one true prophet," a dogma which proclaims that "there is no development but merely a constant repetition of the one and the same religion,"[43] that each messiah to appear in history bears the spirit of all previous prophets.[44] Friedlaender claimed that this doctrine inspired such idiosyncratic figures as Abu Isa and Sabbatei Ṣevi. With characteristic irony, but no documentation, he suggested that Jacob Frank used it to "raise the disloyalty toward one's religion to a full-fledged philosophic doctrine."[45] One problem raised by this fascinating exposition is that it did not indicate the route by which this and other religious teachings traveled from paganism to Shiism to Judaism and, within Judaism, the place where they were hidden for hundreds of years until certain sectarians rediscovered them. In fairness, it must be admitted that this issue has confronted many intellectual historians. For example, scholars and polemicists have long searched for a bond between the Sadducees and the Karaites.

Another problem pivots on the problematic link that Friedlaender established between the various Jewish exponents of this dogma, a heretical belief in a connection between their ministries and those of Jesus and Mohammad. With no compunction he presumptuously entered the mind of Sabbatei Ṣevi: "There is little doubt in my mind that when Sabbatei Ṣevi, faced by the punishment of the Turkish authorities, threw down his Jewish cap and exchanged it for the turban, the theory of the One True Prophet lingered in the back of his mind to allay his scruples."[46]

"Shiitic Elements" presents yet another difficulty. At times it extends beyond the boundaries it set for itself, examining practices which have no connection to Shiism. For example, one of the "elements" is "the prohibition of meat and wine," a practice adopted by Karaites, Isaunians, and Yudganites. Friedlaender acknowledged the existence of this prohibition in Persia long before the advent of Islam. However, he failed to establish any connection between Jewish and Shiitic practice. All he did was to assert that Jewish sectarians were "swayed . . . by foreign non-Jewish conceptions."[47]

[43]*JQR*, n.s. 3:236.
[44]Ibid., p. 237. "One spirit indeed speaks through all the prophets."
[45]Ibid., p. 245.
[46]Ibid.
[47]Ibid., p. 296.

The corpus of Friedlaender's writings on Jewish and Moslem heterodoxy offers evidence that Friedlaender was at once hesitant and searching, timid and yet bold. On the one hand, he questioned both the medieval chronicles and the modern critics, carefully scrutinizing the sources upon which they based their conclusions. With great skill, he reorganized old and recently discovered data around new principles. On the other hand, he did not venture the final step; never did he combine all of his insights into a single synthetic work which would engage the attention of the academic world.

Instead, he turned to folklore, an outgrowth of his concern with the entire spectrum of human religiosity. Friedlaender's study of folk culture provided an opportunity to apply the symbiosis thesis to a new area. His work on Maimonides pointed to a reconciliation of Judaism with non-Jewish culture on the traditional basis of rationalist philosophy. Studies of Jewish and Moslem heterodoxies revealed mutual influences in the newly explored area of sectarian religion. Now evidence from comparative folklore demonstrated *do ut des* on the heretofore despised level of popular superstition.

A short article entitled "A Muhammedan Book on Augury in Hebrew Characters"[48] dealt with an item of folk superstition which was admittedly "vulgar" in style and content. Apologetically, Friedlaender maintained that its vulgarity did not render it unworthy of scholarly consideration; it only indicated that it was the product of the people rather than any elite. To demonstrate the value of this book on fortune-telling for serious scholarship, he sought out and compared manuscripts from three different European libraries.

Treating folk culture on a more literary level was Friedlaender's most extensive venture into Semitic scholarship and most ambitious exploration of the symbiosis thesis, his book-length investigation of the Moslem legend of the Khadir entitled *Die Chadirlegende und der Alexanderroman*.[49]

This legend, loosely based upon a koranic episode,[50] concerns a

[48]*JQR*, o.s. 19 (1906): 84-103.
[49]The full title is: *Die Chadirlegende und der Alexanderroman, Eine Sagengeschichtliche und Literarhistorische Untersuchung* (Leipzig and Berlin, 1913); a preliminary study under the title "Alexanders Zug nach dem Lebensquell und die Chadirlegende" had appeared in the *Sonderabdruck aus Archiv fuer Religionswissenschaft* 13 (1910): 92-110; see also Friedlaender's article on Khadir in *Hastings' Encyclopaedia of Religion and Ethics* (1914), 7:693-695.
[50]Sura 18:59-81.

"servant of God" known as "The Green One" (al-Khadir), who accompanied a certain Musa on a journey, performing acts which first appeared outrageously unfair, but which were justified at the end. In popular Moslem folklore, Khadir became a saint who gained immortal life by drinking from the Fountain of Life, and made himself available to travelers and others in need.

Many scholars before Friedlaender had examined this Islamic myth. Among them were Zunz, Derenbourg, Vollers, Rohde, Clermont-Ganneau, Lidzbarski, Goldziher, and Friedlaender's mentor Noeldeke, to whom the book was dedicated. As a rule, their conclusions stood upon two premises. They assumed that every folktale was based on a single motif or set of motives, each of which bears a certain message. Therefore it was the task of the scholar to determine first the origin of each motive and then its meaning.

The second premise reflected the racialist assumptions popular in Friedlaender's day.[51] It was endorsed by a biographer of Mohammad named Aloys Sprenger, who concluded that the Khadir complex of legends was totally pagan in origin, that the personality which it portrayed was "unbiblical and unsemitic."[52]

Implicitly rejecting both of these assumptions, Friedlaender contended that the first premise was not broad enough to encompass the very complex tangle of stories that constituted the legend of Khadir. As for the second, it was disproved by dispassionate examination of the evidence. In caustic language, he indicated the impossibility of isolating a single source of any myth: "Folk-fantasy, which creates folk legend is not mathematics, which operates on the basis of sharply defined units. It is quite fantastic. It is eclectic, snatching up everything it can get hold of, then incorporating these qualities in the character of its heroes."[53] Consequently he insisted that the very question asked by his predecessors, "Who is Khadir?" should be reformulated to read "What are the manifold, often heterogenous components out of which the Khadir portrait is created?"[54]

[51]For a discussion of the racialist theories which underlay the study of folklore during the late nineteenth and early twentieth centuries, see Stith Thompson, *The Folktale* (New York, 1946), passim.
[52]*Das Leben und die Lehre des Muhammad* (Berlin, 1869), 2:466.
[53]*Chadirlegende*, p. 251.
[54]Ibid., p. 252.

The answer was implied in the question. Friedlaender uncovered sources for this legend of eternal life in the folktales and sagas of many peoples: the Babylonians, who fashioned the Epic of Gilgamesh; the Greeks, who attributed eternal life to such diverse figures as the mythical Glaucus and Andreas, the wily cook of Alexander the Great; the Jews, who took comfort in stories about Elijah, the prophet who ascended to heaven in a fiery chariot, as well as the lesser figure of Rabbi Joshua ben Levi;[55] and the Christians, who ascribed Elijah-like (and later Khadir-like) qualities to several of their national saints.

The presentation of Khadir as a syncretic figure embodying elements from both Aryan and Semitic cultures contested the racialist assumptions of contemporary historiography. The thesis, however, was never stated in so many words. Indeed, the book ended not with a conclusion but with a series of appendices, the most important of which was the first, "Towards a History of the Khadir Legend." Here Friedlaender modestly declared that his monograph was anything but the last word on this complex question. "A satisfying and exhaustive solution of the problem requires a serious consideration of the entire cultural orbit with which the Mohammedan folk spirit has come into contact. This is an enormous task, which is beyond the powers of a single individual."[56]

Unwilling to draw conclusions, Friedlaender arranged his subject matter in such a way as to render generalization impossible. As a rule, folklorists of his day organized their data according to a triadic plan. First they isolated distinct motives; then they indicated their appearance in the literature, oral as well as recorded. The final step was to draw conclusions about the nature and significance of each motif.[57] To a certain extent, Friedlaender's "Shiitic Elements in Jewish Sectarianism" followed this pattern. Although it formulated no generalized conclusions, its data were organized along vertical lines. Each of the fifteen sections analyzed a single motif, indicating where it appeared in the systems of the various Moslem and Jewish heterodoxies. The *Chadirlegende*, by contrast, was organized horizontally. Each chapter treated all of the

---

[55]Cf. Adolph Jellinek, *Bet Ha-Midrash*, 6 vols. (Jerusalem, 1967), 5:133-135.

[56]*Chadirlegende*, p. 252.

[57]Cf. Alexander H. Krappe, "Folklore and Mythology," in *Funk and Wagnall's Standard Dictionary of Folklore, Mythology, and Legend*, 2 vols. (New York, 1977), 1:404.

motives found in a single literature: the Pseudo-Callisthenes, the Babylonian Talmud, the Syrian homily, the Koran, the Moslem *ḥadith*, and then all the Moslem authors who pursued the subject.

Despite the singular richness of this monograph, its organizational structure and the absence of conclusions render it a reference book rather than a history. Nevertheless, it sustained several historical propositions underlying Friedlaender's other Semitic studies. The first was apologetic: Jewish creativity did not end with the dispersion of Israel from its land and the canonization of Scripture; Christianity and Islam did not inherit a mantle tossed away by the people which rejected Jesus and Mohammad. To the contrary, Jews not only continued to don the garments of cultural creativity; they even embroidered them with threads of brighter hue and richer texture. Nor did they keep them all to themselves. Among the finest were myths and sagas which found their way into general folk culture.

This led to a second major thesis. In all of his studies of Moslem and Jewish literature, Friedlaender developed the concept formulated by the nineteenth-century Jewish scholars Solomon Munk and his teacher Steinschneider. These men had firmly established the distinctive contribution of Islam to medieval civilization and the role of the Jews in transferring this culture to Europe. Expanding upon this idea, Friedlaender indicated that medieval culture was a river that flowed in two directions, swelled by the waters of many tributaries. Shiism received its intense longing for redemption from the dreams of the Hebrew prophets; it, in turn, contributed elements from heterodox Islamic messianism to the Jewish sects that arose in early medieval Persia. The Islamic Khadir figure reflected soteriological Elijah myths; soon Moslem concepts and terms were applied to the herald of Jewish redemption. Moreover, just as Christian Docetism was an essential component of Shiite Islam, so were Christian traders the bearers of the Glaucus myth to Arabia. Not surprisingly, some characteristics of Elijah-Khadir found their way back to Christianity, where they were applied to the person of St. George.[58]

A third theme pervaded Friedlaender's investigation of sectarianism and folk mythology. In an effort to prove the superiority of Judaism to other religions, he sometimes advanced beyond conven-

[58]*Chadirlegende*, p. 275.

tional apologetics. A fundamental premise underlying Friedlaender's scholarship was the conviction that at the heart of religion was the longing for redemption, formulated classically by the Hebrew prophets. The prophetic hope was first personified in the biblical and aggadic figure of the Messiah, who would bring justice and peace to Israel and the entire world. Yet when Christianity embraced messianism, it transformed a living idea into a static concept. As a result, "the Messianic idea in Christianity was bound, after a short-lived development, to reach its climax and thereby its end."[59]

The messianic idea in Judaism, in contrast, continued to evolve. It was taken up by Jewish sectarians who expressed the longing for redemption in sporadic outbursts of enthusiasm for outrageous characters claiming to be either the Messiah himself or his herald. Though all of their missions were aborted, the very appearance of these figures testifies to the vitality of the Jewish messianic idea. Also indicating its dynamic quality was the part it played in the origins of Islam's messianic sect, Shiism. That the Jewish messianic idea continued its creative growth was also illustrated by the popularity of the Elijah figure. Originally a biblical prophet, a man of the desert who denounced the activities of kings and ascended to heaven in a fiery chariot, he was transmuted by folk imagination into Elijah-Khadir-St. George, who brought hope and inspired faith in the hearts of millions of humble Jews, Moslems, and Christians.

How can we evaluate Friedlaender the Semitist? Not surprisingly, his work remains a model of Germanic thoroughness and critical acumen; later scholars questioned some of his conclusions, but also continued to build larger structures on the basis of his findings.[60] It seems to this writer that for several reasons Friedlaender's scholarship deserve a wider reading public than it has received: the heuristic observations about multiple causation of past events, the indirect but devastating attack upon the prejudices of other historians, the early exposition of the symbiosis hypothesis, and, finally, the writing itself, which was often ironic, yet peculiarly uplifting. That its reputation has not grown with time is probably the product of two factors. The first, it must be repeated, was

[59]*PP (1919)*, p. 144.
[60]See the article "Al Khadir," by A. J. Wensinck, in the *Encyclopedia of Islam* (London and Leyden, 1927), 2:361-365.

Friedlaender's failure to synthesize his findings into a single, comprehensive monograph. Of no less consequence was his dispassionate attitude toward sectarian heterodoxy, messianology, folk mythology, and superstition. Unlike Martin Buber, his contemporary, and Gershom Scholem, who began to publish soon after his death, Friedlaender did not attach to these phenomena any profound significance; he certainly would have disputed Buber's contention that they were the most genuine repository of Jewish religiosity.[61] Instead, he sustained Louis Ginzberg's conclusion that, in the final analysis, it was Halakha and the institutions that supported it which determined the direction of Jewish life. Friedlaender's lifework in Semitic studies argued for a sensible (and I would say authentic) balance between the halakhic and the aggadic strains of Judaism. Additional evidence of this unfashionably conservative strain in his thinking was the esteem with which he treated the medieval historians. It was of a piece with his advice to his students to consult Kimche for insights into the Bible.

Friedlaender's statement to Harry Friedenwald that he "belonged" in Semitics studies was unquestionably true. However, he was not content to remain a narrow specialist; he became, instead, a scholar concerned with the broad range of Jewish history. His public lectures seethed with excitement about the totality of the Jewish historical experience; his popular articles and books were governed by a faith in the usability of the past. Thus Friedlaender's reputation did not rest upon his Semitics scholarship, but upon his analysis of historical periods which yielded lessons for an American Jewish community seeking continuity with the past and struggling for viability.

[61]Martin Buber, *Tales of the Hasidim: The Early Masters* (New York, 1947), p. 3.

Chapter 5

A Fresh Assessment of Jewish History

> The Jewish settlement in America is from its birth an offshoot of our great center in Russia, and when the old mother is in bad and difficult circumstances she is drawn hopefully to her young daughter in the land of the free. We are strongly bound to that part of our national family that has moved across the sea. It is bone of our bone and flesh of our flesh. Our strength is the greater in that, in our war for liberation, we have two positions, we will receive him properly; but in the event of the worst possible extremity, the second position will be left for Jacob and the "remaining camp will be able to escape."
>
> —*Simon Dubnow*

> If the spiritual history of the Jew in the Diaspora is holy ground, because it represents the triumph of the few over the many, of the weak over the strong, of the spirit over the flesh, it is doubly holy ground in the case of Russo-Polish Jewry. For it is in Poland and Russia that the culture of Diaspora Judaism has found its most perfect manifestation.
>
> —*Israel Friedlaender*

Friedlaender's Judeo-Arabic studies uncovered two dynamic and vitalizing forces in Jewish history. Emanating from the dominant ideal of Judaism was the first, the quest for justice. The prophets of Israel set before the adherents of Judaism and her daughter religions a luminous goal: "to fill the earth with justice, even as it is now filled with injustice." In times of exceptional distress, this unfulfilled dream erupted in heterodox challenges to the religious establishment and messianic outbursts. It was these periods of upheaval which awakened Friedlaender's scholarly interest. However, he realized that Jewish survival has depended upon a second factor, the diversion of prophetic enthusiasm along regular ritual, legal, and social channels. If his serious scholarship seized upon the exotic manifestations of religion, his lectures and treatises directed to the public at large followed the less dramatic trends. As a popularizer of Jewish history, Friedlaender centered attention upon the stable periods of diaspora life, shamelessly idealized in two important essays.

"The Problem of Judaism in America" (1907) established a paradigm for emerging American Judaism in the culture of medieval Andalusia. *The Jews of Russia and Poland* (1915) examined the immediate past of the Russian Jewish immigrants. During the eight years that separated these two works, Friedlaender's historical perspective underwent significant modification. This chapter will document and analyze the shift in the direction of Friedlaender's interest, from mostly serious to entirely popular scholarship, from the glories of medieval Spain to the tortures of contemporary Russia, from the promising potential of American Jewry to the parlous condition which prevailed in his day.

By the time of his arrival in America, Friedlaender had already internalized the *Wissenschaft* understanding of the medieval Judeo-Arabic period as the epitome of what he would call a "union between Judaism and freedom." Exemplifying this perception is a series of essays he devoted to the life and thought of Moses Maimonides, the most prominent representative of that civilization. The second year of Friedlaender's settlement in America, 1904, was the seven-hundredth year since the death of the great philosopher. To commemorate this anniversary, Friedlaender delivered an important Seminary lecture.[1]

It is noteworthy that in the same year, Ahad Ha-am published a lengthy disquisition on the same topic. A comparison of the two essays will once again illustrate the divergence of Friedlaender's historical perspective from that of his Odessan mentor. The thesis of Ahad Ha-am's essay on Maimonides was evident from the title of his essay, "The Supremacy of Reason." It measured Maimonides

---

[1]"Moses Maimonides," *PP*, pp. 113-145.

according to a fixed standard of rationality and concluded that this great Jew, unlike most historical figures, met the mark. For he subordinated everything to reason, including religion. "Religion is not above reason, but below it: just as the masses, for whom religion was made, are below the perfect man. Reason is the supreme judge; religion is absolutely subordinate to reason, and cannot abrogate one jot of its decisions."[2]

Friedlaender's essay on Maimonides demonstrated significant differences from the thought of Ahad Ha-am in the same areas as his discourses on the prophets. The first was his commitment to the methods and values of German historical scholarship. Unlike Ahad Ha-am's philosophical disquisition on the great philosopher, Friedlaender's lecture breathed life into the historical person of Moses ben Maimon. It portrayed a strong-minded great soul who suffered the pain of exile and the loss of dear ones, who experienced the joy of raising a late-born son to maturity, along with the burden of serving the sultan and the Jewish community of Fostat as a physician. All of this provided a background for an analysis of Maimonides' exegetical, halakhic, and philosophic works.

Because of his great respect for Ahad Ha-am, Friedlaender rarely criticized him in public; the two men discussed their divergent views on the prophets only in private correspondence.[3] However, in an obscure bibliographic publication,[4] Friedlaender responded in print to the older man's essay on Maimonides. He praised it as a venture into *Wissenschaft* scholarship, but criticized it for disobeying an important rule of historical writing. "This construction ascribes motives to Maimonides which are essentially modern and therefore an anachronism."[5] What was anachronistic, in Friedlaender's opinion, was the view that any medieval thinker could possibly subordinate religion to reason.

This was an unmistakable illustration of a second deviation from Ahad Ha-am, the secularist philosopher who minimized the role of the Jewish religion. In his view, Judaism had merely provided a protective shield for the Jewish nation. Thus his 1904 essay virtually ignored any religious motivations which might have inspired Maimonides and maintained that the medieval philosopher

---

[2]"The Supremacy of Reason" (Kohn ed.), p. 255.
[3]Ahad Ha-am, *Igrot*, 5:57.
[4]"Some Ahad Ha-am Publications," *PP (1919)*, pp. 423-430.
[5]Ibid., p. 428.

had ventured into biblical exegesis and the codification of Jewish law in order to legitimize the rationalistic assumptions of the *Guide to the Perplexed.*[6]

Friedlaender, on the other hand, considered religion the dominant force in historical Judaism. He was convinced that the ability to commune with God characterized the ancient prophets, that the record of their contact with the Divine in its biblical and exegetical forms inspired every generation of believing Jews, even the most sophisticated. Thus, in response to Ahad Ha-am, Friedlaender argued that Maimonides never envisioned any incompatability between the text of the Bible and the practice of Jewish Law on the one hand and the truths of Aristotle on the other.[7]

Friedlaender published two more essays on the man whose writings had been the subject of his doctoral dissertation.[8] It was evident that Maimonides was no mere object of analysis, but a personal model: a scholar of impeccable style as well as solid substance, a community activist concerned with the physical and spiritual welfare of his people, a man whose primary task was "pedagogic," inspiring the people to sustain their faith in God and their loyalty to suffering Israel. Above all, Friedlaender admired Maimonides' success at reconciling Judaic and secular culture.

It was the conviction that the modern Jew was capable of living creatively in two worlds that inspired Friedlaender's most memorable public address, "The Problem of Judaism in America." The speaker posed an important rhetorical question, expressed in two ways. First, realistically: "Is there no hope for the Jews to participate in the life and culture around them and yet remain Jewish?" Then, metaphorically: "Is Judaism actually like a gas, which can only be kept by the grip of iron and evaporates when allowed to escape from its prison?"[9]

To answer the question in the negative and thus affirm the possibility of a "Judaism of freedom and culture,"[10] he indicated

[6]See Section 2 of "The Supremacy of Reason" (Kohn ed.), pp. 247-260.

[7]*PP (1919)*, pp. 428-429.

[8]"Maimonides as an Exegete," a discourse first rendered in England in 1906 and published in *PP* (1919), pp. 193-216; and "Maimonides as a Master of Style," an essay first published in a German collection of essays on Maimonides, *Moses ben Maimon* (Leipzig, 1908), 1:429-438. Translated into English for *PP* (1919), pp. 217-228, it was later translated into Hebrew by I. Zidman and published in *Leshonenu* 6 (1935): 291-300.

[9]*PP*, p. 169.

[10]Ibid., p. 177.

that "the Jews took an honorable and energetic part in the economic, social, and political development of the Eastern, as well as the Western, Califate."[11]

After citing the names and accomplishments of such versatile Spanish luminaries as Ibn Nagrela, ibn Gabirol, and, of course, Maimonides, he concluded, "Thus the great Jewish-Arabic period irrefutably shows that Judaism *is* compatible with freedom, and that a full participation in the life of the nations may very well be reconciled with a deep attachment to Judaism and a vigorous activity in its behalf."[12]

The essay closed with a ringing apostrophe which for decades would remain the embodiment of the Jewish-American dream.

We perceive a community great in numbers, mighty in power, enjoying life, liberty and the pursuit of happiness: true life, not mere breathing space; full liberty, not mere elbow room; real happiness, not that of pasture beasts; actively participating in the civic, social and economic progress of the country, fully sharing and increasing its spiritual possessions and acquisitions, doubling its joys, halving its sorrows; yet deeply rooted in the soil of Judaism, clinging to its past, working for its future, true to its traditions, faithful to its aspirations, one in sentiment with their brethren wherever they are, attached to the land of their fathers as the cradle and resting place of the Jewish spirit; men with straight backs and raised heads, with big hearts and strong minds, with no conviction crippled, with no emotion stifled, with souls harmoniously developed, self-centered and self-reliant; receiving and resisting, not yielding like wax to every impress from the outside, but blending the best they possess with the best they encounter; not a horde of individuals, but a set of individualities, adding a new note to the richness of American life, leading a new current into the stream of American civilization; not a formless crowd of taxpayers and voters, but a sharply marked community, distinct and distinguished, trusted for its loyalty, respected for its dignity, esteemed for its traditions, valued for its aspirations, a community such as the Prophet of the Exile saw it in his vision: "And marked will be their seed among the nations, and their offspring among the peoples. Everyone that will see them will point to them as a community blessed by the Lord."[13]

[11]Ibid., p. 170.
[12]Ibid., p. 172.
[13]Ibid., pp. 183-184.

The year 1907, when he wrote and delivered "The Problem of Judaism in America," was also the time of Friedlaender's first major personal disappointment, the loss of the Dropsie position. Perhaps because of this, he never again expressed a vision of American Judaism that was quite so glowing, quite so optimistic. Nevertheless, as time went on, he continued to promote the Judeo-Arabic model for Jewish modernity as well as other perceptions borrowed from German Jewish historical scholarship. In the course of time, however, these perceptions were supplemented and eventually all but supplanted by newer ones which rested on different assumptions.

Moses ben Maimon served as Friedlaender's personal model; another figure, however, exerted a more direct influence upon his historical outlook. *Wissenschaft des Judentums* was the matrix of Friedlaender's general purview of Jewish history, but the historical and philosophical works of Simon Dubnow were the source of most of his notions about specific areas of Jewish historiography. They became the rock upon which he constructed his own historical edifice.

The two men never met personally, yet their relationship, which extended over a period of twenty-two years, produced a rich literature, consisting of letters, translations, and original writings.[14] To initiate contact with the older historian, Friedlaender wrote Dubnow a letter requesting permission to translate his "Essay on the Philosophy of History" into German. Permission was granted. Pleased with the results,[15] Dubnow assigned Friedlaender the German translation of two of his "Letters on Old and New Judaism."[16] Friedlaender soon became the English translator and summarizer of Dubnow's Russian Jewish history. To this we shall return later in the chapter.

It was not sufficient to publicize Dubnow's historical message;

---

[14]Two works deal with the relationship between Friedlaender and Dubnow. One is Koppel S. Pinson's essay "Simon Dubnow: Historian and Political Philosopher," which introduces his edition of Simon Dubnow's *Nationalism and History: Essays in Old and New Judaism* (New York, 1970). The other is Moshe Davis's publication of the correspondence between Friedlaender and Dubnow, under the title "Jewry, East and West."

[15]The translation was published under the title *Ein geschichts-philosophischer Versuch von S. M. Dubnow* (Berlin, 1898). Henrietta Szold translated Friedlaender's introduction and German translation into English (Philadelphia, 1903). Thus, in a special sense, Friedlaender and Dubnow arrived in America in the same year. (See Pinson, *Nationalism*, pp. 253-324.)

[16]Published under the title *Die Grundlagen des National-judentums* (Berlin, 1905) with an eight-page introduction by the translator. See Pinson, *Nationalism*, pp. 73-115.

Friedlaender proceeded to analyze it as well. In the preface to the first of his translations, the twenty-two-year-old student lavishly praised the work for its scientific objectivity and attractive style. He also discovered it in the old *Wissenschaft* virtue of establishing a bond between Jewish and general history. Finally, he commented upon its social usefulness. He was certain that it would "arouse enthusiastic interest"[17] on the part of Jewish readers of varying background and education in the survival of Judaism. It is noteworthy that at the beginning of his academic career, Friedlaender found in Dubnow's writings qualities which would later distinguish his own literary creations.

The major thesis of Dubnow's essay, the spiritual nature of the Jewish people, was borrowed from the thought of the preeminent nineteenth-century Jewish historian, Heinrich Graetz. Although Dubnow would later change his emphasis from the spiritual to the sociological, Friedlaender never did, as their correspondence over a later translation would indicate.[18] Ever the ardent devotee of Ahad Ha-am, the Historical School, and the early Dubnow, he would continue to advance this concept in his essays, public lectures, and class discussions.

Also instrumental in the shaping of Friedlaender's historical outlook was Dubnow's periodization. The older historian utilized the language of geology and divided the Jewish past along three major "stratifications": the primary, or biblical, period; the secondary, or spiritual-political, period (Second Temple); and the tertiary, or national-religious (talmudic), period. Jewish history after 500 C.E. consisted of four "composite formations." The first three witnessed the successive hegemony of Oriental, Sephardic, and German-Polish Jewry. The last was "the modern period of enlightenment."[19]

Friedlaender's own discourses on Jewish history hewed to Dubnow's division of postexilic history into periodic hegemonic centers.[20]

Equally influential upon Friedlaender's historiography was a related problem raised by Dubnow, and, indeed, by all Jewish intellectuals of his day, the assimilation of Jews into the host

[17]Pinson, *Nationalism*, p. 255.
[18]See Davis, "Jewry, East and West," p. 24.
[19]Pinson, *Nationalism*, p. 272.
[20]See *Aspects* and *SE*.

culture which, in every European country, came in the wake of
Emancipation. It was Dubnow who introduced the term "isolation"[21] to characterize the attitude of those Jews who, in an effort to
preserve their identity, turned their backs on the outside world.
Following Dubnow, Friedlaender established a dichotomy between periods of Jewish history marked by isolation (also called
"nationalism" and "Nibdalism") and those which manifested the
opposite quality of assimilation. Here is how he defined the terms:
"We may formulate Assimilation as the tendency of a people to
become *similar* to the other nations, and Nationalism as the endeavor to retain its identity, to be *different* from other nations."[22]
This is followed by a moral judgment. "The former is mostly
unconscious, or semi-conscious, because it means *yielding* to nature;
the latter is generally conscious, because it involves *resistance* to
nature. Hence, apart from other considerations, Nationalism is
morally superior to Assimilation."[23]

It was on this scale that Friedlaender weighed all periods of
Jewish history, beginning with the biblical and extending through
the medieval and early modern hegemonic centers. In most cases
the "good" periods were characterized by "isolation"; their heroes
were men who adhered to this principle. "Bad" periods were
marked by rampant assimilation, promoted by errant leaders. Thus
the "bad" era under the Israelite and Judean kings who assimilated
pagan notions of political supremacy and Baal worship was followed by the golden age of the prophets, who separated the people
to enable them to become a beacon of morality for their neighbors.
The subsequent "bad" period of exile was followed by the "good"
one in which the leaders of the returning remnant, Ezra and
Nehemiah, forced the men of Judah to send away their foreign
wives and children, in order to insure that they would remain
"*Nibdalim*, 'separated' from the inhospitable environment."[24]

The Maccabees inaugurated the next "good" period; they fought
"not for the political supremacy but for the spiritual supremacy of
the Jewish people." If Friedlaender idealized the sons of Mattathias
as symbols of religious isolation, he portrayed their royal descendents as the embodiment of assimilation. "The later Maccabeans

---

[21]In the second of his *Letters on Old and New Judaism*. See Pinson, *Nationalism*, p. 113.
[22]*PP*, p. 35 (IF's emphasis).
[23]Ibid., pp. 35-36.
[24]Ibid., p. 37; *Aspects* III, 8.

who were contaminated by Pagan culture, and in some cases were entirely de-Judaised, did not understand this self-restraint of their victorious predecessors and, imperialists that they were, they began to extend the dominions of their power by means of conquests."[25]

Friedlaender's evaluation of later Jewish history also assumed a Dubnowian perspective. It will be remembered that Dubnow divided post-talmudic Judaism into four "composite formations" of hegemonies, each of which became, for several centuries, "the center of gravity of the scattered Jewish people."[26] That Friedlaender freely adopted this idea is evident from his classroom discussions and popular addresses. One popular lecture series organized Jewish history into six "significant epochs." The penultimate lecture dealt with the Spanish-Arabic period; the final address treated Ashkenazic Jewry of the late medieval and modern periods. Like the Russian historian, Friedlaender discussed them in sequential order, without mentioning that the Jews who left Spain in the late Middle Ages were seldom the same people who settled in Poland during the same period. Predicated upon the same assumption was a magazine article addressed to the general American public.[27] It began: "The expulsion of the Jews from Spain in 1492 transferred the center of Judaism from the Iberian peninsula to the ancient Empire of Poland."[28] Like Dubnow, Friedlaender virtually ignored the existence of Jewish life in places that did not qualify as "hegemonic centers."

Moreover, Friedlaender's analysis of post-talmudic history, proceeded upon the hypothesis that periods of isolation alternated with periods of integration. Thus the four periods of Geonic, Sephardic, Askenazic, and post-Enlightenment Jewry demonstrated a definite rhythm: isolation, assimilation, isolation, assimilation. However, in his early writings, the "assimilation" of the second, the Sephardic period, was qualified considerably. Because Sephardic Jewry managed to embellish the tents of Shem with the beauty of Japheth, it was a worthy precursor to the new American community. "The Problem of Judaism in America," as we have already

[25]Ibid., III, 13-14.
[26]Pinson, *Nationalism*, p. 272.
[27]Appearing in the *New York Times Magazine*, January 14, 1917, under the title "The Problem of Polish Jewry."
[28]Reprinted in *PP*. See p. 148.

noted, envisioned the United States as a fifth hegemonic center, modeled neither upon the "isolation" of its Ashkenazic matrix nor upon the "assimilation" of post-Emancipation West European Jewry, but upon the "Judaism of freedom and culture" of medieval Spain. Implied in this synthesis of Central and East European historiography was a rejection of the recent past of every American Jew, whether he hailed from Central or Eastern Europe.

In the final years of his life, much of Friedlaender's youthful optimism waned. He retained the Dubnowian periodization, but modified his evaluation of the various historical epochs. Events in the world at large and in the American Jewish community precipitated this change. The overwhelming political fact of the period was, of course, World War I, which erupted volcanically, evoking pained surprise on the part of American Jewry (and most other people as well). The sufferings of millions of Austrian, Polish, and Lithuanian Jews, living in an area suddenly transformed into a war zone, created panic among their kinsmen in America. This, combined with the need to assert independence from the German Jewish *shtadlanim*, generated the factional dispute over the creation of an American Jewish Congress. Every American Jewish organization was affected by the war: the Zionist Federation, the Kehillah, the Bureau of Education, the youth movements, the American Jewish Committee. Active in all of them, Friedlaender was called upon ever more frequently to explain current policy.

It was natural for a disciple of Dubnow and adherent of Historical Judaism to consult the past. Under the burning pressure of war, the Spanish "Golden Age," which heretofore had appeared so appropriate a model for American Jewry, became almost irrelevant. After 1914, Friedlaender focused upon the actual situation of contemporary Jewry and its current needs.

He had long been convinced of the need for an English-language history of the East European experience rooted in the insights of Simon Dubnow. During the time when the Judeo-Arabic era still engaged his attention, he had briefed the Jewish Publication Society on the merits of such a project. Twice, in 1906 and 1907, he recommended to the Publication Committee that someone undertake a summary rather than a direct translation of Dubnow's words.

The committee accepted Friedlaender's suggestion, but made no specific plans for the project until 1910. In December of that year,

Friedlaender wrote a personal letter to Dubnow with a proposal for a manuscript to "cover about 500 pages octavo and . . . contain about 175,000 words."[29] A year later, Dubnow agreed to undertake the assignment, but only after 1913.[30] In October of that year, Friedlaender, in the capacity of reader for the JPS, received the first part of the manuscript, but he had not yet decided to become its English translator.

His initial reaction to the work reflected the "spiritual" perspective of both of his Odessan mentors. In a book intended for American readers, he suggested, the external conditions of Russian life, "particularly the economic and political oppression,"[31] should be minimized; it should focus instead upon "the mental makeup of the Russian Jew, his beliefs, characteristics, inclinations, ideals, his position and significance within the Jewish people."[32]

Dubnow responded with an explanation for his selection of subject matter and organization. Nevertheless, he granted permission to Friedlaender and Friedlaender alone to delete whatever materials he considered superfluous.[33]

Before he received this letter, Friedlaender had not yet made up his mind to undertake the translation; the above sentiments apparently influenced his decision to do so in April 1914. The first installment arrived in time for Friedlaender to launch the enterprise during the following summer in England. As he initiated the project, he did not realize that this would be his last opportunity to receive Dubnow's manuscripts without having to deal with the bureaucratic, often senseless actions of an autocratic government mired in war. The onset of hostilities changed everything. First, the two men, who had previously corresponded in Hebrew, had to alter their medium of communication. Now Dubnow wrote in Russian; Friedlaender in English. More significantly, Russian censorship slowed down both the transmission of the manuscripts and the remission of payment.

Further complicating the undertaking was Friedlaender's discovery that the work was too cumbersome to be published in a single volume. With the aid of Henrietta Szold, his friend and long-

[29]Davis, "Jewry, East and West," p. 19.
[30]Ibid.; from a letter dated December 26, 1911. The printed text reads "1901," clearly a typographical error.
[31]Ibid., p. 24. Letter dated October 29, 1913.
[32]Ibid.
[33]Ibid., p. 28.

standing secretary of the JPS, he subdivided the project first into two and then three volumes. He also reorganized Dubnow's opus into shorter chapters than those designated by the author, to suit the taste of the American reader. The Jewish Publication Society published the three volumes in 1916, 1918, and 1920. (Prefacing the last of the trio was a short note of regret at Friedlaender's untimely death.) It should be noted that, although Dubnow included some of the materials selected by Friedlaender for translation in other works, his *History of the Jews in Russia and Poland From the Earliest Times Until the Present Day* was published only in Friedlaender's English version.

Clearly, the opus was undertaken in a spirit of service to the community shared by publisher, author, and translator. To accentuate its importance, the Publication Society issued the first volume before its long-planned Bible translation. Dubnow himself maintained that Friedlaender had urged him to take on the assignment with the following "argument": "the desire to connect the American branch of Jewry, which is continually developing and occupying an important place in the future of our people, to its ancient root in the east of Europe."[34]

Actually, Dubnow was one of the few European intellectuals willing to attach significance to American Jewry. The discussion of this subject which closes his "Thirteenth Letter" must therefore have greatly appealed to Friedlaender, the more so because of its striking[35] biblical allusion.

> The Jewish settlement in America is from its birth an offshoot of our great center in Russian, and when the old mother is in bad and difficult circumstances she is drawn hopefully to her young daughter in the land of the free. We are strongly bound to that part of our national family that has moved across the sea. It is bone of our bone and flesh of our flesh. Our strength is the greater in that, in our war for liberation, we have two positions, we will receive him properly; but in the event of the worst possible extremity, the second position will be left for Jacob and the "remaining camp will be able to escape."[36]

As early as 1907, Friedlaender had proclaimed: "America is fast becoming the center of the Jewish people of the Diaspora."[37] The

[34]Davis, "Jewry, East and West," p. 20.
[35]And, for the post-Holocaust reader, eerily prophetic!
[36]Pinson, *Nationalism*, p. 240.
[37]*PP*, p. 179.

devastation wrought by World War I made him painfully aware that what he had previously considered a distant eventuality might actually come to pass in his own day. Other civic leaders shared his perception of the acute need to establish an emotional bridge between the immigrants and their relatives on the other side of the ocean with whom they had lost contact. Therefore they called upon Dubnow's translator to lecture and write on the subject of East European Jewry. Friedlaender, responding with alacrity, delivered a series of three lectures in 1915, which he straightway submitted for publication.[38]

From Friedlaender's correspondence, it is clear why this ordinarily cautious scholar decided to concentrate on a subject in which he had done no original research. Under the pressure of the war, he made a personal reassessment of Russian Jewish life.

> I left Russia twenty-one years ago. I remember how deeply I resented the conditions of the Russian Jewish environment, its narrowness, its ignorance of modern life, its rightlessness, its misery, above all its grinding, hopeless [. . .] poverty, made doubly intolerable by the comparative comfort, enjoyed personally. But after having observed modern Jewish life at so close a range in Germany, in England, and in America, I have come more and more to admire [. . .] of the Russian Jew which enables him to live a human life, a life marked by wonderful intellectualism and idealism amidst such inhuman conditions.[39]

With the reevaluation of East European Jewry came the need to console denizens of Dubnow's "remaining camp" in America. The Introduction to *The Jews of Russia and Poland* informed Friedlaender's readers how his book would help them respond to the suffering of their Russian kinsmen.

> But while we are waiting in agonies of suspense, let us not become a prey to inactive stupor. Let us take care that when the horizon has cleared and our unfortunate brethren from afar apply again for advice, we are able to give them a clear unequivocal answer, an answer that is not prompted by the passing whims of the moment, but one that is

---

[38]Friedlaender did not want the JPS to print a popular version of Russian history to compete with the scholarly opus of Dubnow that he was in the process of translating and editing. The book was published by Putnam's, under the title *The Jews of Russia and Poland: A Bird's-Eye View of Their History and Culture.*

[39]From rough copy of a letter to Lee Kohns, headed "Palisade, N.J., Nov. 5, 1915." *FP.* Dots are inserted where handwriting is illegible.

based on the foundations of our past and is fully in accord with our
historic development.[40]

Which Jews would constitute the audience for this volume?

I have not written for scholars but for the people at large who may
desire to inform themselves, in a concise and none too laborious a
manner, about this important and timely subject.[41]

This was a view which Friedlaender had long held. It had moti-
vated his earliest translations of Dubnow and Ahad Ha-am, and
was formally expressed in his review of the first volume of the
Jewish Encyclopedia.[42]

Its popular character notwithstanding, *The Jews of Russia and
Poland* reflected its author's grounding in German and German-
Jewish *Wissenschaft*. Its basic presupposition, indicated by the title
of the work, was that the totality of Judaism is manifest only in its
history. Here Friedlaender followed Graetz, who, in turn, drew
upon the Hegelian idea that the history of a thing reveals its
character. Also from Graetz was the separation of Jewish history
into "external" events, usually characterized by suffering, and
"internal" culture, marked by devotion to Jewish learning.

Friedlaender's book was divided into three parts, the first two of
which dealt with the political and economic conditions of East
European Jewry. The third section was entitled "The Inner Development of Russo-Polish Jewry." To introduce this chapter, Friedlaender constructed an elaborate biblical metaphor of the relative
value of "external" and "internal" Jewish history.

The student of Jewish history, who, wearied by the uninspiring
vicissitudes of the external life of the Jew, turns away to enter the
sanctum of his spiritual existence, cannot but experience a spark of that
sublime relief which was felt by the great Jewish lawgiver when after
his wearisome wanderings in the desert he suddenly beheld the Divine
presence in the midst of a thorn-bush. We, too, have been wandering
through the dreary wilderness of external Jewish history in the lands of
the Slavs. We saw the buds of Jewish hope parched by the heat of
hatred or swept away by the storms of persecution. We beheld Israel as

[40]*JRP*, p. 2.
[41]Ibid., p. vii.
[42]IF, "Ha-insiklopedia Ha-yehudit," *Ha-shiloah* 8 (5661—1901): 259-260.

an unattractive thorn-bush, dry, leafless, and prickly, a true product of the desert. But suddenly our disappointment is turned into enchantment. For a Divine fire is seen bursting from the unsightly plant, wondrously transfiguring its graceless forms, and a mysterious voice is heard calling: "Put off thy shoes from off thy feet, for the place whereon thou standest is holy ground."[43]

The chapter on inner development graphically illustrated the transformation of Friedlaender's historical vision. In an effort to reconstruct the religious, social, and intellectual milieu of the Russian Pale, Friedlaender utilized three tactics: hyperbolic praise, sympathetic explanation of institutions, and apologetics.

The man who as a professional scholar refrained from creating historical syntheses of subjects in which he was expert arrived at easy generalizations about Russian Jewish history with the enthusiasm of a gifted amateur. Chapter 3 was less a dispassionate overview of the inner development of Russo-Polish Jewry than an outpouring of love for his subject. The following, it proclaimed, were the principal "characteristics of Polish Judaism":

> If the spiritual history of the Jew in the Diaspora is holy ground, because it represents the triumph of the few over the many, of the weak over the strong, of the spirit over the flesh, it is doubly holy ground in the case of Russo-Polish Jewry. For, it is in Poland and Russia that the culture of Diaspora Judaism has found its most perfect manifestation.
>
> Polish Judaism is the worthy successor of Talmudic Judaism. Were it possible for the ancient sages of Palestine and Babylonia to join hands, across the chasm of time and space, with the Talmudic celebrities in the lands of the Slavs; were Rabbi Akiba or Rabbi Meir of the second century to commune with Rabbi Moses Isserles or Rabbi Solomon Luria of the sixteenth, or were Abaye and Raba of Babylonia to confer with the authors of the *Shakh* and *Taz* who lived in Poland and Lithuania,—they would doubtless return to their eternal rest with the blissful consciousness that the heritage left by them was in safe and trusty hands. Those who condemn Polish Judaism condemn Talmudic Judaism or, more correctly, condemn Diaspora Judaism altogether.[44]

What about the hegemonic center that, in the schemes of Dubnow and Friedlaender, flourished between the talmudic and Russo-Polish eras?

[43] *JRP*, p. 157.
[44] Ibid., pp. 158-159.

But, while fully appreciating and even zealously emulating the shining example of Jewish-Arabic culture, we must not forget that its versatility was purchased at the cost of originality, and that the genuine and unadulterated form of post-biblical Judaism is to be found in those less shining and less fascinating ages in which the Jews were free from outside diversions.[45]

It will be remembered that, in the first decade of the century, Friedlaender had praised Maimonides and Ibn Gabirol for their ability to integrate external factors into Jewish culture. In the second decade these became "outside diversions"! The change in perspective undoubtedly reflected Friedlaender's personal experience in American Jewish life. By 1915 Russo-Polish Jewry represented qualities far more formidable than mere "versatility." These were the ancient values of Torah and *avodah*, upon which Friedlaender dwelt at some length, mentioning the third element of the mishnaic trio, *gemillut ḥassadim*, only once. This omission undoubtedly stemmed from his conviction that while American Jewry excelled in philanthropy, it was sadly wanting in Jewish learning and piety. As a foil to the current situation, Friedlaender accentuated the virtues and minimized the failings of the European *Kahal*, the Jewish community organization composed of fiscal, religious, and judicial agencies. His motive, obviously, was to furnish an historical background for the New York *Kehillah*, which he hoped, would bring the terrible fragmentation of America's largest Jewish community to an end. It need hardly be added that the emphasis on the *Kahal* was taken from Dubnow, who assigned deep significance to this instrument of Jewish autonomy.

If Friedlaender was a conservative who took pains to vindicate established institutions, he was also a liberal who justified the abandonment of features of traditional Jewish life which no longer had resonance for modern people. In a long article which recapitulated the position of the book, he wrote:

The peculiar attire which is still worn by the masses of Polish Jewry and is an eyesore to the Poles is nothing but the ancient Polish national costume which the Poles themselves subsequently discarded in favor of a more modern form of dress. The characteristic pieces of the traditional Polish-Jewish costume are still known by their ancient Polish

[45]Ibid., p. 161.

names, and the peculiar fur cap, the so-called *Shtraimel*, which is regarded today as an unmistakable token of Jewish orthodoxy, can be shown to have been worn at one time by the Christian clergy of Poland.

The same applies to a more important, perhaps the most important, aspect of the Polish-Jewish problem, the peculiar vernacular which the Polish Jews brought with them centuries ago from their German homelands and, in their overwhelming majority, continue to speak until today. Ever since their dispersion the Jews have been a bilingual people. While remaining faithful to their ancient national tongue, the Hebrew, as the vehicle of their religious and spiritual self-expression, the Jews have always spoken the language of the nation in whose midst they dwelled.[46]

Here Friedlaender employed his historical training in the service of modernity. In the process, he impugned obscurantist Hasidim and Yiddishists of every hue.

Friedlaender lauded the accomplishments of Russo-Polish Jewry and glowingly described its institutions, but he did not ignore its defects. Several sections of the book are apologetic in nature. If he attributed the fine qualities of European Jewry to the excellence of the Jewish tradition, he indicated that their faults were the results of external circumstances beyond their control. When first the Polish and later the Russian government abolished the *Kahal*, Jewry began to degenerate.

With the collapse of Jewish self-government Polish Talmudism which, with all its subtleties, had never lost its contact with reality, is now deprived of the vivifying breath of practical life and becomes gradually petrified in lifeless casuistry. Polish intellectualism degenerates into scholasticism. The *pilpul* method, originally used as a mental stimulant, is turned into logic-chopping and theory-mongering, which engulfs the whole being of the Polish Jew, laying its impress even on his mode of expression and gesticulation.

As the hostility of the outside world grows in fierceness and extensiveness, the Polish Jew withdraws more and more into the protective shell of his inner life. Talmudism becomes to him a sort of oxygen helmet which enables him to breathe in a stuffy atmosphere, but also produces upon him the abnormally exhilarating, nerve-racking effect of artificial respiration. In spite of all the influences of Cabbalistic mysticism, the mentality of the Polish Jew grows, if I may use the expres-

---

[46]*PP*, pp. 154-155.

sion, at the expense of his emotionality. While in the classic period of
rabbinic tradition the ideal Jewish characteristic was found to consist in
a "good heart" (*Pirke Aboth*, ii, 13), the quality most admired among
Polish Jews is now *a guter Kopf*, "a good head," or *an offener Moiakh*, "an
open brain." This hypermentality leads to combativeness, insincerity,
and intellectual snobbishness. Such, however, is the fate of every plant
which has been detached from its soil and has been deprived of its
natural conditions of development.[47]

In two paragraphs, Friedlaender has taken the Jewish reader from a
description of his ancestors' failings to an explanation of their origin
to a hint at a Zionist solution.

Friedlaender imputed most of the faults of the Polish Jew to his
relationship with the *szlachta*, the Polish nobility.

> He could not help looking upon the Pan as the only guardian of
> authority and the only representative of government, and if the Polish
> Jews of today are credited with qualities of a very opposite kind, if, to
> repeat Brandes's characterization of the Poles, they are found to be
> "obstinate, combative, and quarrelsome, recognizing no higher law
> than their own will," if rhetorics seem to take the place of activities, if
> even the forms of parliamentary procedure are turned into a weapon of
> anarchy, if the lack of self-restraint, in a word, the spirit of *nie
> pozwalam*, is still stalking abroad in the councils of Polish Jews, we have
> no right to regard these failings as being characteristically Jewish, or
> even characteristically Polish-Jewish, but we have to consider them one
> of the many excrescences of our Diaspora life, which, to be sure, it
> must be our duty to cure, but to cure not with clumsiness and violence,
> but with patient and loving hands.[48]

This long and complicated sentence placed the blame for Jewry's
shortcomings on the environment, thereby assuming a position
which, since the time of Christian Wilhelm von Dohm (1781), had
characterized one attitude of modern liberalism toward the Jews.
Its last clause adopted Dubnow's position of making Jews aware of
their faults and committed to their elimination.

It is clear that *The Jews of Russia and Poland* used history as a
vehicle which would carry American Jewry along a course other
than the one it had been riding. Like all of Friedlaender's ventures

[47]*JRP*, pp. 186-187.
[48]*JRP*, p. 25.

into the public arena, its object was to inspire in American Jews the will to maintain the best qualities of their tradition.

The Jews of Russia and Poland appeared at a time when Friedlaender's single scholarly article on a biblical subject was in progress, when his major projects in Semitic scholarship had already been completed. After 1915, he continued to produce lectures and articles characterized by plentiful and appropriate illustrations from the usable past, biblical, medieval, and modern. However, this reflected his background, not his current inclinations. For Jewish history now became a source from which to draw rather than a subject for pedantic research. Increasingly, Friedlaender's interests and energies focused upon the current religious and social problems of American Jewry and the promise of Zion restored.

Part Three

THE PUBLIC FIGURE

Chapter 6
The Exposition of Conservative Judaism

Just as according to the Latin proverb, "Nature refrains from making demands, moving slowly but surely towards the attainment of its ends," so, too, in the domain of spiritual life. There are no sudden transformations, every change being the result of a slow and natural development and coming to maturity in the fullness of time. Those who seek to hamper or to further this natural growth by artificial, unnatural means are bound to meet with failure and to achieve the very reverse of what they had aimed at.

—Israel Friedlaender

Israel Friedlaender was a vigorous man whose restless energy flowed along the two channels of scholarship and communal endeavor. During his first years in America he was able to achieve a workable balance between the academy and the public forum. The onset of the Great War, with its perilous consequences for world Jewry, however, engendered a modification of priorities. Gradually, he relinquished scholarly research in favor of current problems. The change was probably unconscious; if Friedlaender thought of it at all, he regarded it as a temporary measure for the duration of the crisis. Yet this shifting of priorities is largely responsible for the fiasco of the Red Cross Mission and the disaster of his untimely death.

As a communal activist with an academic background, Friedlaender concentrated on three fundamental issues: the optimum form and content of modern Judaism, the social and cultural dimensions of American Jewish life, and the implementation of the Zionist dream. This chapter will investigate the first of these matters; subsequent ones will examine the others.

Even before his migration to the United States, Friedlaender supported the trend within *Wissenschaft des Judentums* known as Historical Judaism.[1] As the only full professor at the Jewish Theological Seminary comfortable with general audiences, Friedlaender was called upon to clarify this religious tendency, known in America as Conservative Judaism. Strange to say, the opportunity was extended by the primary opponents of the movement. For it was the Eastern Council of Reform Rabbis, led by Stephen Wise, which engaged him to articulate the philosophy of the Conservative movement. Friedlaender delivered a set of five addresses entitled "Aspects of Historical Judaism" at the cathedral of Reform Judaism, New York's Temple Emanu-el, during the spring of 1917.[2]

Friedlaender's lectures pursued two related objectives. The first was a practical one: to express in coherent fashion the ideology of the movement. For at least six years, he had recognized the need for such a formulation. In 1911, during the organization of the United Synagogue, he had written to Rabbi Herman Rubenovitz: "It seems to me that such a task cannot be performed collectively, but by a single man, who would weave into one system the salient beliefs of the Conservative Jews of today."[3]

The man to do this was, obviously, Solomon Schechter. And indeed, his essays, many of which had first been delivered as public lectures,[4] did convey an impassioned, if unsystematic exposition of the fundamentals of the movement. But Schechter never outlined a coherent theory of Conservative Judaism. Cyrus Adler, who succeeded him as president of the Jewish Theological Seminary, pointedly opposed any formulation of the Conservative philosophy.[5] There is no record of his reaction to Friedlaender's decision to do so just eighteen months after Schechter's death.

[1] See "Autobiography, 1903."
[2] The dates were April 22, 23, 30, May 7 and 14, 1917. Four are in *FP*. The fifth one is missing. The archives contain a letter on JTS stationery by Bernard Heller dated June 26, 1917. Heller stated that four lectures were returned to him, but not the fifth.
[3] On January 24, 1911, *Rubenovitz MSS*.
[4] *SJ*, vols. 2 and 3; *Seminary Addresses*.
[5] See Adler's essay "The Standpoint of the Seminary," in *Letters, Papers, Addresses* (Philadelphia, 1933), pp. 251-263.

Friedlaender's second objective was polemical. Not only would he demonstrate where Conservative Judaism differed from Orthodoxy on the right and Reform on the left; he would vindicate the position of his party. In 1917 Friedlaender was at the height of his intellectual powers. His aptitude for disputation, moreover, had been sharpened in a number of controversies dealing with educational, communal, and Zionist matters. As a former colleague and an intellectual heir of the first Seminary president, he was well equipped to carry on the debate with the other branches of Judaism on his own terms.

He certainly did not mince words. In one lecture he compared Orthodox Judaism to a "sort of Christian Science that tries to cure the patient by denying the disease."[6] Later he changed the image, describing the movement as an "ostrich, who instead of braving the danger, simply tries to hide its eyes from the danger."[7]

But his worst epithets were reserved for his hosts, the leaders of Reform Judaism, none too gently described as "Paulinians" and "Jewish assimilationists with an inclination to suicide."[8] The Reform rabbis who invited Friedlaender to speak, therefore, deserved a good deal of credit both for granting him the opportunity to present the platform of his movement and for rewarding him handsomely for his efforts.[9] For every lecture provocatively challenged their philosophy and practice of Judaism.

Preceding Friedlaender's formulation of Conservative Judaism was a diatribe against both Reform and Orthodox Judaism for refusing to accept the principle which nineteenth-century historians and social thinkers called *Entwicklung*. That Ahad Ha-am also endorsed this idea was a fact which Friedlaender noted in his translation of the Russian Jew's essays.[10] According to this concept, nations are creatures of nature. As such, they undergo growth and development; they live through "stages," and obey "laws" which determine the process of maturation. They are also products of history, manifesting new tendencies in response to the challenges

---

[6]*Aspects* IV, 4.

[7]Ibid., p. 5.

[8]Ibid., II, 3; IV, 5.

[9]He was paid $500 under the "Adolph Lewisohn Lectureship."

[10]See the Introduction to Friedlaender's translation of Ahad Ha-am's *Al Parashat Derachim, Am Scheidewege* (Berlin, 1913), pp. 1-9, translated into English under the title "Ahad Ha-am as Evolutionist," *FP*, Box 16. The quotation at the head of this chapter was taken from this essay.

of specific historical situations. However, if the nation is to remain true to its nature, these responses must reflect the original "genius" of the nation.

Employing biological imagery, Friedlaender defined Historical Judaism as "the conception of Judaism which regards Judaism in the same light as it does the phenomena of nature." Like any creature of nature, this organism did not emerge suddenly but developed slowly. Therefore the only way to ensure the survival of Judaism in the modern world is for its fate to be controlled by the party which understands, which "believe[s] in development." Friedlaender contended that Orthodox Judaism was "static, emphasizing the stationary character of Judaism," while Reform Judaism was "dynamic, laying stress on the progressive nature of Judaism." While admitting that both qualities were necessary, he pointed out that they were sufficient only in combination. It was his contention that of all the trends, Historical Judaism alone successfully captured the proper balance. To express this idea, he introduced the first of several paradoxes. Historical Judaism would ensure Jewish survival because it "believe[d] that, like every organism, Judaism is static and organic, stationary and progressive, at one and the same time, constantly changing, yet remaining essentially the same throughout the ages."

Continuing the biological metaphor, Friedlaender compared the leaders of the modern religious movements to two physicians endeavoring to cure the same patient.

> I may say that while some of you believed that the sickness of Judaism can only be cured by a radical operation, I am convinced that such an operation is unnecessary and even dangerous, and that all the patient needs is proper care and treatment which would enable him to regain his innate powers of resistance and reject in a natural and painless way the injurious elements which at present endanger his health and his very life.

This clever analogy, conveyed two very different messages. Even as it commended the Reformers for attempting to cure the contemporary malaise of Judaism, it suggested that their methods were dangerously radical.

It was necessary, Friedlaender argued, to understand Judaism on the basis of three intertwined, unchanging ideas rooted in the soul of the people. These ideas were monotheism, ceremonialism, and nationalism, contemporary formulations of the essential unity of God, Torah, and Israel postulated in the Zohar. Here Friedlaender deviated from the theology of one of the founders of Historical Judaism. Heinrich Graetz had posited a tripartite definition of Judaism, consisting of "Torah, the nation of Israel and the Holy Land."[11] God was present only implicitly, in the "mystical relationship" between the three. For his failure to make explicit reference to the deity he had been roundly criticized by Zacharias Frankel,[12] another founder of the movement. When Graetz dealt directly with the issue of monotheism, he designated transcendence, in opposition to "pagan" immanence, as the distinguishing Jewish conception of the deity.[13]

For Friedlaender, however, both were essential to Jewish monotheism. His familiarity with classical Jewish philosophy as well as the enormous value which he ascribed to the emotional element within Judaism engendered an unwillingness to dismiss the notion of an immanent God. Utilizing the familiar Hegelian triad, he suggested that Jewish monotheism reflects the animistic thesis of a deity which filled "every tree, every stone" and the Greek philosophical antithesis of a transcendent First Cause. Yet, he pointed out, the Jewish God is not a synthesis of the two, but an unblended mixture, leavened by the added ingredient of "a moral and ethical force leading men out of the depth of material existence to the lofty heights of the spirit." Rather than solve the problem of immanence vs. transcendence he expressed it as a paradox, following a classical tradition: "The distinguishing feature of the Jewish conception of God and of Jewish Monotheism is ethical Monotheism—the conception of one God over and above nature and humanity, and yet part and parcel of it."

The theological issue gave rise to an historical question. Friedlaender knew that since the time of Isaiah it had been a fundamental axiom of Judaism that the God of Israel directs the course of human history. Modern secular history, on the other hand, assumed the human capacity to ascertain natural causes for the sequence of past

---

[11]Heinrich Graetz, *The Structure of Jewish History and Other Essays*, trans. and ed. Ismar Schorsch (New York, 1975), p. 71.
[12]Zacharias Frankel, *Zeitschrift fuer die religiosen Interessen des Judentums* 3 (1846): 89-90.
[13]Graetz, *Structure*, p. 69.

events. David Biale has pointed out that this issue bedeviled the greatest Jewish historian.

> One might even argue that the very notion of an extra-mundane God precluded an immanent historiography. A transcendent God is a force outside history which somehow plays the guiding role in historical events. A totally immanent history would unfold without outside interference. According to Graetz's definitions, immanent history would be "pagan." If Jewish history is guided from outside history, then historiography would have to take suprahistorical forces into account: historiography would no longer be an account of the immanent interplay of historical forces. Abraham Geiger's criticism of Graetz, that his history lacked an "inner driving force," was therefore correct, if for the wrong reasons: Graetz's historiography was guided by an external theological principle just as his conception of Jewish history was not entirely immanent.[14]

Aware of this problem, Friedlaender posed the following question: How can the people who subscribe to Historical Judaism account for Jewish survival, "this most conspicuous feature of Judaism altogether"? Again he responded to the issue with a paradox: "Miracle though it be, the survival of the Jewish people has its historical causes." In contrast to Ahad Ha-am, Friedlaender believed that Jewish existence was directly attributable to God's guiding presence. But he was also aware that this conviction was not enough. Since this miraculous survival occurred on the plane of history, it was necessary for Jews to utilize every critical tool which would further their understanding of the Jewish past. This was a faith which Friedlaender shared with all the members of the Historical School, from the founders, Zunz, Graetz, and Frankel, to his colleagues Ginzberg and Marx, to his secularist mentor, Simon Dubnow.

If we discount the polemical tone, it is evident that there was little in this argument with which the Reformers could disagree. Like Friedlaender, they, too, were committed to Jewish survival, monotheism, *Entwicklung*, and the critical study of history. It was for this reason that Friedlaender devoted most of his attention to the two remaining aspects of Historical Judaism, ceremonialism and nationalism, both of which had been eliminated from his opponents' radical reformulation of Judaism.

---

[14]David Biale, *Gershom Scholem*, p. 21.

Friedlaender was aware that the Reformers' arguments against ritual observance were both philosophical and historical. The founders of the movement had internalized the Kantian critique of Judaism as a heteronomous, positive religion. To justify their rejection of talmudic law, they argued that Jews who submitted to it possessed no true inwardness. American rabbis who upheld these views considered many traditional prayers, institutions, and laws "out of harmony with the modern age."[15]

Kaufmann Kohler, like Ahad Ha-am, admitted that Jewish law had ensured the historic survival of the Jewish people. However, he did not share the respect for its present structure which marked the Russian essayist's "Flesh and Spirit." Indeed, this radical Reformer ascribed no present value to Halakha; to him it merely "foster[ed] hair-splitting causistry and caus[ed] petrification of religion."[16] For this reason he suggested that the content of Judaism was wholly and adequately expressed in its doctrines, some of which had to be recast in modern terms. The most significant of these was the notion of messianic redemption. No longer should Jews, comfortably settled in the new American Zion, long to return to the Holy Land. It was, instead, their mission to build Jerusalem in America's green and pleasant land. The severance of ritual observance from religiosity and Jewish nationality from the Jewish religion were, then, the two major matters of dispute between the Reformers and their traditionalist opponents.

In order to justify the retention of the second aspect of Historical Judaism, ceremonialism, Friedlaender drew upon insights borrowed from three nineteenth-century founders of the Historical School, Frankel, Graetz, and Michael Sachs. Their understanding of the relationship of the Jewish people to talmudic law was grounded in German nationalistic historiography and the romantic tendency to appreciate religion as an expression of emotion.

Following the German legal historian Savigny, Frankel regarded legal institutions as the distinctive expressions of a nation's soul. Their development could not be understood as a logical process but as an organic one, occurring slowly and unconsciously over a long period of time. Thus the ultimate authority for Jewish law was not revelation but the Jewish people, who found in it their particular

[15]Julian Morgenstern, *As a Mighty Stream* (Philadelphia, 1949), p. 136.
[16]Kaufmann Kohler, *Jewish Theology Systematically and Historically Considered*, ed. Joseph L. Blau (New York, 1968), p. 47.

expression of righteousness. In Ismar Schorsch's words, "The ultimate arbiter of the holy was the *Volk* itself. As long as it still possessed a vibrant religious consciousness, it represented a source of indirect revelation. Its piety exercised a legitimate veto over religious schemes imposed by a self-selected, rationalistic elite."[17] For this reason, the sanctity of any given ceremony depended upon its long-time usage by the Jewish people and upon the fact that it was still cherished.[18]

This, in all likelihood, was the source of Schechter's felicitous phrase "Catholic Israel," which he defined as "the living body . . . best able to determine the nature of the Secondary Meaning"[19] (of Scripture), i.e., endowed with the right to interpret Jewish law.

Complementing Frankel's reliance on the people as the determining factor of the holy in Judaism was Graetz's rationale for continued adherence to Jewish law. We have already taken note of his designation of transcendence as an essential principle of Judaism. Pondering this matter, Graetz asked how Jews managed to bridge the enormous distance between themselves and the Creator. He concluded that their religion provided the means; the Jewish people had always found its way to God through obedience to the Torah, its constitution. By adherence to its laws, "the abstract, ideal teachings are immediately put into practice."[20]

A third founder of the Historical School provided Friedlaender's argument with another important feature. This was Michael Sachs, who explicitly stated an attitude that was implicit in the systems of Frankel and Graetz. Vigorously resisting the Reformers' reduction of Judaism to a series of propositions, he maintained that the Jewish spirit assumed its truest expression in the beautiful poetry of the medieval *paytanim* and the sentimental tales of the Midrash. It was his contention that these outpourings of the human heart reflected an immediacy to God lacking in the philosophical traditions revered by his Reform opponents.

With these arguments in his arsenal, Friedlaender set out to establish the binding power of Halakha. Craftily, he suggested that the Reformers' perception of Torah as "law" was borrowed from

[17]"Zacharias Frankel and the European Origins of Conservative Judaism," *Judaism* 30 (Summer 1981): 348.
[18]Ibid., pp. 348-349.
[19]*SJ* 3, pp. 62-64.
[20]Graetz, *Structure*, p. 69.

the New Testament. "This has had a terrible effect upon us because law implies legalism and formalism. We all have respect for the law but few of us love it. It states a lack of sincerity, a lack of inwardness and the lack of emotion when our Judaism is branded as a religion of law."

Next, he took it upon himself to redefine the concept of Torah by drawing upon an earlier argument. He posed two questions about the connection between monotheism, the first aspect of Historical Judaism, and ceremonialism, the second. The first was epistemological: How does the Jew perceive God? The second was practical: How does the Jew reach God?

In answer to the former question he asserted that the Jewish conception of God is intuitive. "It is a religious sense. The Jew senses the Divine. This sense is a great gift, the greatest gift that can be vouchsafed to man, the greatest gift that was vouchsafed to Israel."

To explain the concept of religious intuition, Friedlaender ingeniously summoned two diverse but equally weighty arguments. The first, which originated in medieval Jewish rationalism, employed *a priori* reasoning to arrive at a self-evident truth (which, however, was self-evident only to Jews).

> The Greeks . . . first looked at nature, and by analyzing nature they gradually and methodically arrived at the idea of God. . . . The Jews first looked at God and from God they looked down upon nature. . . . The Jewish thinkers of the Middle Ages were entirely right and substantially correct when they maintained that the Jewish revelation anticipated the results of Greek philosophy. To quote a simile of Saadya, the Greek philosophers merely counted out the sum which the Jews knew long beforehand.

Probably because the Reformers utilized rationalistic arguments to justify rejection of Jewish law, Friedlaender then advanced a second and, for him, more satisfactory interpretation of Israel's vision of God. It originated in the conviction of the romantics that reason was an insufficient means of achieving metaphysical truth. In this spirit, Friedlaender suggested that the Jewish attitude toward God "cannot be purely logical and purely analytical, it must be primarily emotional. The consciousness of God, communion with the Divine, must find such emotional expression. It is the

knowledge of God . . . it is love of God." Here he repeated an
argument that he had previously advanced.

> It is remarkable indeed that the only Hebrew expression which in any
> way approaches what in modern languages we call religion is *daath
> elohim*, the knowledge of God.[21]

There is no question that these statements, written in the tradition
of Michael Sachs, were directed against the predilection of contemporary Reform rabbis for systematic formulation of Jewish beliefs.
They also call to mind Schechter's position; the Seminary president had described the "saints" of Judaism from biblical to modern
times as men and women characterized more by "inspiration and
enthusiasm" than "ideas, ideals, [and] mere organization."[22]

Following Schechter, assuming the offensive even more aggres-
sively, Friedlaender challenged the Reform rabbis. In their attempt
to "squeeze the religious essence into lozenges,"[23] he deftly suggested, it was they who became "formalistic and legalistic." Their
"theoretical and logical presentation about God," he asserted, did
not take into account the essential characteristic of Jewish religiosity, which remains intuitive communion with the Supreme Being.
Most adept at this extraordinary feat were the prophets of Israel.
To insist that the literary prophets provided not only an ethical
ideal but also a *religious* standard was Friedlaender's way of attack-
ing the Reform movement in a very sensitive area. For its leaders
claimed a legacy of prophetic rather than rabbinic Judaism.

If dogma was unimportant, how did Friedlaender account for the
fact that Maimonides,[24] his favorite historical personality, and
Schechter,[25] his academic associate, had outlined the doctrines of
Judaism? In the Temple Emanu-el lectures, he simply replied that
any Jew who systematically formulated Jewish religious principles
labored under foreign influence.

After establishing the intuitive nature of the Jewish perception of
God and the inadequacy of doctrine to contain it, it was now
necessary to ascertain the means by which the Jew reaches God.

[21]MJ 1 (Jan, 1915): 38
[22]*SJ* 2, p. 150.
[23]*Aspects* II, 6. Friedlaender's actual wording: "The religious sense is omnipresent, it
cannot be squeezed into lozenges."
[24]See Maimonides, "Introduction to Perek Helek," in his *Commentary to the Mishnah*,
Tractate Sanhedrin (Hebrew), ed. M. D. Rabinowitz (Tel Aviv, 1948), pp. 132-146.
[25]See Schechter's essay "The Dogmas of Judaism," *SJ* 1, pp. 147-181.

Cleverly, Friedlaender analyzed the problem and posed its solution in a single figure of speech. "The consciousness of the Divine is like a balloon which lets itself to the winds—it needs a ballast if it is to remain in contact with the earth." Traditional ritual practice provided the ballast. To defend the laws and customs of Judaism against the Reform critique of "ritualism" and "formalism," Friedlaender advanced psychological and historical arguments borrowed from his German predecessors. One reflected Graetz's assertion of the need to connect an earth-bound people to its transcendent God. Imparting his own flavor, Friedlaender formulated a statement which brings to mind the theological paradox with which he expressed the nature of the deity. "This concept of an abstract God must be materialized in concrete institutions and in concrete human groups."

The next argument was utilitarian. In rich detail, he enumerated the life-serving value of the customs and ceremonies of Judaism, which are pedagogical, social, and national as well as religious. He pointed out that they actually sanctify human life. Here he reiterated a favorite theme of his popular lectures: the lowlier the human activity, the more it requires sanctification through *mitzvot*.[26]

Having demonstrated the practical value of Jewish ceremonialism, Friedlaender advanced to the theoretical plane. To prove that "Jewish ceremonialism is Judaism itself," he challenged the Orthodox view of revelation while he mustered historical arguments against them and the Reformers.

Once again he propounded a paradox: "The whole mental activity of the Jew must be seen as emanating from divine authority, and the specific practices are the result of a long historic development." This statement paralleled his description of Jewish survival as "a miracle with historical causes." It also illustrated the difference between the Historical School's vindication of Jewish ceremonialism on the one hand and the positions of Reform and Orthodox Judaism on the other. The first clause cemented the "indissoluble bond" between God and Torah, monotheism and ceremonialism, implicitly censuring the Reformers' attempt to sever it; the second clause assailed the extreme Biblicism of some Reformers and the unhistorical perspective of the Orthodox spokesmen.

Friedlaender accused the former group of denying the validity of

[26]See outlines of two lectures on ceremonialism addressed to the Jewish Welfare Board on August 19, 1918, *FP*, Box 7.

laws governing Jewish life which were talmudic in origin. Much as he cherished every word of the biblical text, he shared Alexander Marx's opinion that "we are much more Talmud than Bible Jews."[27] However, Friedlaender maintained that the authority of the talmudic precepts does not proceed from Scripture alone.

> Not only are the Post-Biblical commandments equally binding and in some cases even more binding than the Biblical Commandments, but we have several examples which clearly show that the binding force of the *Mitzvot* was based upon the divine authority in the general sense outlined above, rather than in a restricted sense of a direct command of God to Moses. For example, the observance of Hanukkah, a post-Biblical law. In other words, the acts of Jewish life, as far as they were designed to embody the religious element, are regarded as divine and therefore authoritative.

The concept of "divine authority in the general sense" was a critique of Orthodoxy fundamentalism. To take literally the mishnaic concept of "Torah from Heaven" was, in his view, to accept a "limitation," an "artificial compression of a point of view which is far more comprehensive." It is probable that Friedlaender himself did not believe in literal revelation. He never discussed the issue in personal theological terms; instead he treated it from an historical perspective.

> No Jew prior to Maimonides, not even during the Jewish-Arabic period, in spite of its many thinkers, ever denied the Divine origin of the Pentateuch, or doubted the correctness of the facts reported by it.[28]

> [Maimonides] counts the belief in the Divine origin of the Bible among the fundamental Articles of Faith.[29]

Without denying the truth of the Sinaitic revelation, Friedlaender nevertheless reduced its significance. Carefully, he expanded the concept of "divine influence" to include revelation to biblical non-Jews as well as Jews. He also indicated that, according to the rabbis, the *Ruaḥ ha-kodesh*, the Holy Spirit, also permeated post-biblical and rabbinic literature. The superior sanctity of the Penta-

---

[27] A. Marx, "Friedlaender the Scholar," p. 350.
[28] *PP*, pp. 139.
[29] *PP (1919)*, pp. 195-196.

teuch, then, reflected not its *origin*, but the people's profound regard for it.

If the sacredness of a particular ceremony was derived from the people's adherence to it, it followed that the final arbiter of Jewish law was the Jewish people. Like Zacharias Frankel, the source of this notion, Friedlaender carried a conservative idea to a liberal conclusion.[30] For if popular usage rendered a custom or ceremony holy, the reverse was also true. When the people no longer honored the custom or observed the ceremony, it was modified. Change in the law became legitimate, however, only when carried out in the name of the people and in the spirit of organic development.

A remarkable feature of the Temple Emanu-el addresses was the absence of technical terms. Friedlaender occasionally quoted Schechter, but he named no European founders of Historical Judaism, nor did he cite passages from their writings. His disputation was rooted in the German concepts of *Entwicklung, Volk, Geschichte, Wissenschaft,* and *Vernunft,* but he burdened his partially lay audience with no German terms.[31] He did not even reiterate such English phrases current in Conservative circles as Frankel's "positive-historical Judaism" and Schechter's "Catholic Israel." On the one occasion in which he used a German word, *Kultur,* an English cognate, he found it necessary to explain it carefully, incidentally apologizing for submitting his audience to the language of the enemy.

Actually, there was no need for Friedlaender to employ the terminology of others. The quotations cited above illustrate the skill of this foreign-born and foreign-educated speaker at coining an appropriate English phrase and inventing an apt image to illustrate a point. The metaphor of the two physicians with which he opened the series was an admirable contrivance, adroitly celebrating the developmental approach to the Historical School while condemning Reform radicalism. The image of balloon and ballast was a graceful means of conveying the notion that observance gives form to religious feeling. A speaker of disarming ingenuity, Friedlaender enhanced his arguments with familiar images from literature and current events. A case in point was the utilization of the figure of

[30]This insight was borrowed from Schorsch's essay "Zacharias Frankel."

[31]Friedlaender was disappointed that the Eastern Council of Rabbis was sparsely represented at his lectures. The bulk of his audience, as he wrote to Stephen Wise, consisted of "the normal elements with which any speaker is acquainted." April 27, 1917, *FP.*

Robinson Crusoe in the negative sense: to demonstrate how ancient Israel did *not* live in seclusion, totally separated from its Near Eastern neighbors. Another was his comparison of newly emancipated Jewry to soldiers emerging from the trenches.

The last example may help explain why the lecture series was never published.[32] Its references were often so topical that they bore little relevancy for the postwar generation. A more significant shortcoming resulted from their polemical nature. In his eagerness to guard the "vineyard" of Jewish law and nationality, Friedlaender contradicted an important message of his Semitic studies. Implied in his scholarly writings was the perception that ideas are not the product of the Semitic or the Aryan soul; instead they flow freely from one group to another, enriched in the transmission. Yet, to dispute the Reform view of Jewish law, he shamelessly glorified the uniqueness of Jewish religiosity expressed in the observance of Halakha. It should be noted, however, that even the ultrarationalist Reformers, following Geiger, believed in a Jewish racial predisposition to monotheism. We can only conclude that when Friedlaender debated the Reformers, he preferred to repeat the nineteenth-century arguments rather than integrate his own twentieth-century findings into his discussion.

In general, these lectures displayed a retreat from rationalism inconsistent with the body of Friedlaender's thought. In the effort to characterize the Jewish perception of God as intuitive, he described Jewish philosophy as a Greek import, foreign to the Hebrew psyche. An odd statement, indeed, from a man known as the principal exponent of Maimonides' philosophy on American soil.

At the Seminary, Friedlaender instructed students in Jewish philosophy as well as history and Bible. He introduced one course with the inquiry whether there is such a thing as Jewish philosophy. Answering his own question in the negative, he maintained that philosophy, unlike Judaism, reduces everything to abstract formulas. Here, as in the public address, he insisted that, throughout Jewish history, systematic formulation of dogma appears only under the pressure of alien influence. He concluded his introduc-

---

[32]Herbert Bentwich wrote to George Dobsevage of the JPS about the "proposed issue of the essays and addresses of the late Professor Israel Friedlaender," September 28, 1920, *FP.* However, nothing came of the proposal.

tory remarks with the wry comment: "Now that I have demonstrated that there is no Jewish philosophy, I shall begin my course in Jewish philosophy."[33]

Boaz Cohen recounted this anecdote as evidence of his professor's "characteristic humor."[34] The wit, however, betrays a lack of clarity in Friedlaender's thought. His scholarly writings and some other popular lectures glowingly described periods of history when Jews assimilated the high philosophy of their environment. These, he maintained, adorned their lives, imparting a rich quality to their Judaism. All of this was abandoned to prove a point to the Reformers.

In truth, ambivalence toward Jewish rationalism was typical of the Historical School. On the one hand, its proponents were aware of the historic roots of rationalism in Hebrew prophecy as well as Greek philosophy; they know that its principles underlay the most profound Jewish literature. It was equally clear that it was the Age of Reason which set the scene for Jewish Emancipation and, ultimately, their own entrance into Western society. On the other hand, they were romantics, who conformed to European historical and nationalist patterns of thought, as exemplified by such modern Jewish thinkers as S. D. Luzzatto. Following Luzzatto, they rejected precision in thought as Hellenism or "Atticism"; they glorified the emotional and poetic elements of Judaism by excluding the rational.

Actually, it was unnecessary to abandon rationalism on either philosophical or historical grounds. The contemporary philosopher Jacob Agus has detected the flaw in confusing the life of religion with philosophical efforts to express the underpinnings of religion in logical form. "Acceptance of the total pattern of religious life as the subjective home of one's spiritual existence by no means precludes the truths of objectivity."[35] Moreover, the Historical School, from its inception, embraced all the historical trends within Judaism, the rational as well as the mystical, the philosophical as well as the halakhic. An important emphasis in Schechter's writings, this idea was reiterated in Friedlaender's lectures which were not polemical in nature.

Despite these flaws, Friedlaender's public addresses are impor-

[33]Boaz Cohen, "An Appreciation," p. 6.
[34]Ibid.
[35]Jacob Agus, *Dialogue and Tradition* (New York, 1971), p. 560.

tant for their presentation of four questions which troubled all serious modern Jewish thinkers:

1. Are the Jews subject to the laws of history?
2. Which aspects of Judaism are essential and unchanging, and which have changed and will continue to change?
3. Is the modern age of Emancipation the culmination of Jewish history or a break with it?
4. Are the Jews a race or a religion?

It should be evident that none of these questions received an unqualified, unambiguous answer. Friedlaender made no attempt to resolve the paradoxes of Jewish history; in fact he savored them.

A good example is the way in which he dealt with the first of these problems. It will be remembered that he found room both for divine guidance and for human endeavor. However, unlike his medieval subject Maimonides, he made no effort to achieve philosophical reconciliation, preferring, instead, to indicate his position with the statement of a paradox.

As to the second question, we have seen that Friedlaender accepted the Historical School's idealistic assumptions about an unchanging core of Judaism as well as its organic, developmental approach. His argumentation also proceeded upon an additional postulate, one which understood historical change as a clashing of opposites which resisted full reconciliation. For had his attitude toward Jewish history been totally developmental, he would have shared in the prewar faith in progress. Like his opponents, the Reformers, he would have welcomed Emancipation without qualification.

Friedlaender acknowledged the material benefits of Emancipation but warned American Jews of its hidden dangers. What the Reformers perceived as release from the burdensome rituals of Judaism, Friedlaender understood as a threat to its very survival. His advocacy of slow "medical" change rather than radical "surgery" was intended to assure the continuity not only of the Jewish religion but of Jewish history as well.

In answer to the fourth question, it is evident that Friedlaender, like the nineteenth-century founders of Historical Judaism and his influential contemporaries Dubnow and Ahad Ha-am, was a nationalist historian, who could not and would not separate the

Jewish religion from the people who developed it. We shall presently return to Friedlaender's third "aspect" of Judaism, nationalism, which is so intimately bound up with the first two. Here it is sufficient to note that, unlike many Zionists, he demonstrated an awareness of the moral problems which nationalism posed to a world racked by chauvinism.

In elucidating the position of the Historical School, Friedlaender first clarified the issues separating his party's philosophy from that of the other two and then directed a frontal attack. Against the Reformers, he uncovered the indissoluble historic bond between ethical monotheism, ceremonialism, and Jewish nationality. Against the Orthodox, he used history to justify changes in religious practice. The result was a clarification of Schechter's thesis that religious authority was vested in "the collective conscience of Catholic Israel as embodied in the Universal Synagogue."[36]

The religio-national character of Judaism and the indispensability of the historical approach to understand its past and to ensure its future were two credos which Friedlaender cherished throughout his life. In the pages ahead, we shall see that if his conception of Historical Judaism remained constant, his application of its principles assumed new forms as he responded to the changing world about him.

[36]*SJ* I, p. xviii.

Chapter 7
A Social Thinker

> The general culture of the land stands before us like an iron
> wall, and we shall be cracked like a nutshell if we attempt to
> run our heads against it. The only solution left to us is that of
> adaptation, but an adaptation which shall sacrifice nothing that
> is essential to Judaism, which shall not impoverish Judaism but
> enrich it, which . . . shall take fully into account what the
> environment demands of us, and shall yet preserve and foster
> our Jewish distinctiveness and originality.
>
> —*Israel Friedlaender*

H. Stuart Hughes's important study of the period in which
Friedlaender flourished establishes the premise that the last decade
of the nineteenth century and the first three decades of the twentieth witnessed a complete reorientation of European social thought.[1]
Hughes focuses upon two significant concerns of social philosophers of the 1890s, the decade of Friedlaender's education. One
was a painful awareness of living in what came to be know as the *fin
de siècle*, the period of the demise of the old society, "coupled with
agonizing uncertainty as to what the forms of the new society
might prove to be."[2] The other was the provocative challenge to the
legacy of the Enlightenment, faith in the ability of reason to solve
human problems. Out of this matrix emerged the new disciplines

[1]Hughes, *Consciousness and Society.* See above, chap. 4, n. 17.
[2]Ibid., p. 14.

of psychology and sociology, which probed the nonrational motives prompting human behavior and the unconscious forces which lay at the base of society. The founders were the social philosophers who comprised a "cluster of genius," Freud, Weber, Durkheim, Pareto, Bergson, and Jung. These men revolutionized the very definitions of man and society.

Similar issues confronted Jewish social thinkers of the period. Communicating Jewish *fin de siècle* malaise, they frequently employed the term "the Jewish question." Deceptively simple, this tidy expression put into words the commonly held fear for the continued viability of Judaism and Jewry. With the significant exception of the spokesmen for religious Reform, Jewish philosophers of the turn of the twentieth century were disappointed with the failure of the high expectations introduced by the Enlightenment. The intervening "century of progress" had not lived up to its promise of freedom from humiliation and persecution. The majority of Jews still lived in autocratic, benighted czarist Russia, scene of government-sponsored anti-Jewish legislation, anti-Semitic publications, and acts of violence. In Western and Central Europe, where Jews enjoyed civil and political rights, the 1880s and 1890s witnessed a growing acceptance of the legitimacy of anti-Jewish speculation and agitation. Even the U.S. government was besieged with demands for legislation to stem the flow of immigration from Eastern (and Southern) Europe.

People concerned with the perpetuation of traditional Judaism agonized over the deleterious effect of Emancipation on the inner life of the Jews. Among Jews who had achieved the rights of citizenship, they discovered widespread defection, either through outright conversion or through abandonment of the distinguishing marks of Judaism in the synagogue service, personal observance, and intellectual pursuits. Consequently, a cohort of Jewish social philosophers tried to erect a new foundation for Judaism, and cultural life. This Jewish "cluster of genius" included such figures as Herzl, Ahad Ha-am, Dubnow, Buber, and Berdychevsky. A generation younger than most of these thinkers, Friedlaender absorbed their ideas about the human condition and the nature of Jewish society and culture. That he realized that America was not free of the Jewish question is indicated by titles of many of his essays: "The Problem of Jewish Culture in America," "Religious

Problems in New York City," "The Problem of Judaism in America," and "The Problem of Jewish Education in America."[3]

Friedlaender's social thought revolved around a single issue: the perils of emancipation. His public discussions often centered upon the question: How can the branch of Jewry newly settled in America reap the benefits of Emancipation and, at the same time, retain its Jewish integrity? Wrestling with the problem, Friedlaender consulted familiar sources, Historical Judaism and the Odessan philosophers; he also dipped into new ideas promoted by another "cluster of genius," the American social philosophers of his day.

As a champion of modernity, Friedlaender could not help but welcome the opportunities granted to Jews newly awarded economic rights and civic equality. But he distinguished carefully between the benefits which Emancipation conferred upon Jews and the dangers which it posed for Judaism. In article after article, lecture after lecture, he reminded his audience of three unwholesome consequences of this phenomenon: fragmentation, assimilation, and materialism.

Without question, this analysis revealed a debt to Ahad Ha-am and Dubnow. Ahad Ha-am's early essays touched upon all three of these points. "Slavery in Freedom" (1891) suggested that the Jews of the West, though outwardly emancipated, were, in truth, locked in the fetters of slavery. One kind of bondage was "moral slavery," illustrated in the Reform movement's denial of Jewish nationality.[4] "Imitation and Assimilation" (1894) dwelt upon a second, equally pernicious product of emancipation, the danger of Jewry "being split up into fragments."[5] Moreover, Jews who "depart from their prototype"[6] would soon fall victim to a third hazard posed by modern life, the abandonment of their spiritual heritage and its replacement with the materialistic values prevailing in the industrial nations. According to Ahad Ha-am, there was only one way for Jews to enjoy the fruits of modernity and yet retain their

---

[3]"The Problem of Jewish Culture in America," *Maccabean*, 6 (June 1915): 120-122. "Religious Problems in New York City" was a lecture probably delivered in the period prior to the establishment of the *Kehillah* (1909). *FP*, Box 9 contains notes for it, but no text. No date is given. Friedlaender published "The Problem of Judaism in America" and "The Problem of Jewish Education in America" in *PP*. The latter essay, *PP* (1919: 279-307) was not reprinted in the second edition.
[4]*Selected Essays of Ahad Ha-am* (1970), p. 190.
[5]Ibid., p. 122.
[6]Ibid.

integrity and spirituality. This was the route of "competitive imitation";[7] by which Jews would selectively adopt elements from the environment and employ them creatively to enhance their Judaism.

In the first decade of the twentieth century, Dubnow also questioned the benefits of Emancipation. For him, as for Ahad Ha-am, this putative solution to the Jewish problem created greater problems than it solved. In their struggle for Emancipation, West European Jews adopted the insidious position of the Reform movement: "Many were convinced that Jewry as a nationality was already dead and that nothing was left for it but to merge with all mankind, or, since mankind is divided into various nations, to become absorbed into other national bodies and retain only its religious traditions in greater or lesser degree."[8] His verdict on this type of assimilation was severe. It was "psychologically unnatural, ethically damaging, and practically useless."[9] As a diaspora historian, Dubnow did not dwell upon the problem of fragmentation. But he demanded Jewish national rights as a means of cultivating the spiritual character of Jewry in contradistinction to the materialistic outlook of the nations among whom they lived.

Like Ahad Ha-am and Dubnow, Friedlaender disputed the Reformers' solution to the Jewish question. Instead of strengthening Judaism with modern ideas, he argued, Reform Judaism discarded historic traditions, substituting for them a weak imitation of Christianity. Borrowing Ahad Ha-am's terminology, Friedlaender accused his opponents of practicing "imitative adaption" rather than "competitive imitation."[10] In the process, they created "a bland oppressively boring religion," comparable to "distilled water, which was perfectly pure but entirely tasteless."[11] The result: assimilation, defection of the young, internal fragmentation of the American Jewish community accompanied by dissociation from the European matrix, and the abandonment of traditional Jewish values for the material goals of the marketplace.

Friedlaender's public discussions focused upon these three injurious consequences of emancipation; he participated actively in

---

[7]Ibid., p. 120.
[8]Dubnow, *Nationalism and History*, p. 134.
[9]Ibid., pp. 134-135.
[10]*Aspects* IV, 6.
[11]Ibid., IV, 13.

programs designed to overcome them. How did he attack the first problem, that of fragmentation? Early in his career, the fledgling historian cleverly employed the tool of historical irony to dramatize this issue. In 1901 he incorporated the following insight into his review of the first volume of *The Jewish Encyclopedia:* "In the dark Middle Ages, when robbers and brigands lay in ambush along the roads, ready to pounce upon travellers, the Jews of various lands knew one another, recognizing their mutual responsibility more than the Jews of today [who live in] the age of railroad and electricity."[12]

Deliberately, Friedlaender minimized the efforts of West European Jews to alleviate the physical suffering of their East European co-religionists. Caustically, he accused the Alliance Israélite Universelle of betraying its own motto, *Kol Yisrael Ḥaverim* ("All Israel are brethren"). The organization, he claimed, was not based upon feelings of fraternity, but rather upon one-sided philanthropy. "The Jews are *Aḥim le-tzarah,* 'brethren in distress,' but they are not *Ḥaverim,* comrades, working shoulder to shoulder for a common goal. And their hands are not clasped. Their symbol should be rather a pair of hands that are open; the one to give help, the other to receive help."[13]

In Friedlaender's opinion, this snobbish frame of mind was detrimental to the spiritual well-being of Western Jewry. He compared the behavior of "enlightened" Jews toward their "unenlightened" co-religionists to that of Germans to Frenchmen.

> Goethe described the attitude of the Germans towards the French in the famous epigram:
> > The German does not like the Frenchman,
> > But he likes to drink his wine.
>
> The attitude of the European and American Jews towards the Jews of Russia is the exact reverse of it. The European and American Jews feel keenly for their Russian brethren. They are deeply interested in their fate; they collect, with unparalleled generosity, enormous sums to alleviate their distress—in fact, the whole public life of the Jews outside of Russia is dominated by their solicitude for the Russian Jew. But—his

---

[12]*Ha-shiloaḥ* 8 (1901): 261 (my translation). This same idea is repeated in "Palestine and the Diaspora" (1917), where the new age is defined as that of "steam, electricity, and aeroplanes" (*PP,* p. 324).

[13]Ibid., p. 323.

wine they do not drink. They flatly refuse to accept anything from him. They barely know what he is able to offer them.[14]

In America, he went on to say, the "uptown Jews" displayed a "one-sided generosity" toward the "downtown Jews," refusing to taste the "wine" of their fine traditional culture. To make matters worse, some of the more acculturated immigrants were following this dangerous example.

Out of the conviction that the solution to the polarization of American Jewish life lay in communal organization, Friedlaender helped Judah Magnes, a close friend, establish the Jewish Community of New York, the New York "Kehillah." The two men, who had first met as students in Berlin, shared the ideals of cultural Zionism and Historical Judaism; they also cherished the conviction that only a democratically run communal polity could successfully coordinate Jewish life in New York City—religious, educational, and communal—in a single rational system. In 1908, after Police Commissioner Bingham's notorious defamation of New York's Jewry in the respected *North American Review*,[15] they set out to convince people of the necessity of communal organization.

In a lecture entitled "Religious Problems in New York City," Friedlaender described the current situation as one of *"Hefker."* He complained that ritual slaughter and circumcision were performed without standards or supervision and that Jewish education was confined to schools that were unattractive, unhygienic, and administered by *melamdim* with no understanding of American children. For these problems Friedlaender proposed the following solutions: to "establish religious authority, to define religious practice and theory," and "development from congregational to communal Judaism."

The New York Kehillah was launched in 1909, with Magnes at the helm and Friedlaender as a member of its executive committee.[16] Although it was already declining at the time of Friedlaender's death, he always believed that it was the best solution to the organizational difficulties of America Jewry.

Equally serious, in his opinion, was a second unfortunate conse-

[14]Ibid., p. 275.
[15]Theodore A. Bingham, "Foreign Criminals in New York," pp. 383-394.
[16]See the definitive study of the New York Kehillah, Arthur A. Goren's *New York Jews*, chaps. 1, 2, and 3.

quence of Emancipation, the problem of assimilation. Of all the Kehillah's efforts to standardize Jewish life in New York, it was the Bureau of Jewish Education, established in 1910, that excited Friedlaender's imagination and mobilized his energy. For he firmly believed that only a Jewish educational system set up on a sound pedagogical basis would prevent the assimilation of the children of the ghetto. This was a conviction which he shared with Samson Benderly, the Palestine-born, Baltimore-based Jewish educator whom he met early in his sojourn in America, probably through their mutual friend Harry Friedenwald. Benderly was appointed director of the Bureau of Jewish Education of New York City; Friedlaender became chairman of its board of trustees. It was his duty to countersign all vouchers and checks of the bureau, to keep track of the agency's manifold activites, and to report on them annually to the parent organization, the Kehillah.

Benderly introduced many revolutionary innovations; he insisted that the physical plant of each school be spacious and hygienic, that the teachers be proficient in English, and that they utilize the newest pedagogical tools, which included the controversial *Ivrit be-Ivrit* method of instruction.[17] As the reigning intellectual of the bureau, Friedlaender was called upon to legitimize these innovations before two tribunals. The first was the general American public. At the request of Magnes and Benderly, he composed a long report entitled "The Problem of Jewish Education in America," which was submitted to the Department of the Interior in 1913. This extensive treatise placed the policies of the bureau in a broad historical perspective, relating them to the history of American Jewry, the educational system of Russian Jewry, and the current condition of the East European immigrants. It then offered a detailed description of the activities of the Bureau of Jewish Education during its first three years.

Championing a cherished Jewish ideal or revered Jewish institution before the non-Jewish public was an activity which afforded Friedlaender much satisfaction. By contrast, his association with Jewish organizations gave rise to more pain than pleasure. A case in point was his defense of the Bureau of Education before certain Jewish groups. On various occasions, spokesmen of the three

[17]See Nathan Winter, *Samson Benderly*, especially chap. 7: "The Bureau of Jewish Education in New York City to 1916," pp. 65-89.

branches of American Judaism criticized the agency and at times censured Friedlaender for supporting it.

Prominent Reform Jews disapproved of the bureau's emphasis on Hebrew. Why, asked Lee Kohns, a business and civic leader, teach American children the Hebrew language; why not concentrate instead on the abstract principles of Judaism in which he (Kohns) was instructed in his youth?[18]

To questions of this nature Friedlaender always had a ready answer: Hebrew was the language in which Jews had prayed and studied for centuries. It was the Jewish people's link to the past as well as to the future in the new Palestinian center, which would unite all Jews who shared a common culture.[19]

It was necessary to reply to the criticism of the Reform Jewish establishment, for the bureau and, indeed, the entire Kehillah enterprise were dependent upon their financial support. Friedlaender's responses to their queries followed objective ideological lines and never affected his relations with such men as Kohns and Jacob Schiff, which were cordial but never intimate. However, in his capacity as spokesman for the bureau, he also confronted two other groups of Jewish leaders whose values he shared and whose respect he craved.

One group consisted of the rabbis and principals in charge of the *hedarim* and Talmud Torahs of the Lower East Side and Brooklyn. Despite the fact that the bureau assigned their schools a central place in the system, many of them were uneasy with the policies of the organization. Akiba Fleishman, principal of the Machzikei Talmud Torah, the oldest and largest institution of its kind in New York City, disputed Magnes's and Benderly's right to impose uniform educational standards upon all schools and to determine which schools should be accepted into the system.[20] Friedlaender's elegant defense of bureau policies contrasted sharply with Fleishman's dull recitation of questionable statistics and faulty grammar (e.g., "The *Ibrit be-Ibrit* method . . . does not work good in *golus*"). Despite the serious nature of the controversy, Friedlaender disarmed his readers with a light and bantering tone. On the issue of the number of children lacking Jewish education, he

[18]Kohns to IF, *FP*, June 4, 1914.
[19]This is the thesis of his essay, "Hebrew as a 'Mother-Tongue' and as a 'Father-Tongue,' " *Maccabean* 30 (August 1917): 317-318.
[20]*American Hebrew* 90 (February 23, 1912): 496.

quoted Mark Twain on "the three kinds of lies, viz. lies, damned lies and statistics."[21] Friedlaender demonstrated the pressing need for more Jewish schools, defended the *Ivrit be-Ivrit* method of Hebrew instruction, and insisted on the bureau's prerogative to establish physical and educational standards for all affiliated schools.

Neither man addressed the issue which lay behind Fleishman's bitter criticism of the Kehillah's policies and personnel. This was the fear on the part of the Orthodox rabbis that the organization of the Jewish Community of New York would relieve them of their most reliable source of social control, the education of the young. It is at any rate unlikely that Friedlaender thought along such lines. His perspective on Jewish life was generated in the clear waters of Ahad Ha-am's essays and Dubnow's *Letters*, not in the muddy stream of New York's ghetto politics. From his point of view, the administrative and pedagogic policies of the Kehillah and the bureau were the most rational means of serving "the needs of Judaism." If they would halt the assimilation of the young and unify the community around a common program, then they were appropriate. Friedlaender would go through life arguing on principle, seldom perceiving the hidden agenda, the power struggle which swirled about him.

Although the criticism of the Orthodox leaders offended Friedlaender, he realized that if he worked *for* them, he was not really one *of* them; his university education and modernist ideas set him apart. However, his defense of the bureau also led to controversy with men whose basic ideology he shared. The "most unkindest cuts of all" were those administered by Solomon Schechter and Cyrus Adler.

These men were far from pleased with the Kehillah's effort at communal organization. As the first and second presidents of the Jewish Theological Seminary, they hoped that their institution, through the rabbis and scholars it trained, would become the focal point of the educational as well as the religious endeavors of American Jewry. Toward this end, Schechter established the Seminary's second branch, the Teachers' Institute, intended to produce educators and committed to the organization of American Jewry along congregational lines and strongly tied to the Seminary.

[21]In the same issue, "Reply from Professor Friedlaender," pp. 496-497.

Like the Kehillah, which shared its birthdate of 1909, the Teachers' Institute was funded by Jacob Schiff. Its first faculty consisted of the two Seminary instructors who exhibited an interest in the education of the very young, Israel Friedlaender and Mordecai M. Kaplan.

It was during Schechter's sabbatical leave of 1910-11 that the Kehillah organized the Bureau of Jewish Education under the leadership of the dynamic Samson Benderly. During this period Friedlaender and Benderly became fast personal friends, settling their families in suburban Palisade, New Jersey.[22]

Neither Kaplan nor Friedlaender was in total agreement with Benderly's personal philosophy of Judaism, which Kaplan designated as secular Ahad Ha-amism.[23] Devoted to cultural Zionism, they nevertheless interpreted Judaism along religious lines. Yet both youthful scholars were caught up in the excitement of Benderly's promise to arouse the Jewish consciousness of the children of the ghetto through the use of new pedagogical techniques. In contrast to this dazzling prospect, the ideological differences between them and Benderly seemed insignificant, the possibility of a dispute with the Seminary administration remote.

For the first two years of the bureau's existence, Friedlaender encountered few problems in serving two masters, the Seminary in the capacity of professor in both branches and the bureau as chairman of the board of trustees. Indeed, in 1912, the two positions seemed to dovetail. For in January of that year Benderly proposed that his most promising students, bright young men such as Isaac B. Berkson and Alexander M. Dushkin, spend part of each day at the Teachers' Institute.

It was on this occasion that Schechter's bitter feelings against the bureau came out into the open. What really angered him was the knowledge that these students would not matriculate into the Seminary's rabbinical school; instead, they would enroll in Columbia University's Graduate School of Education. There they would sit at the feet of Dewey and Kilpatrick rather than Ginzberg and Marx. At the termination of their studies, they would not receive rabbinical degrees but the more prestigious Ph.D. There loomed the distinct possibility that these young men, rather than the rabbis

[22]IF lived in Fort Lee, Benderly in nearby Englewood.
[23]*Kaplan Journals*, October 4, 1914.

he trained, would assume the leadership of the American Jewish community, that the Kehillah, rather than the Jewish Theological Seminary, would become the dominant Jewish institution in New York.

Friedlaender, to his chagrin, became a buffer between his revered master Schechter and his trusted friend Benderly. Because of his position as chairman of the bureau's board of trustees, Schechter heaped personal abuse upon him, accusing him of supporting an organization which competed with the institution they both served.[24]

Patiently, Friedlaender responded to each of Schechter's angry outbursts, vindicating the particular program of the bureau currently under attack. In a ten-page letter, written at the beginning of the controversy, he explored the issue in great detail. Typically, he ignored the political source of the problem, preferring to dwell on the noble purpose of the bureau. There is no conflict between them, he wrote, because they pursue different objectives. "The one concerns itself with elementary Jewish education; the other laboring on behalf of higher Jewish learning."[25] However, he insisted, their overall objectives are the same. "They both endeavor to strengthen the Jewish consciousness, to spread the knowledge of Judaism and to stimulate the interest in things Jewish."[26] Therefore, he suggested a course of action, which was eventually accepted. "To avoid friction, and mutual interference, it is, in my opinion, essential that the two institutions should be entirely independent of one another."[27]

Even after Schechter acceded to Friedlaender's suggestion, he continued to indicate his displeasure with the professor's continued participation in the activities of the Kehillah and the bureau.

> The real point at issue is the welfare and development of the Seminary and institutions connected with it. . . . You are a member of our staff just as I am, and you must decide for yourself how far compatible or incompatible the plans of your Bureau are with the activities of the Seminary Teachers Institute.[28]

[24]Schechter to IF, February 15, 1912, October 7, 1912, October 9, 1912, *FP*.
[25]*FP*, January 24, 1912.
[26]Ibid.
[27]Ibid.
[28]*FP*, February 15, 1912.

However, since Schechter never actually compelled Friedlaender to resign from his bureau position, the latter continued to function as chairman of its board of trustees, unhappily absorbing the verbal abuse of his president.

Later in 1912 Schechter sent Friedlaender another reproachful letter denouncing yet another bureau policy. He claimed that the bureau had rejected the application of a Seminary graduate for a position as school superintendant (principal) "to make place . . . for someone recommended by the Bureau."[29] Once more he reminded Friedlaender where his loyalty should lie; "This collides with the interests of the Seminary."[30] Once again Friedlaender was put in the position of vindicating the Bureau of Education. In a lengthy response, he denied that the agency monopolized teaching positions, insisting that each school controlled its own hiring policy.[31]

Though he never wavered from his support of the bureau, Friedlaender suffered greatly from this unpleasant interchange. Later he wrote,

> My association with the Bureau has in one sense been a source of suffering, I might also say torture, to me. Professor Schechter has not only frowned upon my connection with the Bureau and has times out of number given me drastic proofs of his displeasure. He has on a number of occasions openly charged me with being a traitor to the Seminary.[32]

Friedlaender communicated this uneasy sentiment in a letter composed in June 1915, a few months before Schechter's death. This time he defended the Bureau of Jewish Education before a second Seminary representative, Cyrus Adler. Although these two men were attached to the same institutions and worked together on the *Jewish Quarterly Review*, they were often at loggerheads. Adler's incisive grasp of institutional politics contrasted sharply with Friedlaender's naiveté. In 1907 he had managed to secure the presidency of Dropsie College, a position which Friedlaender had coveted. After Schechter's death, he would replace him as administrator of the Seminary rather than Friedlaender or Ginzberg, who had heretofore been considered the heirs apparent.

[29]*FP*, October 7, 1912.
[30]Ibid.
[31]October 13, 1912, *FP*.
[32]IF to Adler, June 7, 1915, *FP*.

"A traditionalist of the antiquarian type,"[33] Adler was concerned more with religious observance than other facets of Jewish culture. As an adherent of the old policy of *stadlanut* to promote Jewish interests, he distrusted the Kehillah and remained a non-Zionist to the end of his days.[34]

Like Schechter, Adler disapproved of Benderly's philosophy and methods, which he indicated in a scathing letter to Friedlaender. It censured the bureau leadership for implementing procedures which would secularize Jewish education. Friedlaender's impassioned response upheld the bureau's educational policies, then went on to accuse Adler of underhanded attempts to weaken Benderly's authority. The letter ended with a bitter metaphor: "Of men like you I expect that they observe the ancient rules of chivalry: that you lift your visor before you attack your opponent."[35]

Not only did Friedlaender repel dangers from without; he also confronted even more onerous internal problems. In his excellent summary of the bureau's first years, Arthur Goren noted that "the optimism of 1912 became the burden of 1914 and the despair of 1916."[36] Not surprisingly, it was a conflict over money which imposed the burden, the bid for power that engendered the despair of the agency's board of trustees. As Friedlaender and the other members of the board—Magnes, Kaplan, Szold, and Marshall—assumed office in September 1910, they displayed unbounded enthusiasm for the renaissance of Jewish life through modern education. A cadre of fervent intellectuals and (with the exception of Marshall) cultural Zionists, they expected to establish policy for the organization. This was not to be. Benderly, known to friend and foe alike as the "czar" of Jewish education, initiated a number of innovative projects, including Hebrew charts and maps, new storybooks, textbooks, and magazines, and audio-visual aids. From the board of trustees he expected not advice but consent. At a time when money for teachers' salaries was difficult to obtain, board members found themselves haggling with Benderly over ambitious projects for which no funds were available. Disillusioned, Henrietta Szold, the treasurer, asked to be relieved of her duty of signing

[33]H. Parzen, *Architects of Conservative Judaism*, p. 98.
[34]I don't think that Simcha Kling disproves this in his "Our Zionist Fathers," *Conservative Judaism* 32 (Fall 1978): 27-32.
[35]June 7, 1915, *FP*.
[36]Goren, *New York Jews*, p. 101.

checks in 1913. By the time its five-year term expired, in 1915, the board of trustees had become a paper organization.

Friedlaender, at this juncture, also submitted his resignation, suggesting that the structure and function of any future committee be spelled out in detail.

Magnes and Benderly refused to accept the resignation, urging Friedlaender to remain chairman until the board could be reorganized. Friedlaender agreed to stay for a while, but soon found that this was a mistake. Two months later, claiming to have "lost all control of the organization," he wrote a second letter of resignation. "I do not exaggerate when I say that I feel like a rider who has been thrown off by his horse and holding to the tail, is dragged along the street, with this difference, that the rider in this case is not allowed to let go."[37]

Again Magnes and Benderly prevailed, convincing Friedlaender to remain chairman of the board in the interest of the bureau. Six more wearisome months would pass before Magnes finally accepted his resignation.

After the resignation, Friedlaender did not lose interest in the bureau's activities. In April 1918 he submitted a statement to the new board of trustees, praising Benderly's accomplishments but censuring his method of conducting the bureau's affairs.

> I am certainly the first to acknowledge with wholehearted admiration the unique abilities and achievements of Dr. Benderly. But a public institution, maintained out of public funds simply dare not—in my opinion—be conducted as a personal concern, without giving the slightest account to the donors, the public, or to their accredited representatives.[38]

After this letter, there is no record of any further contact between Friedlaender and Benderly.

Friedlaender's concern with education as a bulwark against assimilation was not confined to the instruction of young children, nor did it begin in America. During his student days, he had offered lessons in Hebrew and Jewish history to his assimilated German Jewish peers. This practice of informal tutoring continued

[37]December 12, 1915, *FP*.
[38]Under the title "Statement submitted to the Meeting of the Trustees of the Bureau of Education on April 6, 1918," *FP*.

throughout his life. On his own time, he conducted nonregistered courses for Seminary rabbinical students and "Benderly boys" interested in Arabic language and modern Hebrew literature, often in his own home.

His involvement in higher education for young Jews extended far beyond the confines of the Jewish Theological Seminary and environs. Realizing that the future American Jewish community would require not only rabbis and teachers, but knowledgeable and concerned laymen, he focused his attention upon Jewish undergraduates at the various colleges and universities. He served on the governing board of the Intercollegiate Menorah Society, an organization established to promote Jewish learning among college students, and encouraged adult patrons of the organization to donate books.[39] His message to college students was unequivocal: Until contemporary times, educated people invariably determined the direction of Jewish life. As committed Jews pursuing a higher education, you are therefore the rightful leaders of tomorrow. Join organizations established to perpetuate traditional Judaism, support Jewish culture, be faithful to Zion. Above all, pursue Jewish learning, leaving philanthropy to those untutored in the more exalted callings of Jewish life.

It was on the issue of higher education that Friedlaender again came into contact with Lee Kohns. In December 1912, he wrote a letter to this prominent Jewish businessman who served on the board of trustees of the City College of New York. In it he proposed that City College initiate a program of instruction in Semitic languages, especially Hebrew and Arabic. Among his arguments was one calculated to appeal to a practical-minded, socially-conscious "uptown Jew": the inclusion of Hebrew in the curriculum of a public institution would somehow encourage good behavior on the part of the children of the Russian immigrants, thereby preventing the emergence of "an army of Lefty Louies and Gyp the Bloods."[40]

To Friedlaender's regret, this proposal was never considered seriously by either the German-Jewish establishment or the university community. Nevertheless, the letter is important for two reasons. It was another endeavor to bring a *Wissenschaft* idea to

[39]See letter from Magnes, September 3, 1912, *FP*.
[40]December 20, 1912, *FP*.

fruition on American soil. Since the time of Geiger and Zunz, Jewish scholars had recommended the inclusion of Jewish studies in university curricula. Moreover, it foreshadowed the controversy over Americanization during the World War I period, in which Kohns and Friedlaender would figure prominently.

How can we summarize Friedlaender's involvement in Jewish education? It is clear that few men served it in as many capacities and with such lifelong devotion. Yet, if his activities as teacher, professor, dispenser of educational funds, apologist, informal lecturer, and advisor to the young yielded public prestige, they also generated private distress. Because he judged all educational projects solely on the basis of their utility in the struggle against assimilation, his arguments were ineffective against men who pursued partisan interests. Because he remained committed to the communal organization of Jewry and Jewish education, he incurred the displeasure of Schechter, and probably ruined his chances for advancement. Because he insisted that the Bureau of Education be run on a democratic basis, he lost a best friend.

We have observed that Friedlaender labored for the New York Kehillah as a means of ending the fragmentation of American Jewry, that he struggled for Jewish education on many levels to overcome its assimilatory tendencies. In his opinion, Emancipation had spawned yet a third category of Jewish defection, materialism. *The Jews of Russia and Poland*, it will be remembered, idealized the religious and cultural life of East European Jewry. Neither the book nor the survey of Jewish education took into account the fact that many Jews in the old center were beginning to question the traditional modes of piety and learning. Today many historians maintain that it was these Jews who were the most likely to emigrate. Yet, for Friedlaender, it was the American environment that fostered the widespread pursuit of material gain which pervaded the immigrant ghetto. With great apprehension, he "shuddered at the prospect of the 'People of the Book' making way for the 'People of the Ledger.' "[41]

On behalf of New York's "downtown Jews," he redoubled his efforts to salvage traditional modes of Jewish religion and culture in the face of the pressures of American life. This drew him into direct conflict with the leadership of the Educational Alliance, the

[41]*PP (1919)*, p. 449.

institution established on the Lower East Side of New York City in 1889 as an amalgam of the Hebrew Free School Association, the YMHA, and the Aguilar Free Library Society. The sponsors of the community house were civic-minded German Jewish philanthropists who regarded the swelling tide of Jewish immigration from Eastern Europe as a peril and a challenge. It was dangerous because the foreign-looking and foreign-sounding Jews crowding the tenements and hawking their wares on the street revived the old image of the Jew as an uncouth money-grubbing pariah. Since few Americans differentiated between the "downtown Jews" and their "uptown" co-religionists, the new immigration threatened the newly acquired and still shaky social status of the latter group. It was a challenge because, in defiance of their self-definition as adherents to a creed rather than members of a people, Reform Jews took upon themselves the familial obligations of caring for the new immigrants.

The Educational Alliance offered religious and vocational instruction, a library, health facilities, and a "People's Synagogue" based upon German Reform modes. English was the language of instruction in classes for children and adults, while attempts were made to exclude Hebrew, Yiddish, and every form of traditional Jewish culture from the courses of study. The condescending attitude of the sponsors of these programs toward the immigrants is exhibited in the words of Dr. Adolph Radin. Radin founded the Russian-American Hebrew Association "to exercise a civilizing and elevating influence upon the immigrants and Americanize them."[42]

Friedlaender's tenuous association with the Educational Alliance lasted for over a decade. In 1905 he delivered the first of many discourses critical of the institution.[43] Indicating what he called "the assimilatory tendencies of the directors" were cultural programs devoid of Jewish content and a synagogue lacking the trappings of Jewish tradition. Once again Friedlaender reproached the German Jewish magnates for supporting the Alliance out of *noblesse oblige*, never admitting that the immigrants had great treasures to offer them from Jewish tradition.

These sentiments, delivered by a very young professor before the meeting of a Zionist society, aroused very little attention. But when, in 1915, the same man suggested that the Educational

[42]Moses Rischin, *The Promised City*, p. 103.
[43]For a copy of this lecture, I would like to thank Carmel Agranat.

Alliance institute a full program of Jewish culture, he aroused considerable controversy. There were several reasons for this. First, by this time Friedlaender had acquired a certain standing in the community. He had been Schechter's deputy as president of the Jewish Theological Seminary and executive secretary of the Zionist Federation. Known as co-founder of the Kehillah and the Bureau of Jewish Education, he had also become a trustee of the Educational Alliance itself. More important than his status was the emotional climate of the times. He knew that the directors of the Educational Alliance were determined to impose putative "American" values upon the Russian Jews. Now that the world had plunged into war, the issue loomed as even more crucial. Americanization was no longer defined in terms of helping the immigrant adjust to his environment; it became a standard of the loyalty of each subgroup. Although the United States had always been a nation of immigrants, it was only in the quarter-century preceding World War I that large numbers of Americans had pondered the nature of acculturation. The fact that many considered East European Jews to be among the least desirable newcomers to this country had served as the original stimulus for the Alliance's assimilatory policy. With the onset of war, there was a general upswing of jingoistic chauvinism, which found expression in the Americanization movement, "which gripped the nation like a fever."[44] Milton Gordon has defined this phenomenon as "a consciously articulated movement to strip the immigrant of his native culture and attachments and to make him over into an American along Anglo-Saxon lines—all this to be accomplished with great rapidity. To use an image of a later day, it was an attempt at 'pressure cooking assimilation'."[45]

Before the war, only superpatriots like Theodore Roosevelt maintained this position. Yet in 1915, even liberal Woodrow Wilson demanded that new Americans renounce their ancestral ways and adopt the behavior and thought patterns of the Anglo-Saxon majority. "America does not consist of groups. A man who thinks of himself as belonging to a particular national group in America has not yet become American."[46]

Friedlaender realized that statements such as this one vindicated

[44] Milton M. Gordon, *Assimilation in American Life: The Role of Race, Religion and National Origins* (New York, 1964), p. 98.
[45] Ibid.
[46] Quoted in Oscar Handlin, *The American People*, p. 121.

the assimilatory policies of the Educational Alliance (EA) and other ghetto institutions, posing a threat to the viability of Judaism in the New World. If he couldn't take on the president of the United States, he felt duty-bound to explain his opposition to the Jewish agency's program. In order to do this, he had to clarify the distinction between political loyalty and adherence to a cultural and religious tradition. At EA board meetings, in lectures to the general public, personal correspondence, and official memoranda. Friedlaender investigated three issues related to this objective: the demands of American life upon the Jew, the place of Judaism in American culture, and the nature of Jewish adjustment to American life.

During his first years in America, Friedlaender had pondered the first two questions. In 1907 he had proclaimed:

> The freedom enjoyed by the Jews is not the outcome of emancipation, purchased at the cost of national suicide, but the natural product of American civilization. The idea of liberty as evolved by the Anglo-Saxon mind does not merely mean, as it often does in Europe, the privilege of selling new clothes instead of old, but signifies liberty of conscience, the full untrameled development of the soul as well as the body. The true American spirit understands and respects the traditions and associations of other nationalities, and on its vast area numerous races live peaceably together, equally devoted to the interests of the land.[47]

In 1912, Friedlaender told fellow intellectuals of the Achavah Club that America, unlike Europe, demands nothing in return for emancipation. "Here, liberty is not merely one of external life but also of spiritual development."[48]

By "external life" he meant the pursuit of a livelihood, personal liberties, and civil rights. Because American government and society were rooted in Anglo-Saxon ideas of liberty which Friedlaender (like Schechter) admired, there was nothing the Jew had to do to prove himself worthy of economic equality and political freedom. A fortunate combination of liberal Anglo-Saxon principle and favorable circumstance facilitated Jewish "spiritual development." The principle was that the state was never an end in itself

[47]*PP*, p. 180.
[48]"Minute Book," p. 210.

but rather "a means to secure the welfare of the individual and the society."[49] The circumstance was the peculiarly unfinished quality of American culture. Still in the process of formation, it remained open to influences from all inhabitants of the United States, newcomers as well as descendants of Revolutionary War heroes.[50]

Convinced that this country, which espoused Anglo-Saxon ideals and accepted a profusion of ethnic and religious groups, offered a unique opportunity for the development of Judaism, he was equally aware of the need for creative adaptation to the environment.

> What is true of the Spanish Jews of a thousand years ago, is equally true of the American Jews of today. We, too, live in a powerful environment which we cannot, and indeed, dare not disregard. The general culture of the land stands before us like an iron wall, and we shall be cracked like a nutshell if we attempt to run our heads against it. The only solution left to us is that of adaptation, but an adaptation which shall sacrifice nothing that is essential to Judaism, which shall not impoverish Judaism but enrich it, which, as was the case with Jewish culture in Spain, shall take fully into account what the environment demands of us, and shall yet preserve and foster our Jewish distinctiveness and originality.[51]

Thus Jews would earn a living in the great marketplace of America, gratefully pledging political allegiance to the land which afforded them security and freedom. They would willingly adopt the modes of the environment, becoming indistinguishable in the second generation from older Americans in dress, deportment, language, and secular education. However, in addition, they would find cultural sustenance and spiritual solace by cultivating group life and both traditional and modern modes of Jewish expression.

Group life and Jewish culture would set Jews apart, but would not isolate them from the general community. "In the great palace of American civilization we shall occupy our own corner, which we will decorate and beautify to the best of our taste and ability, and

[49]Ibid., p. 205.

[50]On the latter point, four of Friedlaender's colleagues, including Magnes and Kaplan, disagreed, insisting that he "unjustifiably minimized the force of the state idea in American life," ibid.

[51]*PP*, p. 193. This statement of 1914 was cited by Lawrence A. Cremin in *The Transformation of the School: Progressivism in American Education, 1876-1957* (New York, 1964), p. 69, as an early statement of cultural pluralism.

make it not only a center of attraction for the members of our family, but also an object of admiration for all the dwellers of the palace."[52]

Out of this separation would emerge a new type of Judaism that would contribute to Jewish spirituality in particular and American culture in general. Just as Sephardic Jews had introduced poetry and philosophy into Judaism, so would American Jews create a new Jewish culture, one in which art and music would figure prominently.

With admiration, Friedlaender also observed a behavioral pattern which Jews were beginning to adapt from the American milieu. Expansively, he described the "type of the modern American Jew who is both modern and Jewish, who combines American energy and success with that manliness and self-assertion, which is imbibed with American freedom."[53] By acquiring these positive personal characteristics and, at the same time, retaining his attachment to tradition, Friedlaender's idealized American Jew would slough off the poor qualities acquired in centuries of isolation and persecution and become a new man.

We have already indicated how Friedlaender's early optimism about the speedy emergence of an American Jewish center of the Spanish mode faded with the passage of time. Yet his perception of the meaning of American freedom and the position of the Jew in American society never shifted in the face of the draconian Americanization fervor of the "preparedness" era.

How can we explain the differences between his position and that of his colleagues on the board of the Educational Alliance? Why did these prominent Jews favor radical Americanization of the immigrants even before the Great War? The answer lies in the fact that the social philosophies of the Polish-born professor and the German Jewish magnates were guided by fundamentally different assumptions. The perceptions of Friedlaender's opponents were solidly grounded in eighteenth-century rationalism. Through their dual heritage of Reform Judaism and Jeffersonian liberalism, they fully accepted the values of the Enlightenment. They therefore viewed Jewish particularity and insularity as obstacles in the way of serving ideals that were humanitarian, rational, and cosmopoli-

[52]*PP*, p. 183.
[53]Ibid., p. 181.

tan. For them, Hebrew, peculiar religious rites, and, above all, the principle of Jewish nationality served to isolate Jews from the mainstream of American life. This conviction, reinforced by the "pressure-cooking" Americanization of the 1914–18 period, led to the insistence that the emigrés from Eastern Europe Americanize even more rapidly than before.

A different set of presuppositions governed Friedlaender's understanding of the nature of the American system and the position of Judaism in American culture. If the ideas of his opponents originated in the rationalism of the eighteenth century, his were grounded in nineteenth-century romantic nationalism and evolutionism as well as twentieth-century social psychology.

Friedlaender's interest in the psychological dimension of human existence had a long history. His scholarly writings demonstrated a sensitivity to the psychological foundations of Hebrew prophecy, folklore, and the messianic idea in Judaism and Islam.[54] His speeches to lay audiences also revealed an awareness of this phenomenon. For example, a public lecture delivered in 1905 proclaimed, "Human life is not regulated by logical considerations, but by psychological requirements."[55]

Pursuing this theme was another essay written five years later to elucidate the question of Jewish ethnicity. Here Friedlaender asserted that, in this delicate matter, subjective factors are more significant than objective ones.

> As far as our past is concerned the Jews have never regarded themselves otherwise than as a sharply distinguished racial group, as a community which is knit together not merely by the bonds of faith, but also by the ties of blood. Whether the Jews are a so-called pure race, or whether they have experienced, as has every race in history, an influx of foreign blood, is a question which properly belongs into the domain of anthropology, and concerning which the anthropologists hold vague and contradictory views. But this much I believe will be admitted by all, that only very few human races have displayed such jealous watchfulness in guarding the purity of their blood as have the Jews.[56]

The disparity between the German Jews' Enlightenment-based perspective and Friedlaender's psychological approach is clearly

[54]See *PP (1919)*, pp. 139-143; "Heterodoxies," p. 140.
[55]*PP*, p. 252.
[56]*PP (1919)*, pp. 131-132.

manifest in their proposals for the Americanization of Jewish immigrants.

In the early part of this century two theories of Americanization predominated. The first, which sociologists have called "Anglo-Conformity,"[57] strongly appealed to the leaders of the Educational Alliance: Friedlaender's frequent correspondent, Lee Kohns, who now served as chairman of its executive committee; Samuel Greenbaum, president of the organization and justice of the Supreme Court of the State of New York; and Samuel Strauss, a prominent businessman. Such was the tenor of the times that these men occasionally also referred to "the melting pot of American civilization."[58] The use of this phrase indicated familiarity with a second theory of Americanization, popularized by Israel Zangwill in his 1908 play, *The Melting Pot*.

Friedlaender refused to subscribe to either theory. In his opinion, America demanded neither conformity to "the behavior and values of the [Anglo-Saxon] core group" nor "a blending of the respective cultures [i.e., of all Americans] into a new indigenous American type."[59] His seminal essay "The Problem of Judaism in America," written one year before Zangwill's play, was an early effort to propose a third theory of Americanization, that of cultural pluralism, which, according to a contemporary sociologist, "postulated the preservation of the communal life and significant portions of the culture of the later immigrant groups within the context of American citizenship."[60]

In 1915, however, he adopted a new tactic. In order to demonstrate the inadequacies of the philosophy and program of the Educational Alliance, he submitted a memorandum to that body, part of which was subsequently published in the *Survey*, a social work journal.[61] When Friedlaender set out to refute the theories of Anglo-conformity and the melting pot, he did not reiterate the old arguments. Instead, he addressed new issues raised by advanced

[57]See Stewart G. Cole and Mildred Wiese Cole, *Minorities and the American Promise* (New York, 1954), chap. 6.

[58]This phrase appears in a long written response to Friedlaender's Americanization essay, *FP*, Box 9. The letter was not signed; however, it is clear that its author was a director of the Educational Alliance, probably the extremist Samuel Strauss.

[59]This is Gordon's definition of the melting-pot theory in *Assimilation*, p. 85.

[60]Ibid., Gordon's definition of cultural pluralism.

[61]*Survey* 38 (May 5, 1917): 103-108. Reprinted in *PP*, pp. 229-245.

thinkers of the early twentieth century; Stuart Hughes has designated them "the character of individual and group dominance, the sources of social cohesion, the nature and function of religious sentiment."[62]

"The Americanization of the Jewish Immigrant," Friedlaender's essay, confronted an issue which troubled people concerned with the social cohesion of a nation composed of so many diverse strains. At the onset, it established the premise "that the solution of the immigrant problem consists in making the immigrant *cease* to be an immigrant, i.e., in common parlance, in making the immigrant, who is a stranger in our gates, feel at home, and in transforming him into a happy and useful member of the new environment."[63]

This initial statement indicated a significant shift in Friedlaender's position. Here he assumed the posture of a disinterested observer, a "humanitarian, who is interested in the Jews, not on account of his racial or religious kinship with them, but as a section of humanity to which he is bound by no other tie except that of a common mankind."[64]

Friedlaender had previously considered the collective welfare of the Jewish group; in this instance, he focused upon the needs of the individual immigrant.

In this analysis, he reiterated a distinction conveyed in his earlier work, the separation of "external" problems from "internal"ones. To solve the physical problems of the immigrants, he suggested, "We must endeavor to acquaint the newly arrived immigrant with the conditions of the new land and to enable him to fight successfully in the struggle for existence, so that he may obtain and assume his rightful share in the benefits and responsibilities of the country which he has chosen for his abode."[65]

On this issue he was in full agreement with the leadership of the Educational Alliance. It was, however, his perception of the immigrants' spiritual problems and his suggestion for their solution that fueled the controversy with the Alliance directorate. The recent arrival from Eastern Europe, Friedlaender pointed out, had always cherished the values inherent in Judaism—"Jewish learning and Jewish piety, i.e., knowledge of the Jewish religion and the observ-

[62]Hughes, *Consciousness and Society*, p. 24.
[63]*PP*, p. 230 (IF's emphasis).
[64]Ibid.
[65]Ibid., p. 231.

ance of its practices."[66] In America he experienced what future analysts would term "culture shock."

> On arriving in this country, the immigrant discovers that they are not only valueless, but that they are a hindrance, and sometimes a nuisance, in the eyes of his fellow-men. We are horrified by the sight of physical cripples. But were it given to us, by some kind of spiritual X-rays, to perceive the fractures in the souls of men, we would be a thousand times more horrified by the sight of the untold numbers of mangled human souls which are writhing in inexpressible suffering in the midst of our Jewish immigrant population.[67]

Boldly, Friedlaender formulated the solution to immigrant anomie as "the attempt to restore the equilibrium of the immigrant."[68] What is "equilibrium"? "Equilibrium has been defined as 'a condition of equal balance between opposite or counteracting forces.' "[69] The concept originates in physiology: "In the life of the body the most important sense, without which animal life is practically impossible, is the sense of equilibrium, the sense, as has well been said, 'by which we have a feeling of security in standing, walking, and indeed in all the movements by which the body is carried through space.' "[70] It is equally applicable to man's spiritual life.

> In spiritual life the equilibrium of man, with the possible exception of a few geniuses, is the product of the social forces of his environment. As long as man remains within his natural surroundings, he is endowed with this sense of equilibrium—whether we call it habit, tradition, or association—which gives him the feeling of security in all functions of life. For the environment dictates to him his form of speech, shapes his thoughts, colors his sentiments, determines his manners and customs. In the case of the immigrant, i.e., of the man who has been detached from his accustomed environment, this equilibrium is disturbed. He is deprived of the constant, though unconscious, guidance of his social group, and the result is the same as in the life of the body when the sense of equilibrium is impaired: he loses his feeling of security: he reels; he is swayed to and fro by the slightest touch of the new environment; he becomes unnatural and unhappy. Unless he be a man

66Ibid., p. 236.
67Ibid., p. 237.
68Ibid., p. 231.
69Ibid.
70Ibid.

of exceptional ability, the most valuable in him, his personality, the outcome of long years of breeding and training, is destroyed and he is in danger of becoming a moral wreck, a menace to himself and a menace to his neighbors.[71]

What was the source of this challenging and forceful analysis? Despite the fact that Friedlaender placed quotation marks around his definition of "equilibrium," the specific matrix of this notion is difficult to trace. For he never cited a single physiologist or psychologist by name, nor did he use any term more technical than "equilibrium." Yet it is evident that he had either purposely investigated or unconsciously absorbed the ideas of contemporary thinkers who pondered the relationship between man and his environment, between the individual and the group.

From around 1900 European physiologists and psychologists such as Pavlov and Freud had observed that mental processes, like physical ones, are characterized by a striving for equilibrium.[72] In this country, Walter B. Cannon wrote a series of papers which would later be incorporated into his classic, *The Wisdom of the Body*.[73] It was he who popularized the term "homeostasis," defining it as "the coordinated physiological processes which maintain most of the steady states in the organism."[74] Although most of his *oeuvre* dealt with the effect of bodily changes upon the psyche, Cannon also indicated that homeostasis was a useful concept for sociology. Comparing society to the bodily organism, he suggested that economic and social programs be organized to enable the organism to maintain a steady state.

Two other Americans, George Herbert Mead and Charles H. Cooley, dealt with the question which Hughes would later label "the character of individual and group dominance." Both of them maintained that students of society could best understand the individual in a social context. In *Human Nature and the Social Order* (1902), Cooley demonstrated the inseparability of the individual and the social in human life.[75] In *Mind, Self, and Society*, Mead

[71]Ibid., pp. 231-232.
[72]See Sigmund Freud, *Interpretation of Dreams*, authorized trans. and ed. A. A. Brill (New York, 1913), and Ivan Petrovich Pavlov, *Conditioned Reflexes and Psychiatry*, trans. and ed. W. Horsley Gantt (New York, 1941).
[73]Walter B. Cannon, *The Wisdom of the Body* (New York, 1932).
[74]Ibid., p. 24.
[75]Charles H. Cooley, *Human Nature and the Social Order*, rev. ed. (Glencoe, Ill., 1956).

defined consciousness as "that peculiar character and aspect of the environment of individual human experience which is due to human society."[76] Since consciousness is formed in society, he maintained, it follows that when an individual is removed from the society in which he was reared and placed in a strange environment, then he acquires a new sense of self.

"The Americanization of the Jewish Immigrant" can best be understood as an amalgam of Cannon's notion of homeostasis and Mead and Cooley's social theory of consciousness with still-popular evolutionism. Friedlaender utilized these concepts to demonstrate that rapid Americanization, in the sense of stripping the Jewish immigrant of the cultural and religious trappings of his heritage, would destroy the delicate balance of his psyche. It was, he argued, impossible to transform any human being into "a new man" by fiat. Why? "The human soul is not a *tabula rasa*. The impress of centuries is indelibly stamped upon it, and no mechanical process can undo the organic development of many generations."[77]

The language of this statement indicates that Friedlaender, like so many thinkers of his generation, was one of the "transition figures between philosophy and social science" of which Hughes wrote.[78] "The Americanization of the Jewish Immigrant" designated the societal influences which had contributed to the organic development of East European Jewry and indicated how they could be successfully utilized to restore the equilibrium of the Russian Jewish immigrant. The most important influence was religion, which Friedlaender had always regarded as "the cap and cornerstone of Russian Jewish life."[79] In this essay, however, he adopted a sociological frame of reference, investigating what Hughes calls "the nature and function of religious sentiment" in the life of the Jewish community. He asserted that in Jewish life, religion, broadly understood, exercised three important functions: cultural expression, social cohesion, and personal fulfillment.

The first of these was an older idea which Friedlaender had previously expressed and would continue to present to the American public.

[76]George Herbert Mead, *Mind, Self, and Society from the Standpoint of a Social Behaviorist*, ed. Charles W. Morris (Chicago, 1934), p. 171. This book is a compilation of essays written early in the century.
[77]*PP*, p. 242.
[78]Hughes, *Consciousness and Society*, p. 25.
[79]*PP (1919)*, p. 287.

Religion from this point of view is co-extensive with that which in modern parlance goes by the name of social and cultural life. Judaism, in this formulation, regulates practically all the functions of life, even those which the Christian would never think of associating with religion, such as food and drink, as well as the manners and customs of every-day life. As a result of this development, the immigrant Jew possesses his own language, or rather languages. For, while using Yiddish as a vernacular, he employs Hebrew not merely as the language of prayer and study, but also, to a very considerable extent, as a medium of literature and correspondence. Both languages (Yiddish to a lesser degree than Hebrew) are regarded by him as part of his religious tradition. He wears in his homeland his own form of dress, which is no less hallowed by religious associations.[80]

The novelty lay in his perception of the sociological and psychological dimension of traditional Jewish life. Friedlaender was one of the first social thinkers to point out that the Lithuanian *bet ha-midrash* and the Polish *klaus* were not merely religious and educational institutions; they also satisfied the social, spiritual, and recreational needs of the individual Jew.

Social life, in the sense of sociability, strange though it may sound, was perhaps nowhere so fully developed as in the Ghetto. The *Beth Hamidrash*, "the House of Study," and, in the provinces in which the sect of Hassidim ("Pietists") prevail, the *Klaus*, or "Meeting House," formed the social center of the community, where the Jews met day in and day out not only for mental recreation, by studying jointly the sources of Judaism, but also for social entertainment, in the form of friendly chats, and very frequently of common meals, generally accompanied by singing and even dancing. The Jews of the Ghetto lived up, in very truth, to the biblical adage that "man doth not live by bread alone but by what proceedeth from the mouth of the Lord." For while they often lacked bread, they found supreme comfort and happiness in the study and contemplation of the word of God.[81]

Deprived of the security of these social stimuli and forced to transgress religious commandments in the pursuit of a livelihood, the Jews of the Lower East side reacted in one of two ways. The gentler folk often become "mangled souls."

[80]*PP*, p. 234.
[81]Ibid., p. 238.

No one except he who has an intimate knowledge of the conditions of old-fashioned Jewish life in the Ghetto can adequately appreciate the excruciating mental agony which the immigrant Jew must experience when, for instance, for the first time in his life he is forced to violate the God-given command of abstaining from work on the Sabbath day, or to transgress any of the Jewish regulations concerning food, which in his eyes are clothed with the authority of the Divine will. Nor can the outsider fully realize the inexpressibly tragic gap which opens up in the soul of the immigrant when he discovers that what he has held sacred and dear in the past is valueless, and less than valueless, in the eyes of his new neighbors. The result of this conflict is in innumerable cases a complete loss of equilibrium and the destruction of that feeling of moral and mental security without which a man is degraded into a beast, and life becomes a meaningless and brutal discharge of mere physical functions.[82]

These Jews, often the finest and most sensitive of the immigrants, never found peace in America,

They turn away in disgust from the new environment, which is utterly misconceived by them, and—here again I refer to a phrase current among this type of Jewish immigrant—they deprecate the memory of Columbus for having discovered America, where their hopes for a happier and loftier existence have been cruelly deceived.[83]

Others did adjust, but at a great cost. Having never been taught the true meaning of America, they also throw off the restraints of traditional Judaism and were "ready to play the game."[84] What is the nature of this "game"? It is "the hunt after the dollar, the corrupt state of politics, the hankering after publicity; the drift towards materialism."[85]

Anything but neutral on the subject of the two types of Jews, Friedlaender expressed his preference in a long, colorful sentence.

The writer for one, and here again he is speaking purely as a humanitarian, prefers the kaftan-clad old-fashioned Jew, with his unattractive appearance and ungainly manners, whose whole life is dominated by

[82]Ibid., p. 237.
[83]Ibid., pp. 240-241.
[84]Ibid., p. 241.
[85]Ibid., p. 240.

the ideals and mandates of an ancient religion and civilization, whose mind has been cultivated by the subtleties of the Talmud and whose conduct is regulated by the restraints of the *Shulḥan Arukh*, to that modernized amphibious creature, the gaudily attired, slang-using, gum-chewing, movie-visiting, dollar-hunting, vulgar and uncultured, quasi-Americanized "dzentelman."[86]

Just as Friedlaender attempted to frighten Lee Kohns with the prospect of more criminals like "Lefty Louie" and "Gyp the Blood," he now caricatured the "allrightnick" for Kohns and his associates in the Educational Alliance. Each statement was a clever ploy, designed to demonstrate the value of Jewish culture in preventing the coarsening of the moral fiber of the immigrants.

There remained the question of how to deal with the serious problem of materialism. What conditions would facilitate the creation of the new American Jew, who would abhor vulgarity and shun criminality, who would, instead, retain the best features of his ancestors' culture even as he learned to cope with the new environment? For Friedlaender there was only one answer.

The solution of the problem, therefore, must consist in the restoration of his equilibrium, in the recreation of a social environment for him, which, among the puzzling conditions of the new land, would offer him that spiritual anchorage which his former environment had provided for him; in making him again the unit of a social group, the mandates of which he could obey, and in enabling him to regain the sense of security which had formerly guided him in all the functions of life.[87]

Consequently, Friedlaender urged the Educational Alliance to provide a proper "social environment" which would facilitate the restoration of immigrant equilibrium. With this, the published portion of the memorandum came to an end. It was followed by series of suggestions for the implementation of the proposal.

Before we discuss them, it is important to place Friedlaender's advocacy of cultural pluralism in its historical context. The best known of Friedlaender's contemporaries to espouse cultural plural-

[86]Ibid., p. 243.
[87]Ibid., p. 232.

ism was the Harvard-trained, Zionistically-inclined academic
Horace Kallen. His trenchant study, entitled "Democracy versus
the Melting Pot,"[88] was published in the *Nation* during the same
year that Friedlaender submitted his memorandum to the directors
of the Educational Alliance. Close examination of Kallen's treatise
reveals that, despite its broader scope, its concepts resemble those
in Friedlaender's 1907 essay, "The Problem of Judaism in America." Exploring the role of ethnic minorities in the United States,
Kallen concluded that each nationality remained separate, though
not isolated. To illustrate this point, he employed a metaphor
reminiscent of Friedlaender's image of the palace in which Jews
occupy one corner. "Our spirit is inarticulate, not a voice, but a
chorus of many voices each singing a rather different tune."[89]

Since America as yet possessed no uniform culture, it followed
that each nationality was obliged to retain its traditional heritage.
More radical and perhaps closer to Dubnow than the prophetic
peroration at the end of Friedlaender's essay was Kallen's proposal
of a "federation or commonwealth of nationalities."[90]

Kallen's provocative essay surveyed the economic and social as
well as the ethnic stratifications of American life. It suggested what
was then another novel idea, that "pure English Americans" had, in
the course of time, become just one of many minorities inhabiting
the United States. However, it barely touched upon the psychological and social consequences of extremely rapid Americanization.
Nor was this the concern of Randolph Bourne, the young scholar
whose article "Transnational America," published in 1916, presented the United States as a model for a postwar world in which
many nations would live in concert.[91] The only social scientist of
note to consider these factors was the innovative philosopher and
educator John Dewey. In an article entitled "Nationalizing Education," published a year after Friedlaender's Americanization essay,
he argued that children of various ethnic and religious groupings

[88]Horace Kallen, "Democracy versus the Melting Pot: A Study of American Nationality,"
Nation 100 (February 18, 1915): 190-194; (February 25, 1915): 217-220.
[89]Ibid., p. 217. Similar to Friedlaender and Kallen's notions were those of Judah L.
Magnes. See the sermon delivered at Temple Emanuel in New York on October 9, 1909 in:
Arthur A. Goren, *Dissenter in Zion. From the Writings of Judah L. Magnes* (Cambridge, 1982),
pp. 101-106.
[90]Ibid., p. 219.
[91]Published in the *Atlantic Monthly* 118 (July 1916): 86-97.

should be taught to respect each other in schools and to recognize the contributions of each to American life.[92]

If few social theorists before Friedlaender considered the psychic disorientation of displaced immigrants, this phenomenon did concern the people who came into daily contact with them. Jane Addams, the famous settlement worker who dealt with immigrants of diverse backgrounds in Chicago, was one of the few American intellectuals to decry the psychological consequences of accelerated Americanization. She was disturbed by the alienation of the younger generation from their foreign-born parents, which often resulted in family disorganization and juvenile delinquency. *Twenty Years at Hull House*, published in 1910, expressed the hope that "our American citizenship might be built without disturbing foundations which were laid of old time."[93]

The author whose perception of immigrant anomie most resembled that of Friedlaender was Abraham Cahan. In two brilliant novels, the editor of the Yiddish newspaper *Forward* graphically illuminated the spiritual degeneration of immigrant Jews who underwent galloping Americanization. The hero of *The Rise of David Levinsky* (1917)[94] acquired considerable wealth. However, because he abandoned his original ideals, he achieved neither love nor personal fulfillment. The novella *Yekl: A Tale of the New York Ghetto* (1896)[95] painted an unflattering portrait of Jake, the vulgar, quasi-Americanized "dzentelman" who ultimately was bested by his old-fashioned wife and their gentle boarder, Mr. Bernstein. These two "fractured souls" had long struggled to retain the traditional values even as they deprecated the memory of Columbus. In the end, they gracefully underwent a slow process of acculturation.

Since it is unlikely that Addams, Cahan, and Friedlaender, who traveled in different circles, influenced one another, the similarity of their messages is particularly striking. One thing Friedlaender did share with both of the others: a close personal involvement with the immigrants of whom he wrote. Thus he was not content to

---

[92]John Dewey, "Nationalizing Education," *National Education Association: Addresses and Proceedings of the Fifty-Fourth Annual Meeting*, 54 (1916): 183-189. See also his article "The Principle of Nationality," which appeared in *MJ* 3 (April 1917): 203-208.

[93]Jane Addams, *Twenty Years at Hull House* (New York, 1910), p. 258.

[94]Abraham Cahan, *The Rise of David Levinsky* (New York, 1966).

[95]Idem, "Yekl: A Tale of the New York Ghetto," in *Yekl and the Imported Bridegroom and Other Stories of the New York Ghetto* (New York, 1970).

submit to the directors of the EA a theoretical essay alone; he attached to it a long list of concrete practical suggestions.[96] Most controversial was the proposal that the direction of the organization be taken away from its German Jewish board of directors and placed in the care of the Russian Jews whom it served. In addition, Friedlaender suggested that the school and synagogue be conducted along traditional lines and that Sabbath and dietary laws be observed within the building. He also recommended a full cultural program, including Jewish music and art, more Yiddish lectures,[97] and clubs which would promote specifically Jewish values among children and adults.

Friedlaender's memorandum created an uproar. Kohns, Greenberg, and Strauss wrote him a series of acrimonious letters, disputing his arguments in detail.[98] In the end, the board of trustees refused to countenance the democratization of the EA. However, it did accept several of Friedlaender's proposals, among them an advisory board composed of neighborhood people, lectures and clubs devoted to Jewish issues, and the increased use of Yiddish. The new platform of the Alliance, adopted on February 15, 1916, promised "to carry on the religious work formerly done by the Hebrew Free School Association, and to cooperate with the forces in the City that make for the amelioration and advancement of communal and civic life."[99] It added this statement, which reflected Friedlaender's thinking: "In pursuing these aims, the Educational Alliance shall at all times endeavor to preserve the ideal elements which the immigrants have brought with them."[100]

For the German magnates, these were tactical compromises concluded to sustain the shaky peace between uptown and downtown Jews. However, they never assented to the principle that the best way to Americanize the Jewish immigrants was through religious, social, and cultural activities of strong Jewish content. They could not, because they cherished different assumptions about four fundamental issues: the nature of the Jewish problem, the character of the Jewish immigrant, the relationship between

[96]See *FP*, Box 16.
[97]The Yiddish lectures of Zvi Masliansky had been a popular attraction for many years.
[98]See *FP*, November 1915 to February 1916.
[99]Quoted in Friedlaender's letter of resignation from the Educational Alliance, addressed to Judge Samuel Greenbaum, January 9, 1917, *FP*.
[100]Ibid.

political loyalty and culture, and the proper tempo of acculturation.

At the risk of repetition, it must be emphasized that the theoretical issue separating Friedlaender from the other board members of the Alliance was the definition of the Jewish question. The Reform magnates, like their adversaries, the political Zionists, were preoccupied with the emergence of anti-Semitism in their day. Their solution to the Jewish problem on the Lower East Side—that the immigrants should assume the trappings of the host culture as rapidly as possible—was a sincere effort to render the newcomers less objectionable to a nation now demanding cultural conformity as well as political loyalty. They insisted that rapid acculturation would not only ease the immigrants' entry into American society; it would also keep the doors to America open to other Jews longing to escape the depredations of czarist Russia.

Friedlaender's solution to the Jewish question, on the other hand, proceeded from the axiom that the major problem of the immigrants was internal, not external. Thoroughly convinced that the essence of America was receptivity to all peoples and their cultures, he considered the jingoism of the "preparedness" period a temporary aberration. This explains his decision to focus upon the subjective needs of the individual Jew. What angered the "Yahudim" was Friedlaender's ability to utilize the most advanced concepts of social psychology to support concepts which to them were outmoded and even dangerous.

One of these concerned the character of the Russian immigrant. Friedlaender did not claim that the Russian Jew had no faults; indeed, he listed them in graphic detail: "pettiness, suspiciousness, hyper-sensitiveness and hyper-cleverness, excessive individualism, lack of organizing ability, disregard of externalities, often resulting in uncouthness and uncleanliness."[101]

What he did say was that his positive qualities far outweighed them:

> his extraordinary mental vigor, his unconquerable thirst for knowledge, his boundless respect for learning, his passionate love of liberty, his profound sense of justice, his power to endure suffering, his frugality, his genuine warm-heartedness, and a variety of other virtues which are best evidenced by the fact that his enemies openly justify their cruelty

[101]*PP*, pp. 235-236.

by his enormous superiority over the native population, a superiority which he has been able to maintain in the face of inconceivable misery and persecution.[102]

Many German Jews agreed with this analysis of the Russian Jews' shortcomings; some were even ready to accept the presence of the virtues. However, they disputed Friedlaender's contention that the cause of personal degeneration was transplantation to America. The efforts of the Educational Alliance to Americanize the immigrants proceeded from the premise that the American environment produced a finer Jewish type than the traditional milieu. In 1897, Isidor Straus, founder of the agency, had placed the following statement on the record: "The scope of the Educational Alliance shall be of an Americanizing Educational, Social and Humanizing character . . . for the moral and intellectual improvement of the inhabitants of the East Side."[103] That twenty years had not altered this perspective is indicated by the fact that the argument was repeated in an unsigned letter to Friedlaender, which debated his memorandum, point by point.[104]

Underlying Friedlaender's differences with Reform members of the EA board were two further assumptions. The first concerned the relationship between loyalty and culture. When, in the heat of the presidential election campaign of 1916, both Wilson and Hughes vociferously advocated "one-hundred per cent Americanism,"[105] the more jingoistically inclined EA directors followed their lead. Samuel Strauss charged a group of young immigrants to abandon all ideas that were foreign to American culture, especially the notion that they were members of a race rather than co-religionists. If they refused, he threatened, "America will become a place from which we will have to move on again in our eternal wandering."[106]

Friedlaender's response rebuked Strauss for linking a matter of internal Jewish debate to a question of loyalty to the United States.

---

[102]Ibid., p. 236.
[103]From an address delivered at the annual meeting of the Educational Alliance, 1897. It was quoted in a long unsigned letter to Friedlaender. See above, n. 58.
[104]Ibid.
[105]See *New York Times*, June 8, 1916.
[106]Ibid. Reported in the same issue. The address was delivered the day before.

Whether Judaism was a race or a religion, whether Zionism was justified or unjustified, was an internal Jewish question towards which the various Jewish parties might assume various attitudes; but to tell us that America forbids us to conceive Judaism as a race, or to embrace the Zionist ideal, was to bring up an evil report of *America* which must be energetically repudiated. The immigrant Jews, who felt happy in having escaped Russian tyranny, believed that it was a slander upon this land of liberty to frighten them with the possibility of an American Cossack, who would, like the henchmen of Russian despotism, stick his boots into their souls.[107]

In the same address he brought up yet another issue which distinguished his position from that of the other EA directors. For Strauss and his associates, the rate of acculturation of the immigrants was too slow. Friedlaender was of the opposite opinion.

The environment being friendly, the adaptation to it on the part of the Jews proceeds at a rapid pace. Those unacquainted with the life of Polish Jewry for the last 700 years can scarcely realize the remarkable, almost uncanny, rapidity with which the immigrant Jew is being Americanized. On the contrary, careful observers will be inclined to believe that the transformation proceeds in some sections too rapidly, bringing grave perils in its wake.[108]

The "perils," of course, were those resulting from the psychic dislocation of which he had written in his Americanization essay. There was, at any rate, no question in Friedlaender's mind that the second generation would be "fully and thoroughly Americanized, in the sense of resembling in their whole makeup the rest of the American population."[109]

When the Educational Alliance incorporated some of his proposals into its platform of February 15, 1916, it had seemed to Friedlaender that it was proceeding in the direction of what he called "constructive Americanization." However, the Strauss address, delivered in June of the same year, followed by several harangues in a similar vein at the annual meeting of the agency in January 1917, convinced Friedlaender that it was impossible to

[107]From a newspaper article reporting IF's speech delivered in Yiddish at the People's Synagogue of the Educational Alliance on the topic "Judaism and Americanism." *FP*, Box 9, undated, with no indication of source.
[108]Ibid.
[109]Ibid.

change the direction of the organization. After that meeting, he decided to submit his resignation. In letters to Strauss and Judge Samuel Greenbaum, the president of the Educational Alliance, who partially supported Strauss's view, Friedlaender cited his original reason for joining the board: "The hope that I might in my own small way be helpful in paving the road for . . . mutual understanding [between German and Russian Jews]."[110] Finally convinced that "the EA was a de-Judaising organization,"[111] Friedlaender severed his connection to it.

*   *   *   *

We have seen that Friedlaender, unlike most of his academic colleagues, worked actively in the community to eliminate certain unhappy consequences of Emancipation. To counteract the fragmentation of American Judaism, he supported the Kehillah throughout the years of its active existence. He served it so well that historians of the movement have implied that Magnes considered him his probable successor as the head of the organization.[112] Friedlaender's labors in the diverse fields of Jewish education bequeathed incalculable benefits upon the Jews of New York, young and old. However, these efforts to hold back assimilation resulted in the censure of friends and enemies alike, upsetting his chances for personal advancement.

His most original response to Emancipation American-style was the suggestion that conformity to Anglo-Saxon attitudes and behavior patterns did not help the immigrants avoid the blandishments of American materialism; therefore the only way to endow the American Jew with a healthy mind and a sound spirit was to preserve his communal life and traditional culture within the context of American citizenship. Through their passionate reaction to Friedlaender's Americanization essay, the German Jewish magnates betrayed an as yet unarticulated fear. They sensed that traditional interpretations of Judaism, heretofore dismissed as atavistic, could successfully employ the newer social sciences to legitimize their claims upon American Jewry. Their anxiety, how-

[110]IF to Greenbaum, January 9, 1917, *FP*.
[111]IF to Strauss, January 8, 1917, *FP*.
[112]Goren, *New York Jews*, p. 243; Norman Bentwich, "The Kehillah of New York, 1908-1922," in *Mordecai M. Kaplan Jubilee Volume* (New York, 1953), English sec., p. 84.

ever, was premature. Friedlaender's arguments were too sophisticated for an American Jewish community not yet initiated into the mysteries of sociology and psychology. As a consequence they were largely ignored. The war of words with the assimilationists who controlled the Educational Alliance yielded a baneful lesson. Friedlaender learned that reasonable argumentation, even when rooted in psychological analysis rather than abstract principle, could not prevail in an age racked by jingoism and accustomed to one-dimensional thinking.

In his letters of resignation from both the Bureau of Jewish Education and the Educational Alliance, Friedlaender portrayed himself as a bridge between the "German" and the "Russian" Jews of New York. In actuality, he functioned less as a bridge than as a footpath. In their rush to attack the positions of the other side, the German Jewish establishment and the East European special-interest groups trampled heedlessly over Friedlaender's attempts at mediation. This will become strikingly apparent in the next chapter, which deals with Friedlaender's endeavors on behalf of Zionism.

Chapter 8

Contributions to American Zionism

> Zionism . . . is not an end in itself, an agency for political aggrandizement and the injustice and oppression that goes with it, but it is a means to an end, the physical vessel for a spiritual content, the material agency for the consummation of the great ideals of justice and righteousness.
>
> —*Israel Friedlaender*

Among the proudest legacies of Conservative Judaism is its early and wholehearted espousal of Zionism. To a man, the first faculty of the Jewish Theological Seminary embraced a concept of Judaism which integrated its religious and national elements. Soon after joining the American Zionist Federation in December 1905, Schechter produced a forceful exposition of his pro-Zionist position. However, of all the Seminary faculty, it was Friedlaender who devoted the greatest portion of his time and creative energy both to the theoretical defense of the Zionist ideology and to the day-by-day, year-by-year functioning of American Zionism.

While still in Europe, Friedlaender participated in the Hebrew renaissance and actively supported the Zionist movement. Thereafter, he frequently attended Zionist conferences, including the important Sixth Congress of 1903, where together with his new colleague, Louis Ginzberg, he voted no to the African resolution.[1]

---

[1]According to Cyrus Sulzberger's "An American's View of the Congress," *American Hebrew* 73 (September 11, 1903): 527.

Throughout his sixteen-and-a-half years in America, he remained a functioning Zionist propagandist and activist, thereby generating one of his life's many discordant ironies. The foremost conduit of European Zionist ideas, he nevertheless suffered cruel disillusionment from each venture into the hurly-burly of Zionist politics.

Friedlaender joined the fledgling Federation of American Zionists upon arrival in this country, served as chairman of the Zionist Council of New York in 1905, and headed the FAZ's educational program in 1906. For many years he labored, along with Harry Friedenwald and Henrietta Szold, assembling materials for a Zionist manual.[2] The manual was never published, due to lack of funds; however, some of the articles appeared in the *Maccabean*, the English-language organ of the Zionist Federation. To assure a Zionist future in America, Friedlaender organized Young Judea and was active in the Intercollegiate Zionist Organization. His Zionist activity culminated in the year 1910-11, when he headed the FAZ in the capacity of chairman of its executive committee.

Despite the yeoman efforts of Friedlaender and Henrietta Szold, the executive secretary of the committee, the federation remained feeble and ineffective, unable to recruit a mass following or to reconcile factional differences. Nor could it raise the funds required to carry out its program successfully and still meet the financial demands of the World Zionist Organization. This was not the fault of the Zionist leaders. Historians of American Zionism have noted that prior to World War I, the FAZ was confronted by insurmountable obstacles. The German Jews, for the most part, opposed Zionism; the East European immigrants, though sympathetic, were too present-oriented, busily adjusting to conditions in a strange new land, to devote their energies to what Friedlaender called "a dream of the future."[3]

After the year of stewardship, Friedlaender happily relinquished leadership of the Zionist Federation to the secularists of East European origin, led by Louis Lipsky. Lipsky would direct American Zionism until the ascendancy of Louis D. Brandeis in 1914. Friedlaender continued to wield his pen in defense of the move-

[2]*FP* contain many letters exchanged between the three editors on this subject, 1905-8. See also *Richards MSS* and *Friedenwald MSS*, passim.

[3]From his unpublished address, "Uptown and Downtown Zionism," delivered at the mass meeting of the Qadimah in the Educational Alliance, March 1, 1905. I would like to thank Mrs. Agranat for sending me the text.

ment, in correspondence with such prominent non-Zionists as Jacob Schiff, Cyrus Adler, and Lee Kohns, and in articles in the Anglo-Jewish press. When the Great War erupted, he was once again drawn into official Zionist leadership, serving on the elite Provisional Executive Committee for General Zionist Affairs (PC), organized by Brandeis in August 1914. Under the official title of recording secretary and archivist, he conducted research and saw to it that its results were published. Brandeis, by his own admission, was a neophyte in Jewish affairs and eager to increase his knowledge of Judaism. With exquisite grace, he welcomed Friedlaender's recommendations of modern Jewish authors[4] and sometimes enlisted the professor's services as his ghost writer. For example, along with Leo Motzkin and Eliyahu Lewin-Epstein, Friedlaender prepared an historical survey of the Jewish world situation for Brandeis to deliver at the 1916 convention of the FAZ.

If Friedlaender derived satisfaction from his educational work and pleasure from Brandeis's uncommon ability to recruit new souls for Zion, he nonetheless was visibly uncomfortable with the new focus of American Zionism. In 1916 he complained that his usefulness to the Provisional Committee had become "exceedingly limited" because of his lack of competence in financial and organizational matters.[5]

A crucial event that marked the coming of age of American Zionism brought Friedlaender into conflict with the leaders of the movement. This was the debate over the formation of an American Jewish Congress. At the end of the fateful summer of 1914, Brandeis entered into negotiations with the American Jewish Committee over the creation of a council of Jewish organizations. For nearly two years, a bitter dispute raged between the Brandeis group, which advocated the formation of a Congress, and the non-Zionist leaders of the AJC, notably Schiff, Adler, and Marshall, who favored a conference of existing major organizations. Many contemporaries and most recent historians have understood the Congress dispute as a means employed by the East European followers of Brandeis to challenge the German-Jewish establishment, in other words, a power struggle. At the time, each leader legitimized his position with high-sounding terms. The Brandeis

[4]E.g., Brandeis thanked IF for sending him a copy of his *JRP* with these words, "It's just what I need for my own education." November 8, 1918, *FP*.

[5]IF to Wise, October 5, 1916, *FP*.

group was fighting for "democracy"; Schiff would prevent the surge of anti-Semitism which, he was certain, would result from the formation of a Jewish Congress.

Because of his membership in both the Provisional Council and the American Jewish Committee (the latter by virtue of his position on the Kehillah Executive Committee), Friedlaender was drawn into the conflict. He opposed Schiff's extremism, but did not support the Congress idea when it was first proposed. In his opinion, no issue was worth the price of schism within American Jewry. Moreover, his activities for the Seminary and the Kehillah had brought him into frequent contact with the German Jewish magnates. Unlike Louis Lipsky, for example, he realized that the sorely pressed American Jewish community could not function without their financial resources, and that their years of leadership experience were equally indispensable.

Along with Magnes and Friedenwald, who also belonged to both organizations, Friedlaender championed the position of the committee. In March 1915 he submitted this statement to the Anglo-American press: "I am emphatically of the opinion that the American Jewish Committee is the proper and only agency to call such a conference, and, if necessary, in a more amplified representation, to deal with the problems confronting us."[6]

Two months later, in the wake of the Provisional Council's official support of the opposite position, he offered his major contribution to the Congress debate, a long letter addressed to Brandeis and subsequently published.[7] It was written with two purposes in mind. First, in a determined effort to reconcile the two groups, Friedlaender bathed in light an issue that had heretofore generated only heat. Ignoring the slogans of Brandeis, Lipsky, Adler, and Schiff, he searched for the underlying causes of the conflict. He found them in the social, economic, psychological, religious, and ideological chasm separating the German Jews from the East Europeans.

Better than most of his contemporaries, he realized that the position of each group was largely determined by its reaction to Emancipation. German Jews, eager to prove themselves worthy of

---

[6] *Jewish Weekly* (New York), March 12, 1915.

[7] The unpublished letter, dated June 20, 1915, is found in *FP*. In an abridged version, the essay was published under the title "The Present Crisis in American Jewry" in the December 1915 issue of *MJ*, pp. 265-276. It was reprinted in *PP*, pp. 207-228.

their new liberty and ever-increasing prosperity, denied their Jewish nationality. They discarded the old hopes for restoration in Palestine and defined Judaism as a confession of faith alone. The Russian newcomers, on the other hand, were disappointed with the failure of Emancipation in Eastern Europe and with their relatively slow economic progress in America. They also feared the assimilatory tendencies of the native Jews. Therefore they adopted the opposite position. Disregarding religion, many of them defined themselves as members of the Jewish nation; denying the diaspora, they found the solution to the Jewish question in Palestine alone.

To settle these apparently irreconcilable differences, Friedlaender suggested that the two groups unite around a synthesis of the principles which governed their lives. If American Jewry would accept his new formula, "Diaspora plus Palestine, Religion plus Nationalism," it would then avoid "the permanent schism" which threatened its continued viability.[8]

Friedlaender then turned to his second objective, to persuade the Zionists to withdraw from the fray. Even-handedly, he argued that both organizations had committed serious blunders. If the AJC's high-handed stance had alienated the mass of American Jewry, the Zionists should never have entered the discussions at all. He acknowledged the rights of individual Zionists to express their support for the Congress or any other cause, but argued that the PC and the FAZ, as constituents of an international movement, had no right to do so. A major objective of Zionism was to unite all Jews around a common principle. For a Zionist organization to support a local program was to defeat its very purpose. Alienation of the "classes" might bring ephemeral support by the "masses," but only the former group could provide the funding necessary for the upbuilding of Palestine.

With every reason to be proud of this penetrating and provocative essay, Friedlaender was sadly disappointed when its publication produced polite applause but no real change in the position of either party to the dispute.[9] Each side was bent on victory; few people were ready to listen to a dispassionate analysis or accept any kind of compromise. Nevertheless, he continued to reiterate his

[8]This sentiment appears in the unpublished part of the letter.

[9]See letter of Joseph Jacobs to IF, January 17, 1916, *FP*. Friedlaender's disappointment was also conveyed in his first letter of resignation from the Provisional Council addressed to Brandeis, March 2, 1916, *FP*.

position at meetings of both the PC and the AJC long after the resignation of his confederate, Judah Magnes, from both organizations. He only submitted his resignation from the two organizations on July 3, 1916,[10] when the debate was nearly over, following in the footsteps of the young Felix Frankfurter and his friend Harry Friedenwald. This gesture merely brought him additional trouble. The AJC refused to accept his resignation, insisting that he remain on the committee as long as he was a member of the Kehillah Executive.[11] And the failure of the PC to draft a resolution asking him to reconsider, although probably not intentional, further corroded his relationship with that organization.

When the AJC finally agreed to a Congress, Friedlaender dropped his objections. In 1917 he was elected to attend the postwar congress as the delegate of the United Synagogue.

One founder of the AJC, Cyrus Adler, never acquiesced to the Congress idea; he also remained a non-Zionist. As the leader of the Conservative movement after 1916, it was he who frequently challenged Friedlaender on Zionist issues.[12] To defend Brandeis against Adler's insistence that a Zionist leader should be a practicing Jew, Friedlaender had previously offered the following analysis:

> Suppose that Mr. Brandeis has displayed only a fraction of the zeal and generosity which he devotes to Zionism towards other better favored Jewish causes. Do you for a moment think that his failings in dogmatic or ceremonial Judaism would stand in the way of his being welcomed as a worker, nay, hailed as a leader in Jewish life, not excluding religious movements? Why should a test be applied to Zionism which is considered superfluous in other Jewish causes? Either we must insist that *all* our leaders be "trained," to use your own expression, in the doctrines and practices of Judaism, or we must be charitable and show our indulgence to both types of Jews. Double measure and double weight are not in accord with the spirit of our Torah.[13]

At the United Synagogue convention of July 1-2, 1917, Friedlaender used a similar argument against Adler's objection to a

[10]IF to Wise, July 3, 1916; IF to Marshall, July 3, 1916, *FP*.
[11]Marshall to IF, July 9, 1916, *FP*.
[12]IF to Adler, June 7, 1915, *FP*.
[13]Parzen reprinted the debate at the United Synagogue Convention of 1917 in his "Conservative Judaism and Zionism" *(Herzl Yearbook)*, pp. 315-321.

resolution supporting the Basle Program on the grounds that
resolutions such as this one were not called for in the constitution of
the United Synagogue. Friedlaender was quick to point out that
Adler had offered no such objection to another resolution just
passed, though this issue was also not mentioned in the constitution. It dealt with the deplorable condition of the Jews of Russia. In
each case, he effectively laid bare the true motive behind Adler's
position, the objection to people and programs supporting Zionism.

The final act of Friedlaender's life, his participation in the ill-
starred expedition to the Ukraine, may also be characterized as
Zionistic. For it pursued the purpose of helping Jews to endure
their dreary lot and to preside over their own fate.

Withal, Friedlaender is less frequently remembered for his participation in Zionist activities than for his transmission of Zionist
ideas. Three generations of Conservative rabbis have acknowledged his influence on their Zionist perspective. Along with
Schechter and Mordecai Kaplan,[14] two other disciples of Ahad Ha-
am, Friedlaender set the agenda for a movement that has always
identified with cultural and spiritual Zionism.

To designate Friedlaender a cultural Zionist is not to maintain
that he rejected political Zionism. If he was intellectually drawn to
Ahad Ha-am's theories, he manifested an emotional attachment to
the person and symbol of Theodor Herzl, whose meteoric rise and
fall occurred during his young manhood. An anecdote told Haim
Toren by Lilian Friedlaender toward the end of her life offers
striking evidence of this fact.[15] By a strange coincidence, she met
her husband on the very day of Herzl's death, July 3, 1904. On that
summer afternoon, the very proper Bentwich family sat down to
tea, having despaired of the arrival of their expected guest, a certain
Professor Friedlaender of New York. When the doorbell rang,
Lilian answered it, to discover a disheveled young man who
appeared to be totally disoriented. Approaching her father, the
stranger blurted out, "Herzl is dead; a telegram has just arrived
from Vienna!" Forty-eight years later "Lili" insisted that this was

---

[14]See Mordecai Kaplan's article "Anti-Maimunism in Modern Dress: A Reply to Baruch
Kurzweil's Attack on Ahad Ha-am," in *Judaism* 4 (Fall 1955): 303-312. In a rare public
reference to Friedlaender, Kaplan used Friedlaender's espousal of Ahad Ha-am's philosophy
to prove his case.
[15]See Ḥaim Toren, *Tagim* (Jerusalem, 1972), pp. 160-162.

the moment when she decided that this emotional "gentleman" would become her life's partner. And, indeed, their marriage took place just fourteen months after this memorable first encounter.

This anecdote reveals the depths of feeling which Herzl inspired in the young Zionists of his day. After settling in the United States, Friedlaender transmitted these sentiments to his new friends in American Zionism. On one occasion, he used the person of Herzl as a potent symbol around which to rally the many factions within Judaism.

> Let the memory of our beloved leader, whose spotless figure, freed from the dress of mortality, looks down at us in lofty splendor, be stored up forever in the heart of our nation. Let it become the focus where the stray rays of our hope are gathered. Let it constantly remind us that, despite all dispersion and division, we still are one united people, and that we can be much more so, when our united people will have a united country. Thus the customary lamentation after the departure of the chief of a nation has assumed for us quite a different meaning: Le roi est mort: the King is dead; long live the King—after his death.[16]

Equally symbolic was the name the Friedlaenders bestowed upon their firstborn son. Robert Herzl, always designated by his middle name, was born on December 25, 1906.

All of this, however, did not indicate unquestioning espousal of the Herzlian position. Several of his early addresses and essays, intended to introduce an American audience to Ahad Ha-am and Dubnow, obliquely indicated Friedlaender's opposition to purely political Zionism. Implicit in each was the question: What is the best response to the problems generated by Emancipation? In a lecture delivered in New York in 1905, "Dubnow's Theory of Nationalism,"[17] Friedlaender clarified his position on this issue. First he set up straw men, the formulations of Dubnow's opponents: the "mission" theory of the Reformers, Jewish messianism both in its traditional form and in its recent transmutation into Zionism, even the proposals of the assimilationists. Then, in a single blow, he toppled them all by indicating their lack of appeal to ordinary East European Jews. From a practical point of view, he

---

[16]"Theodor Herzl," *New York Zionist Annual*, December 16, 1906, pp. 41-42.
[17]*PP*, pp. 247-274.

insisted, Dubnow's theory of autonomism, which allowed the Jews to remain subjects of the empires in which they resided while they developed their national culture in small, locally autonomous enclaves, was better suited.to their situation.

Although Friedlaender never personally subscribed to Dubnow's anti-Zionism, he used this essay to polemicize against what he considered to be two far more dangerous enemies to Jewish survival. The first were the "classical" Reform thinkers. Even as he acknowledged the logic of some of their theories, he despised their attempts to parrot Christianity by turning Judaism into a bloodless "church." Second were the Jewish territorialists, who were willing to relinquish, at least temporarily, the goal of Eretz Yisrael in return for a refuge for the persecuted Jews of Russia and Rumania. It is noteworthy that Friedlaender used this opportunity to lash out at the men who only two years before had gained control of the Zionist movement. For Dubnow was also a "territorialist," in the sense that he accepted a European rather than a Palestinian solution to the Jewish question. Yet Friedlaender, the Zionist, preferred the philosophy of the non-Zionist historian to the proposals of the Zionist leaders. Why? Because he thought that Herzl and Nordau, at this point, were willing to compromise away that *sine qua non* of Zionism, "the recognition of Jewish Nationalism."[18]

Forcefully, Friedlaender advanced this argument in several guises during the short-lived ascendancy of territorialism in the early years of this century. On one occasion, he admitted that Herzl, and Pinsker before him, had begun as territorialists, in the sense that "their aim was not the Holy Land, but a Jewish land."[19] At this point, according to Friedlaender's definition, they were not yet full-fledged Zionists, only what he liked to call "philo-Zionists, friends of the Zionists."[20] However, when these two assimilated Jews came into contact with ordinary Jewish people, they then absorbed the genuine Jewish national spirit. Only then did they become full-fledged Zionists. An irony of the current situation, according to Friedlaender, was that some Jews had reversed the process. "Today some Zionists have changed into Territorialists."[21]

[18]Ibid., p. 272.
[19]See "Zionism and Territorialism," an address which Friedlaender delivered before the "Great Beacon," the Order of Ancient Maccabaeans, in London on September 3, 1905. *Agranat MSS.*
[20]Ibid.
[21]Ibid.

What then was Friedlaender's definition of the true Zionist? To answer this question, we must consult two essays written to explain the ideas of Ahad Ha-am.[22] At that time many Zionists viewed Ahad Ha-am as early Protestant Reformers had regarded Erasmus, a "John the Baptist," who cultivated the ideal in its formative stages, yet a "Judas" who betrayed it after its realization as a practical movement. Friedlaender's articles were written to vindicate Ahad Ha-am's criticism of the fledgling *yishuv*. He explained the Odessan's position by his espousal of the principle of evolution.

> The Jewish colonies in Palestine sprang into existence, accompanied by the ardent wishes of the Jewish people which saw in them the beginning of the realization of its age-long dream. Unfortunately, the facts soon proved stronger than the dreams. The foundations upon which the colonies were built were too weak to bear the structure of a degenerated national life. The broad masses of Jewry who had languished in servitude for so many years were far from prepared to carry the national aspirations into life. The colonies failed to prosper because neither the conditions in the Holy Land nor the mental attitude of their founders were favorable to an undertaking which required numerous sacrifices and a vast amount of patient labor. . . . Proceeding from the fundamental premise that all endeavors to transform the Jewish yearning for a home into reality were premature and therefore doomed to failure, he pleads for temporary discontinuation of the colonization work in Palestine, and for the concentration of all the national forces upon the wearisome, and yet far more important preparatory work in the inner life of the people.[23]

For Friedlaender, as for Ahad Ha-am, *teḥiyat ha-levvavot* (the awakening of national consciousness) was at once fuel for the Zionist engine and the destination of the Zionist train. Remarkably, it was for this reason that he cherished the figure of Theodor Herzl, to whom he devoted a section of his public lecture on Ahad Ha-am. Here he pointed out that the dramatic events of Herzl's last years had succeeded in raising the level of Jewish consciousness of the East European masses. Ahad Ha-am's appeal, on the other

---

[22]The first was the Preface to his German translation of Ahad Ha-am's essays, *Achad Ha-am, Am Scheidewege, Ausgewählte Essays* (Berlin, 1904 and 1913). The other, printed in *PP*, pp. 275-298, was originally delivered as a Seminary address.

[23]This is taken from a translation of Friedlaender's Preface, entitled "Ahad Ha-am as an Evolutionist," *FP*, Box 16.

hand, was limited to an elite group of Jewish intellectuals. He concluded: "Were I to name the two men who have had the largest share in shaping the destinies of the modern national movement, I would first mention its father—Herzl, and right afterwards its mentor—Ahad Ha-am."[24]

It is clear, then, that Friedlaender was no blind follower of Ahad Ha-am. Unlike his Zionist mentor and his friend Judah Magnes, Friedlaender never opposed political Zionism. Indeed, after the Balfour Declaration was issued in 1917, he wrote in glowing terms of the "Third Jewish Commonwealth."[25] Nevertheless, he did not regard Zionist politics as the instrument of the physical salvation of the Jews. To Friedlaender it was obvious that America solved the "material" needs of Judaism. Immigration to the United States offered a more effective solution to "the problem of the Jews" than infiltration into Turkish-controlled, bleak and barren Palestine. Because of its vast resources, developing economy, and benign government, this country could quickly accommodate the hundreds of thousands of Jews requiring immediate resettlement. Zionism, therefore, was intended to supply the "moral" rather than the material requirements of contemporary Judaism. "From a philosophical point of view," he suggested, "Ahad Ha-Amism is far superior to Herzlianism."[26] By this he meant that of the two aspects of the Jewish question, it was "the problem of Judaism" which presented the more formidable challenge. To it his life's work was addressed.

In order to create what Hans Kohn has termed "a living and active corporate will,"[27] Friedlaender assumed the role of Zionist educator and propagandist. His lecture "Uptown and Downtown Zionism" (1906) discovered latent Zionism in the heart of every immigrant: "This feeling consists in being aware of the connection with the Jewish people throughout the world, in the love not only of the Jews but also of their spiritual possessions, in the love of the Jewish past and in the hope for a Jewish future, in the love of our holy land and our holy city."

To reinforce subjective Zionist feelings it was imperative to furnish a Jewish education for children and youth and to evoke

[24]*PP*, p. 298.
[25]Ibid., p. 336.
[26]Ibid., p. 297.
[27]Hans Kohn, *Nationalism: Its Meaning and History* (New York, 1971), p. 10.

from their parents "Jewish reminiscences." Once the national consciousness of the Russian Jews was aroused, support of the Zionist movement would follow.

A more difficult task was to bring the uptown Jews to Zionism. Friedlaender insisted that the case for Zion rebuilt was intrinsically so strong that logical argumentation alone would convince them to support Jewish institutions in the Holy Land. Long troubled by the fact that health care often received the support denied worthier causes, he turned the hospital into a metaphor. "He [the uptown Jew] contributes hundreds of dollars towards Jewish hospitals where Jewish patients should be treated. Why not contribute a few single dollars towards the large Jewish hospital where the whole Jewish nation could possibly be cured?"

Arthur Goren correctly points out that Friedlaender and all the cultural Zionists of his day understood education, rather than politics, as the decisive Zionist act.[28] Friedlaender's efforts to teach the Zionist ideology followed the pattern set by the 1905 lecture. In the hearts of immigrant Jews and their adolescent and college-aged children, he attempted to instill an awakened Jewish consciousness. Before groups of assimilated Jews and, later in his career, general audiences as well, he defended the Zionist cause in a systematic fashion.

The Zionist argumentation assumed many forms: personal correspondence and letters written for publication, newspaper and magazine articles, book reviews, reports to organizations, and verbal polemics, both public and private. Unlike his reflections on the relative merits of different historical centers of Judaism, Friedlaender's Zionist philosophy did not undergo significant change during his years in America. To champion cultural Zionism he inveighed against the anti-Zionism of the Reformers and disclosed the exaggerations of the political Zionists.

His principal opponents were the anti-Zionist rabbis and scholars, Kaufmann Kohler, Julian Morgenstern, and David Philipson, and the non-Zionist community leaders, notably Jacob Schiff. At issue was the relationship between religion and politics, Zionism and Americanism. Like his colleague Morgenstern, Kohler insisted that Jews did not possess and never had possessed a capacity for self-government. Political aspiration was, at any rate,

[28]Goren, *New York Jews*, p. 95.

morally inferior to Israel's true calling, that of a religious mission-
ary to the world. In order for Jews to spread the universal
prophetic values of justice and morality, it was necessary for them
to be scattered over the world, not concentrated in Zion. "He [the
Jew] is the salt of the earth, the leaven of the human race, eager to
spread and expand. He has little power of cohesiveness. A Jewish
colony built upon the plan of self-government is bound to end in
failure."[29]

For Friedlaender the absence of Jewish unity was not an
indelible feature of the race, but rather a temporary condition to be
overcome. Jews, he insisted, must remain a separate group or
perish. In an obvious reference to Kohler's simile, he frequently
observed that when salt is dissolved in water, it loses much of its
saltness.[30] On another occasion he employed a different metaphor
to transmit the same meaning: "You might as well talk of being
broadminded when you take a river and pour it deeply into the
ocean."[31] In Friedlaender's view, the perspective of Kohler and his
followers resulted from a misunderstanding of the nature of Judaism and the character of its sacred literature.

The most persistent bone of contention was the question: Are the
Jews a race or a religion? German Jews wholeheartedly embraced
the latter opinion. Against them, Friedlaender asserted that merely
to ask the question was to adopt a Christian perspective. He
produced extensive data from psychology, Jewish law, and religious tradition and concluded that Judaism contains the two elements in indissoluble mixture.[32] From this it followed that a Jew
who prayed for the restoration of Zion or worked for the realization
of this ideal was only acting in faithfulness to his tradition. For
many Reform Jews, however, these were unpatriotic activities.
Because of their upbringing in absolutist Central Europe, many
German Jews feared that Zionism would raise the question of dual
loyalty. Most vocal on this subject was the financier Jacob Schiff.
In the early years of his sojourn in America, Friedlaender took
upon himself the task of answering Schiff's public statements in

---

[29]Kaufmann Kohler, "Self Government Is Bound to End in Failure," *Jewish Comment*,
December 23, 1904.
[30]See *PP (1919)*, pp. 32 and 447. In footnote on p. 32, he noted the New Testament origin
of this idea.
[31]*SE* V, 1.
[32]See "Race and Religion," *PP (1919)*, pp. 431-433 and *Aspects* I and IV, passim.

private letters and circulars to the FAZ.[33] In one long letter he explained the Dubnowian distinction between membership in a nationality and loyalty to the state.

> When Jewish Nationalists speak of the Jews as a Nation, this does not at all imply that they have, or should have, a political government. The word is merely used in the meaning, which it has all over Europe, i.e., in that of a community bound together, not only by the ties of religion, but also by the bonds of common birth (from the Latin *natio*), in the same way as they speak in Europe of a Polish nation.[34]

The tone of his responses to Schiff was fatherly (despite the discrepancy in age) and didactic, indicating respect for the "Jewish heart" of the philanthropist, which was, in his opinion, "staunch,"[35] albeit misguided. However, there was one theme played by all the Reform opponents to Zionism which especially excited Friedlaender's anger. This was the assertion that Zionism was unbiblical in origin and unspiritual by nature.

The spirituality of Zionism was a major thesis of his rebuttal of an article by the American journalist Herbert Adams Gibbons entitled "Zionism and the World Peace," published in the prestigious *Century Magazine*. Following the arguments of the Reform anti-Zionists, yet embellishing them with a Christian design, Gibbons had asked: "Why, then, does Zionism emphasize now the temporal aspect? Why Palestine? Why a distinct nationhood for the Jew? . . . How often has peace been disturbed because men failed to comprehend the universal Zion for all creeds in the words of a Palestinian Jew, who said, 'My kingdom is not of this world.' "[36]

Friedlaender's "Rejoinder," printed later in the same periodical, cited the prophetic tradition to legitimize Jewish nationalism. "The Jewish prophets . . . were both universalists and nationalists, believing in the realization of the universal ideal through the channel of national existence."[37]

---

[33]See IF's letters to Friedenwald, February 19, 1909 and October 1, 1909, *Friedenwald MSS.*

[34]IF to Schiff, April 10, 1911, *FP*.

[35]IF to Friedenwald, February 19, 1909, *Friedenwald MSS.*

[36]*Century Magazine*, January 1919, p. 378.

[37]Ibid., April 1919, p. 804. Friedlaender's article was entitled: "Zionism and the World Peace. A Rejoinder to Herbert Adams Gibbons' Article in the *Century Magazine* of January, 1919."

To reply to the insinuations of both Jewish and Christian anti-Zionists, who maintained that a Jewish state would be inclined to self-glorification, even chauvinism, Friedlaender argued that Zionism, by definition, was never an end in itself. It was rather a means to promote four qualities which were considered desirable in his day. The first was self-reliance. From the inception of the movement for Jewish self-defense, which arose after the 1903 pogroms, Friedlaender praised the Russian Jews who were willing to defend themselves. In 1905 he discovered a connection between this movement and Zionism. "From this conviction which realizes the necessity of self-help for the Jews there is only a short distance— the distance between premises and conclusion—to the idea of Zionism, which demands a legally assured home for the Jews in Palestine."[38] Subsequently, as a founder of Young Judea, Friedlaender cited self-reliance as one of the benefits to be gained from participation in this Zionist youth movement.[39]

For Zionism Friedlaender claimed a second benefit, a means of uniting the generations. Part of the Reformers' rationale for introducing radical change into the philosophy and practice of Judaism was the desire to appeal to the young. Taking this into account, Friedlaender's defense of Zionism implied that this ideology inspired deep emotion in young people, while the blandness of Reform Judaism merely bored them, isolating them from their parents and their heritage.

Ahead of his time, he found in Zionism a third quality, the potential to heal the most disturbing consequence of Emancipation, fragmentation. In a thoughtful article Friedlaender pointed out that it was impossible to reconcile Orthodox and Reform Jews in matters of creed and deed. Therefore the sturdiest bridge between the two groups was

> Jewish Nationalism, which, apart from belief and practice, recognizes the legitimacy of the national element in Judaism, has evolved, or is able to evolve, a whole set of sentiments and interests which both sections, while strongly asserting their individual characteristics, can fully and conscientiously share. Such contact will not effect a reconciliation in the sense of a fusion, but it will lead to something which is far more valuable, to mutual respect and understanding.[40]

[38]Friedlaender, "Jewish Self-Defense," *Maccabean*, December 1905, p. 301.
[39]Friedlaender, "Work of Young Judea," *Young Judea* 1, no. 45 (1909).
[40]IF, "Jewish Nationalism the Bridge," *Jewish Daily News*, Silver Jubilee Number, 1910.

It is reasonable to assume that behind his tireless efforts to win non-Zionists for the cause lay this conviction.

Friedlaender's final argument on the benefits of Zionism was a product of the public debate over the nature of the Jewish commonwealth which the Balfour Declaration of November 1917 seemed to promise. During the Wilson era, the Reform anti-Zionists and their Christian confederates maintained the position that Zionism was undemocratic. Gibbons contended that this movement advanced the rights of a small Jewish minority over those of the large Arab majority. In response, Friedlaender insisted that the very opposite was the case. The Jews were only claiming for themselves the Wilsonian prerogative of self-determination. As for their relationship with the Arabs:

> The Jews, who are of the same race as the Arabs—a kinship cemented by the profound and beneficent influence which their cultures exercised upon one another for many centuries—have genuine sympathy with their aspirations, and look forward to the reestablishment of ancient Arabic glory; but they see no reasons why on the vast expanse of a new Arabic world which is now being set up by the great powers they have no right to claim a little corner in which, in harmony with their fellow-inhabitants, they may rejuvenate the ancient glory of Zion.[41]

Even as he carried on the polemic against the Reform anti-Zionists and their sympathizers, Friedlaender expressed his differences with the political Zionists. On one issue the two groups concurred. American followers of Herzl as diverse as Gottheil and Wise, de Haas and Brandeis, Richards and Lipsky all understood Zionism in terms of aid to suffering Israel. Because it suited their purpose, anti-Zionists such as Rabbi David Philipson and Henry Gibbons sometimes also adopted this position. In April 1917, after the Kerensky government emancipated the Jews of Russia, Philipson issued a public statement which maintained that the Revolution had done away with the need for Zionism.[42] Since Zionism was a solution to the problem of persecution, the rabbi reasoned, now that Russian Jews were no longer oppressed, they did not need Zion as a place of refuge. Friedlaender immediately challenged this

---

[41]"Rejoinder," pp. 808-809.
[42]*New York Times*, April 5, 1917, p. 13.

formulation. On the day after the publication of Philipson's statement in the *New York Times*, Friedlaender's vigorous rebuttal appeared in the same newspaper. Zionism, he insisted, had nothing to do with persecution. Its origin lay rather in the age-long hopes and aspirations of the Jewish people for the return to the Holy Land.[43]

When Gibbons repeated the argument two years later, Friedlaender responded in the same fashion, incidentally informing his audience of the origin of the argument. "Mr. Gibbons is entirely wrong when, possibly misguided by the information of his de-Judaized friends, he repeats the platitude that Anti-Semitism is the source of Zionism."[44]

That Friedlaender's Zionism was linked to his scholarly pursuit of messianism is indicated by the following colorful metaphor. "Modern Zionism," he wrote in 1905, was "a continuation of the Messianic doctrine without its theological eggshells."[45] The very word "messianic" was a two-edged sword. One side of the blade cut into the future, overturning the standards of the past, establishing new ones. In Arthur Hertzberg's analysis, Herzlian Zionism was "messianic" in the sense that it posited a revolutionary total cure to the disease of Jewish landlessness.[46] Friedlaender was one of the first Zionists to articulate this idea. In his critique of the territorialists, he pointed out that "Zionism has always claimed to be the radical, the final solution to the Jewish problem." Territorialism was doomed because it was only a partial response to the "temporary considerations of the moment."[47] To demonstrate that these self-styled Herzlians advanced an anti-Herzlian notion was his way of impugning the hated International Territorialist Organization.

Far more frequently, however, Friedlaender adopted what Hertzberg has called a "defensive" typology of Zionism.[48] He was less concerned with grandiose schemes to normalize the position of the Jew in the world than with the resolution of conflicts raging within the soul of the individual Jew. To accomplish this, he wielded the second edge of the messianic sword with great finesse, driving it deeply into the Judaism of the past. The word "Zionism,"

[43]*New York Times*, April 6, 1917, p. 9.
[44]"Rejoinder," p 804.
[45]*PP*, p. 250.
[46]Arthur Hertzberg, Introduction to *The Zionist Idea: A Historical Analysis and Reader* (New York, 1973), p. 72.
[47]"Zionism and Territorialism."
[48]Hertzberg, *The Zionist Idea*, p. 29.

he maintained, was only a neologism used to describe a movement which was deeply rooted in the biblical, rabbinic, mystical, and philosophical traditions of Judaism. In his romantic vision of Zion restored, Jews would once more live in harmony with the prophetic values of freedom, justice, and righteousness. Liberated from "the influences of the Golus, which still fetter its spirit,"[49] the new Zion would also produce a genuine national culture. For Friedlaender the most noteworthy accomplishments of the current *yishuv* were cultural. He wrote in glowing terms of Boris Schatz, the man who "laid at least the foundation for a Jewish art."[50] Most significant in his eyes was the unprecedented rebirth and rapid development of Hebrew as a living language.[51]

According to Friedlaender's vision, the new Palestine would not only promote ethical and cultural values; it would also restore Jewish spirituality. In his effort to defuse the most dangerous weapon in the anti-Zionist arsenal, Friedlaender introduced the delicate issue of religion. It was obvious that many Zionists had discarded much more than "theological eggshells"; their secular reinterpretation of Jewish messianism had disturbed the inner core, the religious "yolk" at the center of Judaism. This provided an opportunity for non-Zionists such as Adler and Schiff as well as the Reform anti-Zionists and their Christian confederates to brand the movement as anti-religious, a blasphemy against the God of Israel.

Out of heartfelt conviction as well as polemical necessity, Friedlaender developed a philosophy of religious Zionism based upon a reinterpretation of Ahad Ha-am's cultural Zionism. Like the cultural Zionists and unlike the Reform theoreticians under the influence of German idealism, he argued empirically that it is life which produces culture. A letter to Jacob Schiff (which evoked uncharacteristic anger from its recipient),[52] suggested that "a normal Jewish life in Palestine will revive the religious spirit of Palestine."[53]

By using the word "religious," Friedlaender demonstrated his deviation from conventional Ahad Ha-amism. For the founder of cultural Zionism, normalization of Jewish life would bring forth a

[49]*PP*, p. 322.
[50]Ibid.
[51]Ibid., pp. 95-111, 199, 321-322; also treated in the essay "Hebrew as a 'Mother-Tongue' and as a 'Father-Tongue,' " pp. 317-318.
[52]Schiff to IF, June 7, 1918, *FP*.
[53]IF to Schiff, June 6, 1918, *FP*.

new culture that would be modern and secular, while at the same time exhibiting the lofty moral principles first enunciated by the prophets of Israel. Yet, according to Friedlaender, if Jewish life were to be completely "normal," then Jews could no more exist in the rarefied atmosphere of prophetic principle in Zion than they could anywhere else on earth. As in mishnaic times, the "gold bars" would be minted into the small coins of a distinctive historical culture. Since the "gold" was religious in the broad sense of the word rather than narrowly moral or ethical, then normalization of Jewish life would, perforce, result in a culture that would be religious rather than secular.

To respond to non-Jewish as well as Jewish critics of Zionism, Friedlaender advanced his religious interpretation of Zionism in the general press. In the *Century* article, he acknowledged and defended the secular dimension of Zionism, the right of Jews to control their own fate. However, he also maintained that secularism had gone too far. In the modern world, he insisted, the means had to be human, but the end-goal must remain divine. It was on this basis that he offered a rare public criticism of Ahad Ha-am as well as all nonreligious Zionists: "Yet, though refusing to acknowledge the metaphysical basis of the prophetic ideal, they passionately cling to the ideal itself."[54]

In actuality, he protested, Jewish longing for the restoration of the ancient homeland had a religious basis.

> Three times a day the Jew has prayed for the reestablishment of Zion. In joy and sorrow he has remembered its past glory and dreamed of its future splendor. At midnight he sat down on the ground, putting ashes on his forehead to weep for the destruction of Jerusalem and to pray for its rebuilding. And when he went to his eternal rest, his eyes were covered with the dust that was brought from the holy ground.[55]

These words, though undoubtedly heartfelt, were nonetheless the product of an astute observation. If the Jews were moved by references to their common cultural heritage, the way to a Christian's heart was through his Bible.

Two years before, Friedlaender had presented his vision of a restored religious community on the soil of Israel to the secular press.

[54]"Rejoinder," p. 304.
[55]Ibid., p. 305.

Assembled on its hallowed soil, where every footstep re-echoes the religious message of its ancient leaders, neither shut out from the rest of the world by the cramping walls of the Ghetto, nor yet crushed or crippled by the tremendous impact on non-Jewish influences, Israel may work out its own destiny and may become again a potent factor in the religious life of humanity.[56]

From all of these statements, it is clear that Friedlaender fostered a Zionism that was elitist, visionary, and spiritual rather than practical and political. Few of the issues which troubled him were of concern to the political Zionists. Nevertheless, there was mutual respect between the two. The Zionist Organization reissued several of Friedlaender's articles in pamphlet form.[57] For his part, Friedlaender offered his whole-hearted support to the FAZ and the ZOA. Despite his perception of Zionism as both a product of the religious tradition and a means to achieve religious revival, he rejected Mizrachi. In his opinion, the very existence of a "religious" Zionist organization implied that the Zionist mainstream was irreligious.[58] It also jeopardized the unity that the movement was intended to preserve.

One policy of American Zionism, however, incited Friedlaender's vocal opposition. During the waning days of his chairmanship of the Zionist Federation, he denounced the organization's tendency to "negate the diaspora."[59] This idea, he insisted, was not only impractical; it even discouraged young American Jews from joining the organization. Shortly before his death, he again gave vent to this sentiment.

But while believing in Zionism as the ultimate consummation of Israel's hope, and his only safeguard against absorption in the whirlpool of humanity, the writer does not belong to those who champion "the denial of the *Golus*," and are willing to neglect or to sacrifice the bulk of the Jewish people outside of Palestine for the sake of a small minority who are to form the Jewish nucleus in Palestine. Basing his deductions upon acknowledged historical facts, he is convinced that, given the unifying and inspiring influence of a Jewish center in our ancient

[56]The original article, entitled "Zionism as a Stimulus to Jewish Faith," appeared in the *Evening Post* on December 12, 1917, p. 12. See *PP (1919)*, pp. 445-450.

[57]"Zionism and the World Peace," "The Political Ideal of the Prophets," and "Zionism and Religious Judaism."

[58]See "Why I Don't Belong to Mizrachi," in *Dos Yiddishe Folk*, April 4, 1919, p. 4.

[59]Letter to the editor of the FAZ's Yiddish organ, *Dos Yiddishe Folk*, May 26, 1911; reprinted in Friesel, *The Zionist Movement*, as Appendix IV, pp. 206-209.

homeland, Jewish life in the Diaspora may be so shaped as to harmonize both with the age-long traditions of our people and with the life of the nations in whose midst we dwell.[60]

These two long sentences remain Friedlaender's definitive statement of the role of Zion in diaspora life. Having established the viability of the American diaspora, what future role did Friedlaender envision for it vis-à-vis the restored Zion? In the classical formulation of cultural Zionism, a small Palestinian elite would produce a vibrant, authentically Jewish culture; this culture would, in turn, reverse the spiritual malaise plaguing the majority of Jews, who would continue to abide in the diaspora. Yet the latter would be the consumers rather than the producers of Jewish culture.

Was this Friedlaender's prognosis for American Jewry? The evidence indicates a decided ambivalence about the matter. We have noted the dissipation of his early dreams for the rapid formation of an American diaspora along the typology of medieval Spain. Yet even as personal disappointment and advancing years dampened his youthful enthusiasm, he retained his faith in the ultimate potential of American Jewry. In 1915 he represented his optimistic expectations for the portion of Russian Jewry newly settled in the United States with the following striking image:

> We are all acquainted with the wonderful story of the coal, which, as the scientists tell us, is nothing but concentrated sunlight. It is the story of primeval forests, filled with luxurious ferns, which for years out of number had been drinking in the rays of the sun, but, having been buried beneath the ground and excluded from the reviving touch of light and air, were gradually turned into coal—black, rugged, shapeless, yet retaining all its pristine energy which, when released, provides us with light and heat. The story of the Russian Jew is the story of the coal. Under a surface marred by oppression and persecution, he has accumulated immense stores of energy in which we may find an unlimited supply of light and heat for our minds and our hearts. All we need is to discover the process, long known in the case of the coal, of transforming latent strength into living power.[61]

Friedlaender's activities on behalf of such institutions as the Kehillah, the Bureau of Jewish Education, the Menorah move-

[60]*PP*, p. xxii.
[61]*JRP*, pp. 208-209.

ment, and Young Israel were undoubtedly an attempt to generate the potential energy of America's Russian Jewish immigrants. Moreover, on a few occasions, notably in the letter to Brandeis, he referred to the two future centers of world Jewry. However, he frequently went on record with such statements as the following, which placed American Jewry in a secondary, supportive position: "In the Dispersion we can and must aim at the preservation of Judaism, at the adaptation of Judaism, but we scarcely dare hope for a creative Judaism."[62] American Jewry would have to wait for a Simon Rawidowicz to formulate a theory of equal partnership between the Jewish communities of America and Israel.[63]

From Friedlaender's statements it is evident that the notions of his two principal mentors were stamped upon his mind. As a follower of Dubnow, he cherished the contributions of past diaspora communities and respected the vigor and intelligence of his Russian Jewish contemporaries. But he was also the bearer of Ahad Ha-am's more pessimistic notions. Reinforcing them was dismay at the dissension with American Judaism and revulsion against its low educational, religious, and moral standards. We can only conclude that each of Friedlaender's pronouncements reflected the mood of the hour; his basic philosophy held the two notions in tension.

Demonstrating both the complexity of his mind and the vigor of his spirit were his activities on behalf of Arab-Jewish cooperation in the period following the Balfour Declaration. Early Zionist visionaries had portrayed Palestine as a "land without a people awaiting the people without a land." Like Ahad Ha-am and Judah Magnes, Friedlaender was painfully aware that this was simply not the case; Palestine contained a considerable indigenous population that had to be taken into account. In order to impress the ZOA leaders with this fact, he composed a memorandum, entitled "The Arabic Problem."[64] He reminded them of its importance "for the future Jewish commonwealth." "Whatever will be the boundaries of Jewish Palestine, there can be no question that the Hebrew commonwealth will be like a small island in the midst of an Arabic ocean." He urged the Zionist organization to "take a careful survey of these

[62]*PP*, p. 320. According to Bernard G. Richards, Friedlaender wrote a paper supporting this position entitled "We Are in Golus." It is found in the *Richards MSS*.
[63]Simon Rawidowicz, *Babylon and Jerusalem: Towards a Philosophy of Israel's Wholeness* (Hebrew) (London and Waltham, Mass., 1957).
[64]In *FP*, Box 1, n.d.

factors" in order to "prepare a solution for the manifold problems which undoubtedly will beset future Palestine." There then followed a list of four recommendations. Friedlaender designated them "practical needs"; we would call them suggestions for good public relations. Not surprisingly, they were all educational in nature: a Bureau of Information to collect data on all aspects of Arabic life, a periodical devoted to promoting good relations between Arabs and Jews, translation of Arabic classics into Hebrew, and the republication of the works of medieval Jewish writers who wrote in Arabic.

The "Rejoinder" to the Gibbons article, composed during the same period, naively portrayed Semitic "kinsmen" working alongside each other to restore the ancient glory of their respective traditions under the benign guidance of the British Empire.[65] "The Arabic Problem" demonstrated Friedlaender's tougher side. Unlike many "practical" and "political" Zionists, he did not minimize the potential danger of the Arab presence to either the physical well-being or the spiritual advancement of the Jewish people. This awareness was the product of perceptions that were foreign to most of them. As a Semitics scholar, Friedlaender understood the value of Moslem culture and the tenacity of the Arab peoples. As a follower of Ahad Ha-am, he maintained that the restoration of the people to its land must proceed slowly, confronting each obstacle as it arose. As a student of Hebrew prophecy as well, he always insisted that Zionism was but a means through which the Jewish people might achieve greater spirituality as it fulfilled its potential as "a light unto the nations." Behind the suggestions of "The Arabic Problem" lay the perceptions of his earlier essays.

> It is not an end in itself, an agency for political aggrandizement and the injustice and oppression that goes with it, but it is a means to an end, the physical vessel for a spiritual content, the material agency for the consummation of the great ideals of justice and righteousness.[66]

> But while in its form religious Judaism is thus circumscribed within national and territorial limits, its motives and ultimate aspirations are essentially universal.[67]

---

[65]"Rejoinder," pp. 807-808.
[66]Ibid., p. 804.
[67]*PP (1919)*, p. 447.

Once again, the Zionist leaders distributed Friedlaender's memorandum. Once again, they disregarded the substance of the argument, using it as propaganda rather than a program for action. Louis Finkelstein's comment on this aspect of Friedlaender's life merits repetition. "Alas, the vision, so clear to him, seemed absurd to many of his colleagues. . . . Friedlaender, rebuffed by those who could not understand, was broken-hearted, not for himself, but for the future of mankind."[68]

Despite its hyperbole, this statement underlines Friedlaender's anomalous position in American Zionism. Alone among the faculty members of any American rabbinical school, he was prominent in all the major Zionist organizations of early-twentieth-century America. Yet his activities on their behalf yielded him more distress than satisfaction. The major defect of the Federation of American Zionists, its incapacity to recruit a large membership and hence to produce sufficient revenues, led to the cancellation of the Zionist manual, which had occupied almost five years of his (and Henrietta Szold's) time. The creation of the Provisional Zionist Council under the charismatic leadership of Louis Brandeis introduced the needed membership and funding into American Zionism. However, its focus on organizational and financial issues left Friedlaender out in the cold. Moreover, on the two occasions when he desperately required recognition and support, the leaders of the organizations failed to respond, misplacing the letter asking him not to resign from the Provisional Council amidst the turmoil of the Congress dispute, and not backing him wholeheartedly after his dismissal from the Red Cross Commission. Feeling betrayed by his associates of long duration in the Zionist movement, Friedlaender abandoned organizational activity to concentrate upon theoretical issues. Some of his most heuristic reflections on the future of Zionism after the Balfour Declaration were delivered under the auspices of the newly reorganized Zionist Organization of America. Though they brought him honor and respect, Friedlaender was sorely disappointed by the fact that his ideas did not form the basis of any new programs. The Zionist Organization remained "Herzlian" and practical, focusing on rescuing Jews in physical danger and creating a sound economic program under the British mandate. Willing, even eager to publish his Ahad Ha-amist argu-

[68]*PP*, "Introduction," p. xii.

ments, it refused to take them seriously. The leadership of 1919 was no more inclined to heed his admonitions about respecting Arab rights and creating a truly "Jewish" polity than its predecessors of 1911 had been disposed to refrain from "negating the Diaspora."

This is not to say that Friedlaender's Zionist mission to America was a failure. What Friedlaender could not know was that his most important Zionist influence extended to the leaders of the following generation. During the years between 1910 and 1919 they were the young men and women sitting in his classes at the Seminary's Rabbinical School and Teachers Institute and listening to his Menorah lectures on university campuses.

As the stewardship of American Judaism passed from the German Reformers to the traditionalists of East European stock, many of whom were trained at the Seminary, the opposition to Jewish national expression gradually diminished. If the captains of American Zionism during the interwar and World War II periods were— *mirabile dictu!*—Reform rabbis, Stephen Wise and Abba Hillel Silver, their lieutenants were Conservative rabbis and Seminary-trained community leaders. To an incalculable extent, these men were guided by the living words of Mordecai Kaplan and the remembered traditions about Israel Friedlaender. When the Nazi depredations of the 1930s and 1940s rendered a purely "religious" definition of Judaism inappropriate, the opposition to Zionism fell almost unheeded from the ideology of Reform Judaism, like a withered leaf in autumn, and was soon swept into the ash can of history.

Chapter 9

Toward a Philosophy of American Judaism

> The only solution left us is that of adaptation, but an adaptation which shall sacrifice nothing that is essential to Judaism, which shall not impoverish Judaism but enrich it, which, as was the case with Jewish culture in Spain, shall take fully into account what the environment demands of us, and shall preserve and foster our Jewish distinctiveness and originality. Let the cynics in our midst sneer to their heart's content at what they choose to brand as *minhag America*. Jewish learning in this country, like that of our ancestors in Spain, will rise and develop in intimate association with the culture of our neighbors. It will be American in language, in scope, in method, and yet be distinctively Jewish in essence, the proud possession of American Israel and through it in God's own time the cherished property of Universal Israel.
>
> *—Israel Friedlaender*

Of all the personalities with whom Friedlaender came into contact, Simon Dubnow is the man whose life most closely resembled his own. Like the younger man who sought him out, Dubnow was both a creative scholar and a communal activist. Dubnow's theory of autonomism provided a national and secular rationale for sorely-pressed Russian Jews; Friedlaender, his disciple, helped to formulate and implement a national and religious philosophy for their American brothers and cousins. Most chillingly, Friedlaender's cruel and early death in the aftermath of the First World War foreshadowed the equally violent and gratuitous murder of his eighty-one-year-old mentor at the start of the Second.

Both men bore the proud legacy of nineteenth-century Jewish historiography and stood on the shoulders of giants such as Graetz and Steinschneider. Yet as spokesmen for the two major branches of a diaspora Jewry, Friedlaender and Dubnow also reflected the settings in which they operated. They flourished when neoromanticism held European scholarship in thrall and consequently rejected their predecessors' negative evaluation of mysticism and messianism. Less than Dubnow, but more than most analysts of American Jewry, Friedlaender applied psychological and sociological criteria to the study of past and contemporary events. In short, both men broadened the purview of modern Jewish historiography.

How can we evaluate the brief, stormy career of a man who brought to these shores the insights of Dubnow and Ahad Ha-am, Graetz and Frankel, Steinschneider and Noeldeke? At this juncture, it is appropriate to reconsider Morris Adler's assessment of Friedlaender, cited at the beginning of this study. In testing his allegations, two questions must be answered. First, did Friedlaender the thinker, like Maimonides, to whom Adler likens him, achieve a philosophic synthesis of all the partialities of Jewish life and fuse these elements "into a universe and not a multiverse"? And then, did Friedlaender the man achieve the "wholeness," which, in Adler's estimation, was "the central quest of his life"?

In Friedlaender's day, virtually all scholars, and many educated lay people as well, were familiar with Hegel's analysis of the pattern of human history, usually expressed by the formula "thesis, antithesis, and synthesis." Indeed, Friedlaender deliberately structured several of his popular lectures and written essays around this prescription. In each case, he set forth a thesis—which, when challenged by an antithesis, yielded to a greater synthesis. However, close examination of each essay employing this terminology reveals that Friedlaender did not truly support a Hegelian view of history and society. Instead, he utilized the Hegelian nomenclature as a framework around which to organize his own thoughts and convey them to others.

In this country he first employed these terms in his important public lecture on Dubnow (1905). He initiated his discussion with a description of two theories rejected by the Russian historian. The thesis was political Zionism, for which Dubnow considered the Jewish people ill-prepared; the antithesis was assimilation, which would result in the termination of Judaism. Dubnow's synthesis, according to Friedlaender, was his theory of autonomism, which demanded "a separate and independent development of the Jewish nation" within each European country.[1]

In his own popular writings on historical themes, Friedlaender repeatedly employed these terms, modifying the thesis to suit the occasion, while retaining the "antithesis." Throughout history, he maintained, Jews have been subjected to the forces of isolation or nationalism or "nibdalism" on the one hand, and assimilation on the other. How were they resolved? In the heroic era of the Jewish past, it was the prophets of Israel who created the first important synthesis. This was "the political ideal of the prophets," a Jewish nationalism that was at once spiritual ("a kingdom of priests and a holy nation") and universalistic ("the Servant of the Lord for the benefit of mankind").

In subsequent epochs, great Jews from Ezra to Moses Maimonides met new crises by advancing new syntheses. Each leader took into account the novelties of the current condition of Jewry as well as the ideas which flourished in his own day, yet none strayed far from prophetic principle or traditional practice.

Current conditions presented new problems; the antithesis of assimilation became more dangerously attractive than ever before. The effort to meet the economic demands of the American marketplace and the social and intellectual requirements of a dynamic society provoked dramatic reactions. Some Jews embraced a new Protestantized "religion" which rejected the national element of Judaism. Others reversed the process, substituting national feeling for religious devotion.

According to Friedlaender's analysis, religion and nationalism were the thesis and antithesis underlying the Congress dispute of 1914-1916. Parallel to them was another dichotomy, a thesis of diaspora clashing with an antithesis of Palestine. In order to resolve the issue, Friedlaender created what he called a new synthesis: "religion plus nationalism; diaspora plus Palestine."[2]

But was this truly a Hegelian synthesis, as Friedlaender claimed?

[1]*PP*, p. 268.
[2]Ibid., pp. 209, 211, 216.

According to his own definition of the term, "A synthesis . . . equally distant from the thesis and antithesis and yet composed of both . . . [merges the two] into a higher union, which combines the advantages and eliminates the disadvantages of either."[3]

It is evident that the new formula upon which Friedlaender bestowed the title "synthesis" did not meet his own definition of that term. "Religion plus nationalism, diaspora plus Palestine" was an all-inclusive phrase, embracing every element, eliminating none. Rather than being "equally distant" from each point, it merely recapitulated the same four concepts that formed the original problem.

If Friedlaender's formula was not, as he claimed, a synthesis in the Hegelian sense, what, then, was it? It seems to this writer that it was the first tentative step toward a philosophy of American Judaism which was grounded in Jewish sources, yet responsive to its own time and place.

William James was the towering figure of American philosophy in the first quarter of this century. His important lectures on Pragmatism (1906-7) shaped a system that would pervade American thinking for several decades. It was James who championed subjectivity, evaluating concepts for their utility rather than their correspondence to an ideal. Ideas, he insisted, "become true just insofar as they help us to get into satisfactory relations with other parts of our experience."[4] Moreover, an idea remains true only "so long as to believe it is profitable to our lives."[5]

When James examined the great philosophers of the past, he divided them into two "teams." First were the tender-minded idealists; these men lived by principle, espousing such phenomena of the spirit as religion, intellectualism, and monism. In contrast to them were the tough-minded empiricists whose faith was confined to provable fact. They embraced systems that were "sensationalistic, materialistic, irreligious, pluralistic and sceptical."[6]

James searched for a scheme which would be acceptable to people of all temperaments and intellectual inclinations and found it in the system of pragmatism initiated by Charles Sanders Peirce. By his own admission, it was a method rather than a "philosophy" in the traditional sense of the word. The pragmatic method would

[3]"Dr. Friedlaender at Seminary Meeting," *Jewish Exponent*, March 6, 1908, p. 9.
[4]William James, *Pragmatism* (New York, 1955), p. 49.
[5]Ibid., pp. 58-59.
[6]Ibid., pp. 21-22.

lay to rest metaphysical disputes that might otherwise be interminable. The pragmatist would not be constrained to reconcile differences into any overarching system but could be content with an "and" relationship, sometimes even an "or" relationship. He would

> try to interpret each notion by tracing its respective practical consequences. What difference would it practically make to any one if this notion rather than that notion were true? If no practical difference whatever can be traced, then the alternatives mean practically the same thing, and all dispute is idle. Whenever a dispute is serious, we ought to be able to show some practical difference that must follow from one side or the other's being right.[7]

Pragmatic thinking was evident both in Friedlaender's perception of the nature of the Congress dispute and in his plan for its resolution. The major theoretical question underlying the first of his two dichotomies was, Are the Jews a race or a religion? In an early essay on this topic, he acknowledged that, from an anthropological point of view, there was no such thing as a pure race. Nevertheless, from a practical standpoint, the Jews were, indeed, a race, simply because they had always considered themselves as such.[8] Like James, then, Friedlaender indicated that the measure of an idea was not its "truth," but its psychological benefit and social value.

This pragmatic bent of mind was also evident in Friedlaender's letter to Brandeis. Before undertaking an analysis of the dispute over the creation of a Congress, he informed his correspondent,

> I am not one who is a believer in "Peace at any price." Such a policy is a manifestation of cowardice and of lack of conviction. But neither do I belong to the war party which values fighting for its own sake. The only principle that determines me is the *outcome* of the struggle, and the good or evil which may result from it for the development of Judaism.[9]

The body of Friedlaender's epistle indicated his espousal of another notion associated with pragmatism: the refusal to settle for either a tough-minded or a tender-minded perception of the world.

---

[7]Ibid., pp. 42-43.

[8]*PP (1919)*, p. 432.

[9]IF to Brandeis, June 20, 1915, p. 2, *FP* (IF's emphasis). This excerpt is from a section of the letter that was not published.

Friedlaender's "solution" to the theoretical questions raised by the Congress dispute actually pitted two "tender" ideas against two "tough" ones. Time and again Friedlaender had conveyed the notion that religion and Palestine were the historic, imperishable ideals of Judaism, expressing the unbreakable link between God, His people, and the divinely promised land. Diaspora and nationalism, by contrast, were their "tough" challengers, representing the physical situation of contemporary Jewry and the current mind-set of its East European branch. "Diaspora" denoted the actual condition of world Jewry since the Exile; "nationalism" represented the indomitable conviction of political Zionists that Western society had rejected the Jews, who now faced only two choices: total assimilation or return to the ancient homeland.

Reacting to these positions, Friedlaender's maxim, "religion plus nationalism, Palestine plus diaspora" was broad enough to encompass all these modes of Jewish expression, the tender and the tough. Yet, it was, in no sense, a synthesis. For no element of the original thesis or antithesis was eliminated in the face of a new and higher unity. His formula indicated that none was sufficient unto itself, that all of them had to be retained. Yet, each thesis was viable only in tandem with its antithesis. Since the so-called synthesis was created by the word "and," it was the relationship between the elements that counted. The new formula indicated Friedlaender's disapproval of any program for Judaism which promoted half of either dichotomy at the expense of the other.

Philosophies which responded to the demands of modernity by ignoring—or worse, denying—any of these factors were, for Friedlaender, insidious. It is for this reason that he abandoned his normally temperate tone to lash out at Julian Morgenstern, the Bible scholar who denied the political acumen of ancient Israel, and, by extension, the ability of modern Jews to create and sustain an autonomous commonwealth. Friedlaender argued that this was a perversion of historical fact and current reality. It was the ethnic community that had ever preserved the tender ideal of religion and cherished the notion of return to Palestine. To discard this "tough" fact of history in order to pursue a disembodied religious ideal was, therefore, extremely dangerous. It was not only untrue to the Jewish past; it would ultimately "detach Israel from its God and its Torah."[10]

[10]*PP (1919)*, p. 437.

Religion and nationalism were ideals which had to be held in tension, each balancing the other. If Reform Jews broke the tension by rejecting the latter, political Zionists served the same unworthy object when they dwelled upon the national dimension of Judaism, excluding its religious, ethical, and universalistic qualities. "The Present Crisis in American Jewry" impugned the legitimacy of any movement which dared to substitute part of historic Judaism for the whole. Hence, it was not the objective analysis which it purported to be. It was, rather, a tract promoting two interrelated programs.

One was Historical Judaism, slowly evolving into its American form of Conservative Judaism. It admitted God's overall design in the governance of the world and His special concern for the Jewish people and its land, thereby advancing the concept of religion plus nationalism. At the time of the formation of a United Synagogue Friedlaender wrote, "The mainspring of Conservative Judaism, as distinct from Orthodoxy is something which is both more primitive and more sublime; I mean the religious and national Jewish instinct."[11]

This cryptic statement indicated Friedlaender's awareness of the potential danger of Jewish nationalism, which, if left unchecked, often led people to "primitive" expressions of chauvinistic exclusivism. In the Temple Emanu-el lectures, he indicated Historical Judaism's tendency to balance the primitive with the sublime by placing equal emphasis on the ethical message of the Bible.

Spiritual Zionism, the second program espoused by Friedlaender, rode on the horns of a similar dilemma. Like Conservative Judaism, it espoused the "tender," "sublime" prophetic ideals, which it proposed to implement in the soil of a restored Zion. This ideology also displayed a "tough" realistic quality. Following Ahad Ha-am, Friedlaender urged the political Zionists to examine the facts of life in the Middle East before they plunged, willy-nilly, into long-range schemes for the Jewish settlement of Palestine.

Friedlaender was aware that consistency was the hallmark of neither of these philosophies. In popular lectures, he often spoke of "the synthetic tendency of the Seminary," as indicated by its objective: "For it is our institution that seeks to harmonize Judaism with the new conditions of life and to give shape to a modern Judaism which is both modern and Jewish."[12] But his penetrating

[11]IF to Herman Rubenovitz, *Rubenovitz MSS*, Box 1, November 6, 1910.
[12]"Dr. Friedlaender at Seminary Meeting," p. 9.

analysis of the intellectual substructure of Conservative Judaism, the Temple Emanu-el Lectures, indicated that the movement was grounded in a series of paradoxes.

He was equally cognizant of the problem of creating a Zionist state that would be "both modern and Jewish." In his answer to a query by a former student he wrote,

> The problem you mention is one of the most complicated that will confront the Jews when they begin to carry into effect the plans of national restoration. The particular difficulty lies in the fact that on the one hand the tradition of Judaism has constantly upheld the identity of state and religion, whereas modern thought has just as consistently opposed that identity.[13]

Having established the theoretical obstacles hindering the reestablishment of a Jewish commonwealth, Friedlaender nonetheless maintained the faith that in the real world, life would triumph over theory. "I am sure that in the practical working out of our plans this difficulty will be ultimately overcome, as well as many others."[14] This sentence displays the radiant optimism and restless impatience with ideology that are the hallmarks of the pragmatist.

To classify Friedlaender as a pragmatist is not to claim that he ignored the ultimate question. In a private letter written in 1915, he professed enduring faith in a benevolent diety: "I am grateful beyond words that, instead of falling into the attitude of suspicion and cynicism, I have succeeded in discovering this one great Truth, in the one great Goodness manifesting itself in a variety of forms, like the light which breaks in different colors through its prism."[15]

Yet as a scholar and a publicist, Friedlaender preferred to dwell upon the "different colors," the multiple phenomena of historical and contemporary Jewish life. It was axiomatic for an adherent of Historical Judaism to discover the workings of the divine in the history of his people. To accomplish this goal, he would utilize his God-given reason, aided by the tools of modern critical scholarship. Jewish tradition has always considered the study of the classical biblical and talmudic texts an act of worship. In the tradition of Zunz and Graetz, Friedlaender accepted the corollary

[13]IF to Margaret Elfenbein, June 23, 1918, *FP*.
[14]Ibid.
[15]November 5, 1915, *FP*.

that immersion in every period of Jewish history and every mode of Jewish expression was an activity of equivalent piety.

As a champion of evolutionism and organicism, Friedlaender cherished all the products of Jewish development: law and legend, philosophy and folklore, reason and emotion, tradition and innovation. He freely admitted that these modes of expression often existed in tandem, sometimes even in tension with one another. Whether their historical manifestations complemented one another or whether they could only be posed as an unresolvable paradox, they constituted the breadth and the truth of Jewish life.

For this reason, Morris Adler's first question must receive both an affirmative and a negative answer. Friedlaender's philosophy of Judaism, as summarized in the formula "religion plus nationalism, diaspora plus nationalism," did exhibit a "comprehensiveness that could embrace the partialities of life." However, because it represented Friedlaender's efforts to embrace all the particulars of Jewish existence throughout the ages and in the current era, it was decidedly not a genuine synthesis.

Nor were his arguments free of flaws. Especially when they dealt with the emotionally charged issue of Jewish nationalism, they displayed noteworthy lapses of fact and logic. For example, Friedlaender devised a pun on the popular Reform definition of the Jewish religion. Judaism, he declared, was both "ethical monotheism" and "ethnical monotheism." It is clear that he coined the second term as a means of expressing the indissoluble bond between the Jewish religion and Jewish nationality. However, this phrase actually approximated his own definition of pre-Israelite Semitic paganism, "the hypostasis of the nation."

A certain fuzziness also marks other arguments advanced by Friedlaender on behalf of Jewish ethnicism. To declare Jews members of a race in opposition to scientific evidence simply because they regard themselves as such may pass the pragmatic test, but it fails most measures of logic. For what is a madman but a person who regards himself as Napoleon, or as the Messiah, or as the last best example of a master race?

Equally confusing was Friedlaender's presentation of Jewish philosophy. It will be remembered that in order to demonstrate Israel's intuitive perception of God, he questioned the legitimacy of Jewish philosophy. However, on other occasions, he celebrated the historical periods when Greek logic and beauty were incorporated into Jewish life and thought. Utilizing abstract terms, he sometimes approved of the eras of synthesis between isolation or nationalism and assimilation. In one lecture, however, he concluded that the Jewish people was best served when it embraced only the first idea. Nationalism, he reasoned, was "morally superior" to assimilation, because it did not yield to nature, but resisted it.[16]

Yet, when Friedlaender analyzed the Jewish religion, he changed the rules. To vindicate the retention of Halakha, he delineated a legal system which has evolved organically and must continue to follow the same route. This creates a problem. For if religion and nationality are inextricably bound together in Judaism, how could the religion have unfolded along natural lines while the nation's development defied natural process?

These are not serious errors; they merely reflect the emotional quality of Friedlaender's polemics as well as his grounding in the vocabulary and conceptualizations of German romantic historiography. Taken as a whole, however, these discrepancies offer additional evidence of Friedlaender's failure to construct a rigorously coherent program.

Friedlaender's life was equally devoid of the harmonious balance which his eulogizers attributed to it. We have seen how the young man mastered the disciplines of philology, philosophy, and history, how the mature scholar broadened his perspective to include the findings of psychology and sociology. And, indeed, it was with great verve that he applied them ably to the study of the Jewish past and the needs of contemporary Jewry. In this sense he was indeed a harmonizer.

However, his personal life was marked by uncertainty and disharmony. Arriving in America recommended by the great European orientalists Noeldeke and Goldziher,[17] Friedlaender never lived up to his early promise as a Semitics scholar. He investigated several *geniza* manuscripts from the Taylor-Schechter collection but managed to complete research only on projects initiated during his Strassburg years. To his friends he indicated dissatisfaction with his role as a teacher of Bible and biblical exegesis coupled with an ungratified longing for a full-time career as a Semitist. At any rate, the strong pull to communal activity in

---

[16]*PP*, pp. 35-36.
[17]The Goldziher recommendation is dated July 12, 1903, *FP*, Noeldeke's recommendation to Ginzberg is unavailable.

education, in Americanization, and in Zionism prevented him from concentrating on scholarship. These endeavors popularized his name among the denizens of the Lower East Side and their counterparts in other sections of the country. However, because of them, Friedlaender incurred the censure of Schechter and Adler, who preferred a faculty unreservedly devoted to academic pursuits.

Before the summer of 1914, Friedlaender's life was precariously balanced between the isolation of the ivory tower and the hurly-burly of public endeavor. In the wake of the European war, it tilted, slowly but decisively, in the latter direction. After completing his *magnum opus*, *Die Chardirlegende*, in 1913, Friedlaender made no significant forays into new Semitics scholarship. Instead, he devoted his efforts to East European Jewry. Rather than investigate new *geniza* documents, he edited, translated, and summarized Dubnow's thoughts on the history of the great Russian center. It was in order to preserve the essential values of this endangered civilization that Friedlaender engaged the powerful Reform magnates in battle over the schools, synagogues, and recreational activities of the Lower East Side. His efforts on behalf of the Hebrew language and the restoration of Zion were intended to sustain Russian Jewry's most recent achievement, to enable what he called "the rays of national revival"[18] to stream forth, unclouded by the afflictions of war.

Despite his prominence as a Jewish leader, Friedlaender never reached his goals. The activities of Benderly on the one hand and Adler on the other curtailed his efforts in Jewish education. The Reform Jewish magnates first accepted his proposals for the revitalization of the Educational Alliance in principle and then promptly undermined them. The American Zionist leaders, under the leadership of Louis Brandeis, solicited his propaganda efforts on behalf of their movement. Yet it was obvious that they regarded the real task of Zionism as organizational and financial, and his work as merely ornamental.

Appointment to the Red Cross Commission afforded Friedlaender the opportunity to translate his zeal for Zion into concrete action. Even after his last-minute ejection from the expedition and his humiliation by the Zionist leaders, he nonetheless continued his efforts on behalf of the restored Jewish homeland in the press and

[18]*JRP*, p. 207.

on the lecture podium. At the same time, events in Eastern Europe increasingly focused his attention on that part of the world. The war had burdened the Jews of czarist Russia with unbearable suffering; the upheavals of 1918 and 1919 only provoked fresh disaster. For Friedlaender, whose consciousness had been permeated with the desperate condition of Russian Jewry for over five years, the security of this community became an obsession, overshadowing even the happiness of his beloved wife and children. How otherwise could we explain his decision to join the Joint's relief mission, an act for which nothing in his previous training had prepared him? We can only conclude that it was the desperate attempt of a highly emotional man to find release from the turbulent feelings that had dominated his being for over a decade. It is obvious that his participation in the mission was at once heroic and foolhardy. Sad to relate, it did not enable Friedlaender to achieve the internal serenity he so desperately sought. His last letters reveal a man once again caught up in circumstances beyond his control, a tortured soul whose only recorded decision, "to concentrate in Zion," is subject to several interpretations.

*   *   *   *

If the circumstances of Friedlaender's death crowned him with posthumous glory, it was the conduct of his life that charted a new direction for American Jewry. For the historian, this man's life is a mirror of his times, reflecting the serious problems besetting American Jewry during the first decades of the twentieth century. Prominent among them was the status of Jewish learning. Long before T. S. Eliot, elitist European Jews bestowed upon their migrating sisters and brothers the dubious title of *Ama Reka* ("Hollow People"), a sorry pun on the continent of their new settlement. It was evident that American Jewry reserved most of its honors for worldly success rather than scholarly accomplishment. Friedlaender, more than any of his colleagues in either modern rabbinical seminary, exerted a sustained effort to reverse these priorities. In order to raise up a new generation devoted to the older values, he devoted countless hours to the deliberations of the Bureau of Jewish Education, the Educational Alliance, and other organizations concerned with youth. In order to transmit the best of traditional and current scholarship to adult American Jews, he traveled frequently to Philadelphia to participate in the deliberations of the JPS. Moreover, in New York and in other cities, he delivered popular lectures which not only disseminated Jewish learning of the highest caliber, but also pleaded for its retention as the supreme Jewish value.[19] His was one of the first voices to advance the rights of the spirit against the demands of the body for Jewish philanthropic funds, suggesting that monies be allocated equally to hospitals and to educational institutions. To grant further status to Jewish studies, Friedlaender even tried to introduce them into the curriculum of City College. These efforts were only marginally successful, but they pointed in a direction to which a more mature American Jewry would return half a century later.

Furthermore, many of Friedlaender's activities dramatized a second challenging problem, the cleavage between the "German" and the "Russian" Jews. This issue lay at the root of the battles which he fought over concrete programs promoting the education and acculturation of the immigrants and the creation of an American Jewish Congress; it also underscored his ideological debates with the Reformers over the interpretation of Scripture and the meaning of Jewish history.

According to the historian Jacob Marcus, 1920, the year of Friedlaender's death, marked the inception of the era in which the two groups would fuse.[20] Friedlaender worked diligently to make the "new American Jew" a reality. With intelligence and moderation, he addressed the important question of the proper language of discourse for the emerging Jewish community. During the last decades of the nineteenth century and the first decades of the twentieth, this issue was a subject of intense controversy. Yiddishists such as Chaim Zhitlovsky, Friedlaender's colleague in the Achavah Club, fostered Yiddish as the common bond to unite all Jews of East European origin. The principal cultural media of the Lower East Side, Yiddish newspapers and theater, seemed to argue their brief. On the other hand, Jews of Central European stock exhibited a certain ambivalence on the issue of linguistic expression. While most members of this community, which included an increasing proportion of native-born persons, adapted English as

---

[19]See "The Function of Jewish Learning in America," *PP*, pp. 185-205.
[20]Jacob Marcus, *Studies in American Jewish History*, p. 12.

the medium of social discourse and business dealings, some of their rabbis and intellectuals preferred to retain German for religious education and serious scholarship.

Friedlaender, like Schechter, cast his lot unequivocally with the English language. This does not mean that he totally abandoned the vernacular expressions of his childhood and youth. We have seen that he continued to carry on some correspondence in German and to complete some scholarly efforts initiated in that language. When asked, he would also address the East European immigrants in the native tongue which they shared. And we must never overlook his abiding love for Hebrew. He ever delighted in introducing young students to the richness of the biblical expression and medieval Hebrew poetry. The modern revival of the language always thrilled him, leading him to sponsor small enclaves of Hebrew readers and writers.

However, even before his emigration from Europe, he made clear his commitment to English as the language of the new American center.[21] His essays and lectures, in form and substance, communicated this message. In all his finished works, the prose flowed smoothly, abounding in idiomatic expressions and bristling with colorful figures of speech.[22] By contrast, Schechter's graceful but highly accented rhetoric was available to general audiences only in written form. Moreover, Brandeis's forceful apology for American Zionism was grounded in American progressivism rather than Jewish tradition. Among contemporary Jewish publicists, only Friedlaender wielded the English language with rhythmic ease, impassioned eloquence, and an aura of authenticity.

To integrate the emerging American Jewish community around traditional cultural and religious values even as it struggled to adjust to "a powerful environment,"[23] Friedlaender introduced the most advanced Jewish thinking, modifying European ideas to suit the circumstances of the new milieu. His writings on the Jewish condition in America relayed two messages. The first, suggested by nineteenth-century *Wissenschaft* scholarship and later taken up by Ahad Ha-am, was that certain modes of culture may be borrowed from the environment as long as they do not lead to absorption into the culture of the host nation. The second, drawn

[21]IF, "The Jewish Encyclopedia," *Ha-shiloah* 8 (1901): 255.
[22]Papers not prepared for publication do not meet the same standards.
[23]*PP*, p. 193.

from Dubnow's philosophy of Jewish history, concerned the worthiness of the diaspora in general and American Israel in particular. Almost alone among traditional Jews, Friedlaender envisioned a glorious future for American Jewry. As the years went on, this hope flickered, but it never disappeared.

To these fundamental messages Friedlaender appended several corollaries, which were soon transmitted by popularizers to the general American public. His seminal essay "The Problem of Judaism in America" proposed two apparently contradictory myths. It established an historical precedent for "a Judaism of freedom and culture"; at the same time, it maintained that the current situation was unique. If the logic was imperfect, the motive was clear. By designating the Judeo-Arabic epoch an historical typology, Friedlaender suggested the possibility of another diaspora in which Jews would be politically emancipated, economically secure, yet remain steadfast to the tradition. The myth of American exceptionalism emerged out of the general perception of the New World as a unique place of freedom, opportunity, and hope; it also reflected a modernist predilection for the new and untried.

Amplifying the declaration of American exceptionalism were two additional ideas. One, which Friedlaender shared with Schechter,[24] visualized Anglo-Saxon culture as hospitable to Jewish culture, since both prompted ideals of freedom and justice. The other vindicated cultural diversity on the grounds that the United States was a pluralistic rather than a monistic society.[25] With Friedlaender's encouragement,[26] Louis Brandeis employed these arguments to legitimize American Zionism.[27] By dedicating his *Theories of Americanization* (1920) to Friedlaender's memory, Isaac B. Berkson acknowledged the debt of his community theory to the historical philosophy of Simon Dubnow transmitted and adapted by Israel Friedlaender.

* * * *

[24]See Schechter's essay on Abraham Lincoln, which compares the American president to the ancient Jewish sage Hillel, in *Seminary Addresses*, pp. 146-168.

[25]*PP*, p. 180; "Minute Book," p. 205.

[26]IF to Brandeis, June 23, 1915, *FP*. In this letter, Friedlaender compared Brandeis's ideas to those of Dubnow.

[27]See Louis D. Brandeis, "The Jewish Problem and How to Solve It," in *Brandeis on Zionism: A Collection of Statements by Louis D. Brandeis* (New York, 1942), pp. 12-35.

Far more popular than Friedlaender's moderate modernism were radical solutions to the problems of the immigrants, such as the creation of a Yiddish-speaking enclave in North America and the replacement of the capitalist system with a socialist utopia or a stateless society. Strange to say, Friedlaender seldom addressed these philosophies. Instead, he chose to do battle with Reform Judaism, to which most American Jewish leaders subscribed, and, to a lesser extent, with secular Jewish nationalism. On one occasion, he suggested that no matter how hard the Reformers tried, they could never amputate the ethnic limbs from the religious body of Judaism. Nor could the secularists accomplish their equal and opposite purpose.

> There are many Jews who deny the racial or national character of Judaism and yet betray in their actions and sentiments a deep attachment to the Jewish people as a racial community. There are others who deny the religious basis of Judaism and yet in their whole spiritual make-up bear the deep impress of the Jewish religion.[28]

But what about anarchists and socialists, who summarily rejected both religion and nationalism? Perhaps Friedlaender dismissed them as lost to Jewish life. It is more likely, however, that he believed that their activites, like those of the secular Zionists, also bore the imprint of the Jewish religion.

Indeed, Friedlaender's willingness to work with all segments of American Jewry developed out of the conviction that neither the Reform "religionists" not the secularists of any stripe understood the source of their own motivation or realized the direction in which they were heading.

> We can work in harmony with the adherents of both religious and racial Judaism as long as they are *not* consistent. After all, the actions of men are not determined by formulas and abstractions, but by natural and historical forces, which, having slowly ripened out of centuries of development, cannot be easily discarded.[29]

For these reasons and because of an orientation that was cultural rather than political, Friedlaender did not confront the socialist

[28]*PP (1919)*, p. 440.
[29]Ibid.

theoreticians of the Yiddish press or the East Side coffee houses. He was convinced that the opportunities of American life would solve the material problems of the Jews in one or two generations. What concerned him was spiritual distress, as he indicated in his characteristically ironic fashion. "Judaism which stood out like a rock amidst the billows of hatred and storms of persecution is melting away like wax under the mild rays of freedom."[30]

Throughout his career he insisted that the most effective method of blocking the lethal effect of those rays was to perpetuate a Judaism that was not a mere creed, but the multifaceted, highly spiritual culture of a regenerated nation. For him, these were manifest in Zionism and Conservative Judaism, two interrelated ideologies which he understood as direct heirs to Historical Judaism, "the course laid down by history [which] follow[s] the mandate of God that speaks through history."[31]

Working for Zionism, Friedlaender was a less successful organizer and publicist than pedagogue. His time-consuming efforts as an officer of the FAZ bore little fruit; his suggestions for disseminating Jewish culture in the diaspora and squarely facing the Arab problem were solicited by the ZOA and then promptly ignored. Most enduring of his contributions to American Zionism was his influence on the college students in the Menorah societies and the future rabbis and teachers who studied at the Jewish Theological Seminary. In the years after Friedlaender's death, Conservative rabbis and educators would use his memory to justify their Zionist activity in the face of the aloofness of the Seminary administration.

As a formulator of Conservative ideology and architect of the Conservative movement, Friedlaender extended several lines of thought which Schechter had introduced to American Jewry. His Temple Emanu-el addresses pursued some of the arguments of Schechter's essay on Geiger. In pleading the case for Zionism, Friedlaender extrapolated upon Schechter's thesis that the movement would serve as a "bulwark against assimilation."[32] Like Schechter, moreover, he excoriated the Bible critics for their ignorance of the Hebrew language and Jewish exegetical literature. Furthermore, his extensive analysis of Briggs's *Critical Commentary on the Psalms*, like Schechter's Ben Sira studies, disputed one

[30]Ibid., p. 166.
[31]*Aspects* I, 4.
[32]Schechter, *Seminary Addresses*, p. 93.

corollary of the Wellhausen hypothesis, the late dating of the
Psalms. Both works demonstrated that certain psalms were written
relatively early in Jewish history.

Most significantly, Friedlaender put flesh on the bare bones of
Schechter's theological position, "an enlightened Skepticism combined with a staunch conservatism which is not even wholly devoid
of a certain mystical touch."[33] "Enlightened skepticism" referred to
the methods of critical scholarship, which often compelled sacred
and historical texts to yield information they did not intend to
impart. "Staunch conservatism" indicated adherence to traditional
religious practice. Friedlaender's lifework illustrated the one; his
spirited defense of Jewish ceremonialism vindicated the other.
Most notably, Friedlaender's choice of subject matter for serious
and popular scholarship and, indeed, his very personality successfully imparted that third elusive quality of the "certain mystical
touch."

Taking stock of a career that came to an end over six and a half
decades ago, we can ascertain the keenness of Friedlaender's insights. The middle-of-the-road philosophies which he endorsed
have endured the test of time, whereas such ideologies as classical
Reform, Yiddishism, territorialism, socialism, and anarchism,
which he either opposed or ignored, have all but disappeared from
the American scene.

As to his personal life, most of its vicissitudes can be traced to
Friedlaender's most characteristic quality, a soaring idealism that
befitted a disciple of Ahad Ha-am. Strange to relate, this idealism
accomplished two contrary purposes. On the one hand, it enabled
him to function as a gifted pedagogue who successfully transmitted
the insights of ancient, medieval, and modern Judaism to a generation of rabbis and teachers, a talented public speaker who lifted the
sights of his audiences, and a communal leader grudgingly respected even by those with whom he disagreed.

On the other hand, that same quality of idealism, when applied
to his personal life, led him from rebuff to disillusion to premature
death. Convinced of the uprightness of his positions on the interpretation of Scripture, the nature of Judaism, and the proper
direction for American Judaism, he considered it sufficient to argue
each case on its own merits. Since he was unwilling to devote equal

[33] *SJ* 1, p. xvii.

energy to institutional politics, he achieved neither the recognition which he deserved not the personal advancement which he craved.

Despite this minor shortcoming, which mirrored his stellar virtues, Friedlaender takes his place in the annals of American Judaism as a conduit and reinterpreter of important European and American ideas, a selfless public servant, and a convincing apologist for Zionism and Conservative Judaism. To his adopted community he donated the vivid insights of a penetrating mind, the unbounded enthusiasm of an ardent soul, and every ounce of his physical and moral strength.

Bibliography

Unpublished Addresses of Israel Friedlaender

Aspects of Historical Judaism. A course of five lectures delivered at Temple Emanu-el, April 22, 23, 30, May 7, 14, 1917. *FP*, Boxes 8 and 12 contain the first four lectures.

"Jewry, East and West," May 6, 1915. Delivered at Kent Hall, Columbia University. *FP*, Box 9.

Significant Epochs in Jewish History. A course of six lectures delivered before the Training Class of the Jewish Welfare Board, August 14, 15, and 16, 1918. Outline and nos. 5 and 6 in *FP*, Box 15.

"Uptown and Downtown Judaism," 1905. Delivered at a meeting of the Qadimah. New York. March 1, 1905. *Agranat MSS.*

"Zionism and Territorialism." Delivered before the Great Beacon, the Order of Ancient Maccabaeans. London. September 3, 1905. *Agranat MSS.*

Published Writings of Israel Friedlaender

An excellent and complete bibliography of Friedlaender's writings was published by Boaz Cohen, entitled *Israel Friedlaender: A Bibliography of His Writings with an Appreciation* (New York: Moinester Publishing Co., 1936). The following is a list of Friedlaender's major published works, in chronological order.

Der Sprachgebrauch des Maimonides. Ein lexikalischer und grammatischer Beitrag zur Kenntnis des Mittelarabischen. Frankfurt am Main: M. J. Kauffmann, 1902.

Die Messiasidee in Islam. Berlin: Druck von H. Itzkowski, 1903. (Reprinted from *Festschrift zum 70 Geburtstage A. Berliner's*, pp. 116-130.)

Achad Ha'am. *Am Scheidewege. Ausgewaehlte Essays.* Authorized translation from the Hebrew. Berlin: Juedischer Verlag, 1904.

"The Arabic Original of the Report of R. Nathan Hababli." *Jewish Quarterly Review*, original series 17 (1905): 747-761.

S. M. Dubnow. *Die Grundlagen des Nationaljudentums.* Authorized translation from the Russian. Berlin: Juedischer Verlag, 1905.

"Zur Komposition von Ibn Hazm's *Milal wa'n Nihal.*" In *Orientalische Studien Theodor Noeldeke zum siebzigsten Geburtstag (2 Maerz, 1906) gewidmet,* vol. 2, pp. 267-277. Giessen: Toepelmann, 1906.

"A New Specimen of Modern Biblical Exegesis." Review of *A Critical and Exegetical Commentary on the Book of Psalms,* by Charles A. Briggs. *American Hebrew and Jewish Messenger* 81 (July 5, 1907): Literary Supplement, pp. 3-7.

"The Problem of Judaism in America: A Lecture." *Jewish Comment* 28 (1908): 193-195, 204-205; (1909): 219-220, 223.

The Heterodoxies of the Shiites according to Ibn Hazm: Introduction, Translation and Commentary. New Haven: Yale University Press, 1909.

Selections from the Arabic Writings of Maimonides: Edited with Introduction and Notes. Leyden: Late E. J. Brill, 1909.

"Abdallah b. Saba, der Begruender der Sia, und sein juedischer Ursprung." *Zeitschrift fuer Assyriologie und Verwandte Gebiete* 23 (1909): 296-372; 24 (1910): 1-46.

"The Political Ideal of the Prophets: A Study in Biblical Zionism." *Jewish Comment* 30 (March 11, 1910): 313, 320-323.

"Shiitic Elements in Jewish Sectarianism." *Jewish Quarterly Review,* new series 1 (1910): 183-215; 2 (1911-12): 481-516; 3 (1912-13): 235-300.

"Muhammedanische Geschichtskonstruktionen." *Beitraege zur Kenntnis des Orients* 11 (1911): 17-34.

"Qirqisani's Polemik gegen den Islam." *Zeitschrift fuer Assyriologie und Verwandte Gebiete* 26 (1911): 93-110.

Die Chadirlegende und der Alexanderroman. Eine Sagengeschichtliche und Literarhistorische Untersuchung. Leipzig and Berlin: B. G. Teubner, 1913.

"The Problem of Jewish Education in America and the Bureau of Education of the Jewish Community of New York City." In *The Report of the Commissioner of Education for the Year Ended June 30, 1913,* 1: 365-393. Washington, 1914.

The Jews of Russia and Poland: A Bird's-Eye View of Their History and Culture. New York and London: G. P. Putnam's Sons, 1915.

"The Present Crisis in American Jewry. A Plea for Reconciliation." *Menorah Journal* 1 (December 1915): 265-276.

"The Present Position and the Original Form of the Prophecy of Eternal Peace in Isaiah 2:1-5 and Micah 4:1-5." *Jewish Quarterly Review,* new series 6 (1916): 405-413.

S. M. Dubnow. *History of the Jews in Russia and Poland from the Earliest Times until the Present Day.* Authorized translation from the Russian. Philadelphia: Jewish Publication Society, vol. 1, 1916; vol. 2, 1918; vol. 3, 1920.

"The Americanization of the Jewish Immigrant." *Survey* 38 (May 5, 1917): 103-108.

"Zionism and the World Peace: A Rejoinder to Herbert Adams Gibbons' Article in *The Century Magazine* of January, 1919." *Century Magazine*, April 1919, pp. 803-810.

Past and Present: A Collection of Jewish Essays. Cincinnati: Ark Publishing Co., 1919.

Past and Present: A Collection of Jewish Essays. 2nd ed., with some deletions. New York: Burning Bush Press, 1961.

Personal Interviews and Correspondence

Agrarat, Carmel. Interviews of March 1, 1978 and August 1982.

Aronson, David. Interview of March 27, 1978.

Finkelstein, Louis. Interview of March 15, 1978.

Friedlaender, Herzl. Correspondence of 1978 through 1984.

Friedlander, Ben-Zion. Correspondence of 1982-83.

Friedlander, Judith. Interviews of August 1982.

Ginzberg, Adele.* Interview of May 17, 1978.

Ginzberg, Eli. Interview of October 19, 1978.

Goldman, Israel.* Interview of March 27, 1978.

Grayzel, Solomon.* Interview of March 7, 1979.

Greenberg, Simon. Interviews of March 28, 1978 and November 18, 1981.

Kadushin, Max.* Interview of November 8, 1978.

Kahn, Alfred. Interview of January 27, 1979.

Kleban, Anna. Interview of March 1, 1978.

Levinthal, Israel.* Interview of September 25, 1978.

Schussheim, Mary.* Interview of May 17, 1978.

Archival Sources

Agranat Papers, Jerusalem, Israel. Privately owned.

American Jewish Historical Society, Waltham, Massachusetts. Louis D. Brandeis Papers; Richard Gottheil Papers; Julian W. Mack Papers; Steven S. Wise Papers.

Central Zionist Archives, Jerusalem, Israel. Ahad Ha-am Papers.

Jewish Theological Seminary, New York City. Cyrus Adler Papers; Harry Friedenwald Papers; Israel Friedlaender Papers; Louis Ginzberg Papers; Journals of Mordecai M. Kaplan; Alexander Marx Papers; Bernard Richard Papers; Herman Rubenovitz Papers; Solomon Schechter Papers; Moritz Steinschneider Papers.

National Archives, Washington, D. C. American Red Cross Papers.

Zionist Archives and Library, New York City. Jacob de Haas Papers and Richard Gottheil Papers.

Published Primary Sources

Adler, Cyrus. *I Have Considered the Days*. New York: Burning Bush Press, 1945.

————. *Jacob H. Schiff: His Life and Letters.* 2 vols. New York: Doubleday, 1929.

————. *Letters, Selected Papers, Addresses: Collected and Published by His Colleagues and Friends on the Occasion of His Seventieth Birthday, September 13, 1933.* Philadelphia: Private printing, 1933.

Ahad Ha-am. *Igrot Ahad Ha-am.* Vols. 1, 3, 4, 5. Jerusalem: Yavne, 1923-25.

American Joint Distribution Committee. *Memorial Meeting: Israel Friedlaender: Bernard Cantor, Carnegie Hall, New York, September 9, 1920.* New York, 1920.

————. *Record of the Special Meeting Relating to the Deaths of Professor Israel Friedlaender and Rev. Dr. Bernard Cantor, July 15, 1920.* New York, 1920.

Blatman, Leon S. "Professor Israel Friedlaender's Relief Mission." In *Kamenetz-Podolsk: A Memorial to a Jewish Community Annihilated by the Nazis in 1941,* pp. 67-75. New York: Sponsors of the Kamenetz-Podolsk Memorial Book, 1966.

Davis, Moshe. "The Human Record: Cyrus Adler at the Peace Conference, 1919." In *Essays in American Jewish History to Commemorate the Tenth Anniversary of the Founding of the American Jewish Archives under the Direction of J. R. Marcus,* pp. 457-491. New York: Ktav, 1975.

————. "Israel Friedlaender's Minute Book of the Achavah Club, 1909-1912." In *Mordecai M. Kaplan Jubilee Volume,* English sec., pp. 157-213. New York: Jewish Theological Seminary, 1953.

————. "Jewry, East and West (The Correspondence of Israel Friedlaender and Simon Dubnow)." *YIVO Annual of Jewish Social Science* 9 (1954): 9-62.

Kaplan, Mordecai M., and Cronson, Bernard. "First Community Survey of Jewish Education in New York City, 1909; Presented at the First Annual Convention of the Kehillah, February 27, 1910." *Jewish Education* 20 (Summer 1949): 113-116.

Leff, M. *Statement by Dr. M. Leff before the America Joint Distribution Committee, March 21, 1921.* New York: American Joint Distribution Committee, 1921.

Urofsky, Melvin I., and Levy, David W., eds. *Letters of Louis D. Brandeis.* 5 vols. Albany: State University of New York Press, 1971-78.

Yaari, Abraham, ed. *Solomon Schechter's Letters to Samuel Poznanski.* Jerusalem: Bamberger and Wahrman, 1943.

Secondary Sources

Addams, Jane. *Twenty Years at Hull House with Autobiographical Notes.* New York: Macmillan, 1910.

Agus, Jacob B. *Dialogue and Tradition: The Challenges of Contemporary Judeo-Christian Thought.* London, New York, and Toronto: Abelard-Schuman, 1971.

————. *Guideposts in Modern Judaism: An Analysis of Current Trends in Jewish Thought.* New York: Bloch Publishing Co., 1954.

————. *Jewish Identity in an Age of Ideologies.* New York: Frederick Ungar Publishing Co., 1978.

Ahad Ha-am (Asher Ginzberg). *Kol Kitve Ahad Ha-am.* Jerusalem and Tel Aviv: D'vir and Hazaah Ivrit, 1947.

————. *Nationalism and the Jewish Ethic: Basic Writings of Ahad Ha-am.* Edited with Introduction by Hans Kohn. New York: Schocken, 1962.

————. *Selected Essays.* Translated and edited by Leon Simon. New York: Atheneum, Temple Books, 1970.

Baron, Salo. *History and Jewish Historians: Essays and Addresses.* Philadelphia: Jewish Publication Society, 1964.

————. *A Social and Religious History of the Jews.* Vol. 5 Philadelphia: Jewish Publication Society, 1957.

Barth, Karl. *Protestant Thought from Rousseau to Ritsich.* Translated by Brian Cozens. New York: Harper and Brothers, 1959.

Barzun, Jacques. *Darwin, Marx, Wagner.* Garden City, N.Y.: Doubleday, Anchor Books, 1958.

Bentwich, Margery. *Lilian Ruth Friedlander: A Biography.* Jerusalem: Rubin Maas, 1957.

————, and Bentwich, Norman. *Herbert Bentwich: The Pilgrim Father.* Jerusalem: Gesher Printing Press, 1940.

Bentwich, Norman. *For Zion's Sake: A Biography of Judah L. Magnes.* Philadelphia: Jewish Publication Society, 1954.

————. *Solomon Schechter.* Philadelphia: Jewish Publication Society, 1938.

————. "The Kehillah of New York, 1908-1922." In *Mordecai M. Kaplan Jubilee Volume,* English sec., pp. 73-85. New York: Jewish Theological Seminary, 1953.

Berkson, Isaac. *Theories of Americanization: A Critical Study with Special Reference to the Jewish Group.* New York: Teachers College, Columbia University, 1920.

Biale, David. *Gershom Scholem, Kabbalah and Counter-History.* Cambridge, Mass.: Harvard University Press, 1979.

"Bibliograph" [Kressl]. "On the Hebrew Writings of Israel Friedlaender." Letter to the Editor of *Hadoar. Hadoar* 56 (December 24, 1976): 123.

Bingham, Theodore A. "Foreign Criminals in New York." *North American Review* 187 (September 1908): 383-394.

Blochet, Edgar. *Le Messianisme dans l'hétérodoxie musulmane.* Paris: Maisoneuve, 1903.

Bourne, Randolph. "Trans-National America." *Atlantic Monthly* 118 (July 1916): 86-97.

Brandeis, Louis D. *Brandeis on Zionism: A Collection of Statements by Louis D. Brandeis.* Washington, D. C.: Zionist Organization of America, 1942.

Brann, Marcus. *Geschichte des juedisch-theologischen Seminars in Breslau*. Breslau, n.d.

Briggs, Charles August, and Grace, Emilie. *A Critical and Exegetical Commentary on the Book of Psalms*. International Critical Commentary. 2 vols. New York: Charles Scribner's Sons, 1906-7.

Buber, Martin. *Tales of the Hasidim: The Later Masters*. Translated by Olga Marx. New York: Schocken Books, 1947-48.

Butterfield, Herbert. *Man on His Past: The Study of the History of Historical Scholarship*. Boston: Beacon Press, 1955.

Cahan, Abraham. *The Rise of David Levinsky*. New York: Harper and Row, Colophon Books, 1966.

———. *Yekl and the Imported Bridegroom and Other Stories of the New York Ghetto*. New York: Dover Publications, 1970.

Cannon, Walter B. *The Wisdom of the Body*. New York: W. W. Norton & Co., 1932.

Cohen, Gerson D. "The Reconstruction of Gaonic History." Introduction to *Texts and Studies in Jewish History and Literature*, by Jacob Mann. 2 vols. New York: Ktav Publishing House, 1972.

Cohen, Naomi W. *American Jews and the Zionist Idea*. New York: Ktav Publishing House, 1975.

———. "The Maccabaean's Message: A Study in American Zionism until World War I." *Jewish Social Studies* 18 (July 1956): 163-178.

———. *Not Free to Desist: The American Jewish Committee, 1906-1966*. Philadelphia: Jewish Publication Society, 1972.

———. "The Reactions of Reform Judaism in America to Political Zionism: 1897-1922." *Publications of the American Jewish Historical Society* 40 (June 1951): 361-394.

Cole, Steward G., and Wiese, Mildred. *Minorities and the American Promise*. New York: Harper and Row, 1954.

Collingwood, R. G. *The Idea of History*. New York: Oxford University Press, Galaxy Books, 1950.

Cooley, Charles H. *Human Nature and the Social Order*. Rev. ed. Glencoe, Ill.: Free Press, 1956.

Cremin, Lawrence A. *The Transformation of the Schools: Progressivism in American Education, 1876-1957*. New York: Knopf, 1961.

Davis, Moshe. *Beit Yisrael be-Amerikah, Meḥkarim U-Mekorot*. Jerusalem: Goldberg's Press, 1970.

———. *The Emergence of Conservative Judaism: The Historical School in 19th Century America*. Philadelphia: Jewish Publication Society, 1963.

———. *Yahadut Amerika be-Hitpatḥutah* [The shaping of American Judaism]. New York: Jewish Theological Seminary, 1951.

Delitzsch, Friedrich. *Babel and Bible: A Lecture on the Significance of Assyriological Research for Religion*. Translated by Thomas J. McCormack.

Chicago: Open Court Publishing Co., 1902.

Derenbourg, Joseph. "Le Prophet Elie dans le Rituel." *Revue des Études Juives* 2 (1881): 290-293.

Dewey, John. "Nationalizing Education." *National Education Association: Addresses and Proceedings of the Fifty-Fourth Annual Meeting* 54 (1916): 183-189.

———. "The Principle of Nationality." *Menorah Journal* 3 (April 1917): 203-208.

Dienstag, Jacob I. "Israel Friedlaender as a Maimonidian Scholar" (Hebrew). *Bitzaron* 25 (October 1956): 30-36.

Dubnow, Simon. *History of the Jews in Russia and Poland from the Earliest Times until the Present Day.* 3 vols. Translated by I. Friedlaender. Philadelphia: Jewish Publication Society, 1916-20.

———. "Israel Friedlaender, In Memory of a Dear Soul." *Ha-aretz*, September 1 and 4, 1922. Reprinted in *Beit Yisrael be-Amerika*, edited by Moshe Davis, pp. 195-200. Jerusalem: Goldberg's Press, 1970.

———. *Nationalism and History: Essays in Old and New Judaism.* Edited with an Introductory Essay by Koppel S. Pinson. New York: Atheneum, Temple Books, 1970.

———. *Weltgeschichte des juedischen Volkes.* Berlin: Judischer Verlag, 1925-30.

Dushkin, Alexander M. *Jewish Education in New York City.* New York: Bureau of Jewish Education, 1918.

Feinstein, Marnin. *American Zionism, 1884-1904.* New York: Herzl Press, 1965.

Fineman, Irving. *Woman of Valor: The Life of Henrietta Szold, 1860-1945.* New York: Simon & Schuster, 1961.

Finkelstein, Louis. Introduction to *Past and Present: Selected Essays*, by Israel Friedlaender, pp. ix-xv. New York: Burning Bush Press, 1961.

———. "Israel Friedlaender." *Universal Jewish Encyclopedia* 4:450-451.

———. "Tradition in the Making: The Seminary's Interpretation of Judaism." In *Tradition and Change: The Development of Conservative Judaism.* New York: Burning Bush Press, 1958.

Frankel, Zacharias. *Zeitschrift fuer die religiosen Interessen des Judentums* 3 (1946): 89-90.

Frazer, J. G. "The Resurrection of Glaucus." In *Apollodorous, The Library*, vol. 1. Cambridge: Loeb Classical Library, 1921.

Freud, Sigmund. *Interpretation of Dreams.* Translated by A. A. Brill. New York: Macmillan, 1913.

Friedlaender, Lilian. "A Chassid's Service to American Judaism: The Work of Israel Friedlaender." *Menorah Journal* 6 (December 1920): 337-344.

Friesel, Evyator. *The Zionist Movement in the United States, 1897-1914* (Hebrew). Tel Aviv University: Institute for Zionist Research, 1970.

Geiger, Abraham. *Nachgelassene Schriften.* 5 vols. Berlin: L. Gerschel, 1875-78.

———. *Was hat Mohammed aus dem Judenthume aufgenommen?* Bonn: F. Basden, 1833.

Gibbons, Herbert. "Zionism and the World Peace." *Century Magazine,* January 1919, pp. 368-378.

Ginsberg, H. L. "New Trends in Bible Criticism: The Broader Historical View." *Commentary* 10 (September 1950): 276-284.

Ginzberg, Eli. *Keeper of the Law: Louis Ginzberg.* Philadelphia: Jewish Publication Society, 1966.

Ginzberg, Louis. "Cabala." *Jewish Encyclopedia* 3:456-479.

———. *Geonica: Texts and Studies of the Jewish Theological Seminary of America.* Vol. 1. New York: Jewish Theological Seminary, 1909.

———. *Students, Scholars, and Saints.* Philadelphia: Jewish Publication Society, 1928.

Goldberg, Abraham. "American Zionism up to the Brandeis Era." In *The Brandeis Avukah Annual of 1932: A Collection of Essays on Contemporary Zionist Thought Dedicated to Justice Louis D. Brandeis,* edited by Joseph Shubow, pp. 549-568. Boston: Stratford Co., 1932.

Gordis, Robert. *An American Philosophy: Conservative Judaism.* New York: Behrman House, 1945.

———. *Understanding Conservative Judaism.* New York: Rabbinical Assembly, 1978.

Gordon, Milton. *Assimilation in American Life: The Role of Race, Religion and National Origins.* New York: Oxford University Press, 1964.

Goren, Arthur A. *Dissenter in Zion. From the Writings of Judah L. Magnes.* Cambridge and London: Harvard University Press, 1982.

———. *New York Jews and the Quest for Community: The Kehillah Experiment, 1908-1922.* New York and London: Columbia University Press, 1970.

Graetz, Heinrich. *Geschichte der Juden von den aeltesten Zeiten bis zur Gegenwart.* 2d ed. Vols. 3 and 4. Leipzig: O. Leiner, 1863-1902.

———. *The Structure of Jewish History and Other Essays.* Translated and edited by Ismar Schorsch. New York: Ktav Publishing House, 1975.

Greenberg, Simon. *Israel and Zionism: A Conservative Approach.* New York: United Synagogue of America, 1959.

———. "Zionism, Israel and the RA." *Proceedings of the Rabbinical Assembly* 37 (1945): 345-348.

Grinstein, Hyman B. "The Efforts of East European Jewry to Organize Its Own Community in the United States." *Publications of the American Jewish Historical Society* 49 (1959): 73-89.

————. *The Rise of the Jewish Community in New York, 1654-1860.* Philadelphia: Jewish Publication Society, 1947.

Hahn, Herbert H. *The Old Testament in Modern Research.* Phildelphia: Fortress Press, 1970.

————. "Wellhausen's Interpretation of Israel's Religious History: A Reappraisal of His Ruling Ideas." In *Essays on Jewish Life and Thought Presented in Honor of Salo Baron,* pp. 299-308. New York: Columbia University Press, 1959.

Halevi, Moshe [Morris D. Levine]. "Ha-shalem be-midotav." *Ha-toren* 8 (July 30, 1920): 3-7.

Halkin, Abraham. Preface to Moses Maimonides' *Epistle to Yemen: The Arabic Original and the Three Hebrew Versions.* New York: American Academy for Jewish Research, 1952.

Halpern, Ben. *The Idea of the Jewish State.* Cambridge: Harvard University Press, 1969.

Handlin, Oscar. *The American People in the Twentieth Century.* Cambridge: Harvard University Press, 1954.

————. *Race and Nationality in American Life.* New York: Doubleday, Anchor Books, 1957.

————. *The Uprooted: The Epic Story of the Great Migrations That Made the American People.* Boston: Little, Brown, 1951.

Hartmann, Edward George. *The Movement to Americanize the Immigrant.* New York: Columbia University Press, 1948.

Hertzberg, Arthur. *The Zionist Idea: A Historical Analysis and Reader.* New York: Atheneum, Temple Books, 1973.

Herzl, Theodor. *The Jewish State.* Translated by Harry Zohn. New York: Herzl Press, 1970.

Higham, John. "Social Discrimination Against Jews in America, 1830-1930." *Publications of the American Jewish Historical Society* 47 (September 1957): 1-33.

————. *Strangers in the Land.* New Brunswick, N.J.: Rutgers University Press, 1955.

Hoffmann, David. *Die wichtigsten Instanzen gegen die Graf-Wellhausenche Hypothese.* 2 vols. Berlin: Druck von H. Itzkowski, 1904.

Howe, Irving. *World of Our Fathers.* New York and London: Harcourt Brace Jovonovich, 1976.

Hughes, H. Stuart. *Consciousness and Society: The Reorientation of European Social Thought, 1890-1930.* New York: Random House, Vintage Books, 1958.

Iggers, George G. *The German Conception of History: The National Tradition of Historical Thought from Herder to the Present.* Middletown, Conn.: Wesleyan University Press, 1968.

James, William. *Pragmatism and Four Essays from the Meaning of Truth.* New York: Meridian Books, 1955.

Janowsky, Oscar I. *The Jews and Minority Rights.* New York: Columbia University Press, 1933.

Jellinek, Adolph. *Bet ha-Midrash.* Vol. 5. Jerusalem: Wahrmann Books, 1967.

Kallen, Horace. "Democracy Versus the Melting Pot: A Study of American Nationality." *Nation* 100 (February 18, 1915): 190-194 and (February 25, 1915): 217-220.

Kaplan, Mordecai M. "Anti-Maimunism in Modern Dress: A Reply to Baruch Kurzweil's Attack on Ahad Ha-am." *Judaism* 4 (Fall 1955): 303-312.

Karp, Abraham J. *A History of the United Synagogue of America, 1913-1963.* New York: United Synagogue of America, 1964.

———. "Solomon Schechter Comes to America." In *The Jewish Experience in America: Selected Studies from the Publications of the American Jewish Historical Society,* edited by A. Karp, vol. 5, pp. 111-129. New York, 1969.

Kling, Simcha. "Our Zionist Fathers: Israel Friedlaender." *Conservative Judaism* 32 (Fall 1978): 27-32.

Kochen, Lionel. "Graetz and Dubnow: Two Jewish Historians in an Alien World." In *Essays in Honor of E. H. Carr,* edited by C. Abramsky, pp. 352-366. London: Archon Books, 1974.

Kohler, Kaufmann. *Jewish Theology Systematically and Historically Considered.* Edited by Joseph L. Blau. New York: Ktav Publishing House, 1968.

———. "Self Government Is Bound to End in Failure." *Jewish Comment* (Baltimore), December 23, 1904.

———. *Studies, Addresses and Personal Papers.* New York: Alumni Association of the Hebrew Union College, 1931.

Kohn, Hans. *The Idea of Nationalism: A Study in Its Origins and Background.* New York: Macmillan Co., 1944.

———. *Nationalism: Its Meaning and History.* New York and Cincinnati: Van Nostrand Reinhold Co., 1971.

Kohn, Jacob. "Israel Friedlaender: A Biographical Sketch." *American Jewish Year Book (1921-1922),* pp. 65-79. Philadelphia: Jewish Publication Society, 1921.

Kohut, Alexander George. "Bibliography of the Writings of Professor D. Moritz Steinschneider." In *Festschrift zum achtzigsten Geburtstage Moritz Steinschneider's,* pp. v-xxxvii. Leipzig: Otto Harrassowitz, 1896.

Krappe, Alexander H. "Folklore and Mythology." In *Funk and Wagnalls Standard Dictionary of Folklore, Mythology, and Legend.* 2 vols. New York: Funk & Wagnalls Co., 1949-50.

Laqueur, Walter. *A History of Zionism*. New York: Holt, Rinehart and Winston, 1972.

Lewis, Bernard. *History Remembered, Recovered, Invented*. Princeton, N.J.: Princeton University Press, 1975.

———. *Islam in History: Ideas, Men, and Events in the Middle East*. London: Alcove Press, 1973.

———, and Holt, P. M., eds. *Historians of the Middle East*. London and New York: Oxford University Press, 1962.

Lipsky, Louis. *A Gallery of Zionist Profiles*. New York: Farrar, Straus and Cudahy, 1956.

Magnes, Judah. "Friedlaender the Student. The Work of Israel Friedlaender." *Menorah Journal* 6 (December 1920): 351-354.

———. *Thirty Years of Zionism*. New York: Nesher, 1927.

Marcus, Jacob Rader. *Studies in American Jewish History: Studies and Addresses*. Cincinnati: Hebrew Union College, 1969.

Margolies, Morris. *Samuel David Luzzatto: Traditionalist Scholar*. New York: Ktav Publishing House, 1979.

Margoshes, Samuel. "Israel Friedlaender." In *Three Zionist Rishonim*, pp. 24-31. New York: Brith Rishonim, November 1961.

Marx, Alexander. *Essays in Jewish Biography*. Philadelphia: Jewish Publication Society, 1947.

———. "Israel Friedlaender, Zionist and Scholar." *Maccabean* 34 (August 1920): 33-35.

———. "Political Ideal of the Prophets." *Maccabean* (March 11, 1910): 313, 320-323.

———. "Friedlaender the Scholar. The Work of Israel Friedlaender." *Menorah Journal* 6 (December 1920): 344-350.

Mead, George Herbert. *Mind, Self and Society from the Standpoint of a Social Behaviorist*. Edited by Charles W. Morris. Chicago: University of Chicago Press, 1934.

Morgenstern, Julian. "The Achievements of Reform Judaism." *Central Conference of American Rabbis Yearbook* 29 (1925): 247-281.

———. *As a Mighty Stream: The Progress of Judaism Through History*. Philadelphia: Jewish Publication Society, 1949.

———. "Jerusalem, 485 B.C." *Hebrew Union College Annual* 27 (1950): 107-179; 28 (1957): 15-47; 31 (1960): 1-29.

———. "The Significance of the Bible for Reform Judaism in the Light of Modern Scientific Research." *Journal of the Central Conference of American Rabbis* 18 (1908): 217-248.

Noeldeke, Theodor. *Beitraege zur kenntnis der Poesie der alten Araber*. Hannover: C. Rumpler, 1864.

———. *Sketches from Eastern History*. Translated by John Sutherland Black. London and Edinburgh: Adam and Charles Black, 1892.

———. "Sufi." *Zeitschrift der deutschen morgenlaendischer Gesellschaft* 48 (1894): 45-48.

Parzen, Herbert. *Architects of Conservative Judaism.* New York: Jonathan David, 1964.

———. "Brandeis and the Balfour Declaration." *Herzl Yearbook* 5 (1963): 309-350.

———. "Conservative Judaism and Zionism (1896-1922)." *Jewish Social Studies* 23 (October 1961): 235-264.

———. "Conservative Judaism and Zionism (1896-1923)." *Herzl Yearbook* 6 (1964-65): 311-368.

———. "The Federation of American Zionists, 1897-1914. In *Early History of Zionism in America,* edited by Isidore S. Miller. New York: American Jewish Historical Society and Theodor Herzl Foundation, 1958.

Pavlov, Ivan Petroveich. *Lectures on Conditioned Reflexes and Psychiatry.* Translated and edited by W. Horsley Gantt. New York: International Publishers, 1941.

Plaut, Gunter, ed. *The Rise of Reform Judaism: A Sourcebook of Its European Origins.* New York: World Union for Progressive Judaism, 1963.

———. *The Growth of Reform Judaism: American and European Sources until 1948.* New York: World Union for Progressive Judaism, 1965.

Poznanski, Samuel A. "Bibliographie." *Revue des Études Juives* 47 (1903): 133-147.

———. "Professor Israel Friedlaender" (Hebrew). *Ha-tekufa* (Warsaw), 8 (1920): 483-488.

Rabinowitz, Saul. *Rabbi Zechariah Frankel: His Life, Times, Books and Academy* (Hebrew). Warsaw: Aḥiasaf, 1898.

Rawidowicz, Simon. *Babylon and Jerusalem: Towards a Philosophy of Israel's Wholeness* (Hebrew). London and Waltham, Mass.: Ararat, 1957.

———. *Simon Dubnow in Memoriam, Essays and Letters* (Hebrew). London and Waltham, Mass.: Ararat, 1954.

Reardon, Bernard, M. G. *Religious Thought in the Nineteenth Century Illustrated from Writers of the Period.* Cambridge, England: At the University Press, 1966.

Rischin, Moses. "The American Jewish Committee and Zionism." *Herzl Yearbook* 5 (1963): 65-81.

———. "The Early Attitude of the American Jewish Committee to Zionism: 1906-1922." *Publications of the American Jewish Historical Society* 49 (March 1960): 188-201.

———. *The Promised City: New York's Jews, 1870-1914.* Cambridge: Harvard University Press, 1962.

Rosenblum, Herbert. "The Founding of the United Synagogue of America, 1913." Dissertation, Brandeis University, 1970.

Rubenovitz, Herman H., and Rubenovitz, Mignon L. *The Waking Heart*. Cambridge: Nathaniel Dame, 1967.

Rudens, S. P. "A Half Century of Community Service: The Story of the New York Educational Alliance." In *American Jewish Year Book (1944-1945)*, pp. 73-85. Philadelphia: Jewish Publication Society, 1944.

Sachar, Howard M. *A History of Israel from the Rise of Zionism to Our Own Time*. New York: Alfred A. Knopf, 1976.

Sanders, Ronald. *The High Walls of Jerusalem. A History of the Balfour Declaration and the Birth of the British Mandate for Palestine*. New York: Holt, Rinehart & Winston, 1983.

———. *The Downtown Jews: Portraits of an Immigrant Generation*. New York: Harper and Row, 1969.

Sarna, Nahum M. "Geiger and Biblical Scholarship." In *New Perspectives on Abraham Geiger*, edited by Jakob J. Petuchowski. New York: Ktav Publishing House, 1975.

Schechter, Solomon. *Aspects of Rabbinic Theology*. New York: Schocken Books, 1961.

———. *Seminary Addresses and Other Papers*. New York: Burning Bush Press, 1959.

———. *Studies in Judaism, First Series*. Philadelphia, Jewish Publication Society, 1945.

———. *Studies in Judaism, Second Series*. Philadelphia, Jewish Publication Society, 1908.

———. *Studies in Judaism, Third Series*. Philadelphia, Jewish Publication Society, 1924.

Schoener, Allon, ed. *Portal to America: The Lower East Side, 1870-1925*. New York: Holt, Rinehart and Winston, 1967.

Scholem, Gershom. *The Messianic Idea in Judaism and Other Essays in Jewish Spirituality*. New York: Schocken Books, 1974.

———. *Sabbatai Ṣevi, The Mystical Messiah 1626-1676*. Translated by Zwi Werblowsky. Princeton, N.J.: Princeton University Press, 1973.

Schorsch, Ismar. "Ideology and History in the Age of Emancipation." Editor's Introduction to *The Structure of Jewish History and Other Essays*, by *Heinrich Graetz*. New York: Ktav Publishing House, 1975.

———. "Zacharias Frankel and the European Origins of Conservative Judaism." *Judaism* 30 (Summer 1981): 344-345.

Schussheim, Morris. "Recollections of Israel Friedlaender." *Proceedings of the Rabbinical Assembly* 9 (1945): 168-175.

Seltzer, Robert. "Coming Home: The Personal Basis of Simon Dubnow's Ideology." *AJS Review* 1 (1976): 283-301.

Shapiro, Yonathan. *Leadership of the American Zionist Organization 1897-1930*. Urbana, Ill.: University of Illinois Press, 1971.

Sklare, Marshall. *Conservative Judaism: An American Religious Movement.* New York: Schocken Books, 1972.

Sochen, Frieda. "Israel Friedlaender, His Approach to Zionism and *Eretz Yisrael.*" *Hadoar* 56, no. 5 (December 3, 1976): 69-70.

Sprenger, Aloys. *Das Leben und die Lehre des Mohammad, nach bisher Groesstentheils unbenutzten Quellen.* 3 vols. Berlin: B Nicholaische Verlagsbuchhandlung, 1869.

Sultzberger, Cyrus. "An American's View of the Congress." *American Hebrew* 73 (September 11, 1903): 527-528.

Szajkowski, Zosa. *Jews, Wars and Communism.* New York: Ktav Publishing House, 1972.

———. "Jewish Relief in Eastern Europe, 1914-1917." *Yearbook of the Leo Baeck Institute* 10 (1965): 24-51.

———. "The Private and Organized American-Jewish Overseas Relief 1914-1938." *American Jewish Historical Quarterly* (beginning September 1967) 57:52-106, 191-254, 285-352; 58:376-407, 484-506; 59:83-138.

Tal, Uriel. *Christians and Jews in Germany: Religion, Politics and Ideology in the Second Reich, 1870-1914.* Translated by Noah Jonathan Jacobs. Ithaca, N.Y., and London: Cornell University Press, 1975.

Thompson, Stith. *The Folktale.* New York: Dryden, 1946.

Toren, Haim. *Tagim (Miniatures; Brief Essays and Sketches)* (Hebrew). Jerusalem: Reuven Maas, 1972.

Tuchman, Hyman, ed. *Ahad Ha-am (1856-1927): The Philosopher of Cultural Zionism. Issued upon the Occasion of His Fortieth Yahrzeit.* New York: Jewish Agency, 1967.

United Synagogue. *Fifth Annual Report.* New York: United Synagogue of America, 1918.

Urofsky, Melvin. *American Zionism from Herzl to the Holocaust.* Garden City, N.Y.: Doubleday, Anchor Books, 1976.

Weber, Max. *The Sociology of Religion.* Translated by Ephraim Fischoff. Boston: Beacon Press, 1964.

Wellhausen, Julius. *Das Arabische Reich und sein Sturz.* Berlin: W. de Gruyter, 1902.

———. *Prolegomena to the History of Ancient Israel.* New York: Meridian Books, 1957.

Wensinck, A. J. "Al Khadir." *Encyclopedia of Islam* 2:861-865.

Winter, Nathan W. *Jewish Education in a Pluralistic Society: Samson Benderly and Jewish Education in the United States.* New York: New York University Press, 1966.

Wohlgemuth, Joseph. "Professor Israel Friedlaender." *Jeschurun* 7 (July-August 1920): 407-411.

Zimmerman, Frank. "The Contributions of Friedlaender to the Study of the Bible." *Proceedings of the Rabbinical Assembly of America* 9 (1945): 162-167.

Zunz, Leopold. *Die gottesdienstlichen Vortraege der Juden, historisch entwickelt.* Berlin: A. Asher, 1832.

*Deceased.

Index